Youth and Sexualities

Pleasure, Subversion, and Insubordination in and out of Schools

Edited by

Mary Louise Rasmussen, Eric Rofes, and Susan Talburt

YOUTH AND SEXUALITIES: PLEASURE, SUBVERSION, AND INSUBORDINATION IN AND OUT OF SCHOOLS
Copyright © Mary Louise Rasmussen, Eric Rofes, and Susan Talburt, 2004.
All rights reserved. No part of this book may be used or reproduced in any manner
whatsoever without written permission except in the case of brief quotations
embodied in critical articles or reviews.

 First published 2004 by
PALGRAVE MACMILLAN™
175 Fifth Avenue, New York, N.Y. 10010 and
Houndmills, Basingstoke, Hampshire, England RG21 6XS.
Companies and representatives throughout the world.

PALGRAVE MACMILLAN is the global academic imprint of the Palgrave
Macmillan division of St. Martin's Press, LLC and of Palgrave Macmillan Ltd.
Macmillan® is a registered trademark in the United States, United Kingdom and
other countries. Palgrave is a registered trademark in the European Union and other
countries.

ISBN 978-1-4039-6488-5

Library of Congress Cataloging-in-Publication Data

Youth and sexualities : pleasure, subversion, and insubordination in and out of schools /
edited by Mary Louise Rasmussen, Eric Rofes, and Susan Talburt.
        p. cm.
    Includes index.

    1. Gay youth—Psychology. 2. Lesbian youth—Psychology. 3. Youth—Sexual
behavior. 4. Homosexuality—United States. 5. School environment—United States.
I. Rasmussen, Mary Louise, 1967- II. Rofes, Eric E., 1954- III. Talburt, Susan.
HQ76.25.Y68 2004
306.76'6'0835—dc22

                                                                2004049588

A catalogue record for this book is available from the British Library.

Design by Autobookcomp.

First edition: December 2004
10 9 8 7 6 5 4 3 2 1

Transferred to Digital Printing 2010

Contents

Contents

Part II: Rethinking Youth Practices

Acknowledgments

One of the more pleasurable tasks in editing a collection such as this is thanking those who made it possible. This collection reflects ongoing conversations, papers, and emails over several years and we would like to acknowledge the international community of researchers, within and outside this collection, who continue to support and foster such work. To all those who contributed chapters to this collection, thanks for providing an erudite and extremely engaging body of work. And, to Amanda Johnson from Palgrave, a big thank you for sponsoring this project. To the queer young people, who are the principal subjects of this collection, you continue to inspire our research and practice in this area. It is our hope that collections such as this will contribute to a more complex picture of these young people's lives. Mary Louise Rasmussen would like to pay special tribute to Susan Talburt and Eric Rofes for their incredible generosity, patience, and knowledge; I couldn't have asked for better companions in this task.

Portions of chapter one, "Intelligibility and Narrating Queer Youth," by Susan Talburt, initially appeared as "Construction of LGBT Youth: Opening Up Subject Positions," *Theory into Practice* Vol. 43,(2) (spring 2004). Copyright 2004 by the College of Education, The Ohio State University. All Rights Reserved. Reprinted with permission.

Chapter eight, "Agency in Borderland Discourse: Engaging in Gay-bonics for Pleasure, Subversion, and Retaliation," by Mollie Black-burn, will appear in modified form as "Agency Borderland Discourse: Examining Language Use in a Community Center with Black Queer Youth" in an upcoming issue of *Teachers College Record*. Printed here with permission of Blackwell Publishing, Ltd. The article is scheduled to appear in volume 107, issue 1 in January 2005.

Introduction

Transforming Discourses of Queer Youth and Educational Practices Surrounding Gender, Sexuality, and Youth

Susan Talburt, Eric Rofes, and
Mary Louise Rasmussen

This book is an intervention into the ways we conceptualize, represent, and work with all young people, but especially with queer youth. At a moment in which some argue that issues of access to public education and safety in peer groups will be the next major civil rights struggle facing schools in the West, we put forward this book as a strategic intervention aimed at altering the very premises that guide the actions of teachers, counselors, youth workers, and researchers. As school systems address bullying, harassment, and legal threats for failing to provide equal educational access, an entire army of professionals is being marshaled to create effective responses to newly identified "problems" related to gender, sexuality, schooling, and youth cultures. The editors of this volume have grave concerns about a range of policies and activities that are emerging internationally and that are intended to "protect" queer youth, create "safe" school cultures, and effectively divide "queer youth" from "straight youth." In this context we deploy the term "queer" to refer to individuals and communities of young people who may identify themselves as not straight.

The concerns we articulate above about policies and activities pertaining to "queer youth" are also informed by queer theory. In *Foucault and Queer Theory* (1999), Tamsin Spargo notes that queer theories "expose and explore naturalized models of gender" (56) and sexualities. In the queer theoretical tradition, our text also tries to undo the cultural understandings that continually reinscribe and naturalize the heterosexual/homosexual binary in the service of "queer youth."

We ourselves have participated in the establishment of programs and services for queer youth; we have engaged in political action related to school-based oppression and violence; we have written academic papers and books that examine the ways in which schools respond—or fail to respond—to gender and sexual diversity. We see schools not as purified spaces nurturing innocent children but as concentrated sites of contestation around issues of power and identity. While we share in many people's commitment to civil society, participatory democracy, and public education, we do not believe that the safety and empowerment of children and youth are enhanced or strengthened when liberal constructs and narrow interventions constitute the entire range of cultural responses to complex social dynamics.

To our minds, the majority of discourses related to adolescence, sexuality, and gender are dominated by liberal understandings of complex matters such as identity, tolerance, safety, and equity. Partially as a result of such discourses, we believe that queer- and heterosexual-identified youth often find themselves in untenable situations, increasingly defined by a dynamic that somehow manages to promote the utility of separating "queer" and "normal" young people. This text aims to critique and undermine this liberal discourse and move it toward radical reinterpretations that have the potential to transform cultural understandings and practices relating to "queer" and "normal" youth communities.

A certain common sense has overtaken public and professional discussion about queer youth, a common sense that frames them overwhelmingly in terms of oppression and victimization. A parallel common sense has overtaken gay and lesbian political activism in the West, one that is driven to mainstream or normalize gay and lesbian people as a strategy for gaining entry into civil society (D'Emilio and Freedman 1997; Vaid 1995; Warner 1999). This volume challenges both of these seemingly commonsensical approaches to social justice. In fact, we believe that the intersection of these two common senses creates a limited context for understanding youth in fully complex ways, constrains analysis of cultural identities and conflicts, and serves effectively as a barrier to transformative practices in and out of schools. The creeping liberalism that repeatedly marshals tropes of victimization and stigma as tactics encouraging support for queer youth emerges out of a broader gay political denigration of institutional multicultural approaches of integrity in favor of an obsession with acceptability. Hence people who are nonheterosexual-identified are expected to beg for liberal, and often only symbolic, forms of support and tolerance (see Kumashiro 2002).

As social conceptualizations and cultural understandings of young people continue to change, we note the creation of an extended adolescence, a constructed developmental stage that is itself problematic (Lesko 2001). While the extension of adolescence has the potential to pose profound problems for all young people, we argue that queer youth are one of the populations that exemplify the conflicts and contradictions inherent in this transformation. Contemporary understandings of youth make it nearly impossible for young people to embrace non-normative identities or take possession of their bodies and their lives. With these understandings reigning supreme, is it any surprise that an entire regime of social service programs, modeled on child-saving concepts, has emerged in the past two decades, intended to "service" and "protect" queer youth? When such cultures insist on seeing "good" young people as asexual, how can there be a lesbian seventh-grader? When society constructs teenagers as the chattel property of their adult parents, how can we talk about a young person's right to forge his or her own gender identity? When schools embrace abstinence-only approaches to sex, how can we begin a dialogue about young people's sexual pleasure?

Normative frameworks, including heteronormative frameworks, are the scaffolding that holds in place an entire system of power and privilege that endeavors to relegate young people, people of color, queers, and women to the symbolic fringes of society. For this reason, we believe that confining talk about youth and institutional change to the seeming "givens" of normative frameworks prevents us from more ambitious goals. We argue for understandings of young people, queer politics, and practices in and out of schools that interrogate the production of identities and practices and challenge social and institutional norms with a view to reforming existing practices. And key to such reform is a revised approach to the agency of children and youth.

To understand youth and the institutions they inhabit as productive of identities and differences is to acknowledge that both are actors, or to imbue both youth and institutions with agency. In the present political moment, it sometimes seems as if we have an easier time accepting the power and agency of cultural institutions, than that of people, particularly young people. Instead of setting up a sociological dichotomy of structure versus agency, our understanding of people and institutions as active constitutes a step against reification of queer youth or of the spaces they inhabit. In other words, neither queer youth nor schools nor cultural practices is narrowly seen as one thing or the other. They are in changing relations and mutually constitutive, resources and responses rather than fixed entities. Yet there is an essentializing tendency at present in social scientific discourse, educational practice, and in gay and lesbian politics to understand subjects and institutions as fixed. Perhaps more importantly in regard to queer youth, this tendency sees both gender and sexuality as inherent or biologic, sacrifices youth self-definition, empowerment, and autonomy in order to garner "a place at the table" (Bawer 1993), and centers mainstream, white middle-class cultural values.

In the following sections of this introductory chapter we lay out our agenda in editing this volume by offering a brief sketch of the current mainstream gay and lesbian political zeitgeist, dominant frameworks for understanding queer youth, and the interventions of this text as a whole and its individual chapters.

Queer Politics

We cannot underestimate the conservative opposition to recognition of lesbian, gay, bisexual, and transgender (LGBT) identities, sexualities, or cultures in schools and the lead the Religious Right has taken in defining public schools' approaches to sexuality in general (Irvine 2002). Yet we cannot capitulate to that conservatism by perpetuating a discourse of queer youth that frames them as victims-in-need-of-tolerance-and-inclusion or as "just like everyone else." D'Emilio (2002) points to a shift in queer politics that is suggestive of a cautionary stance on the part of those who would endeavor to support queer youth:

> Whereas the issues of the 1970s revolved around a demand to be left alone, those of the 1990s call for recognition and inclusion. Instead of a core outlook captured by the phrase "here we are," the agitation around family, school, and work puts forward a different demand: "we want in." If the former appears as a simple statement of fact that can be realized through visibility and the creation of public communities, the latter demands both action and response. It requires, for its realization, a strategy of winning allies, of building support outside the community from the people—heterosexuals—whose lives too will inevitably be changed by the full inclusion of homosexuals in the core institutions of American society. (97)

This search for allies all too often results in the desexualizing of the mainstream LGBT movement as it searches for normalcy and respectability (Warner 1999). While normalization might enable greater inclusion in educational spheres, it also reflects a series of strategic compromises that have enormous ramifications for queer youth. First, it allows normative cultural values to leak over into queer spaces and drive out the queerest of the queers. For example, those queers who organize their sexual practices or gender performances outside the range of heteronorms can be seen as recalcitrant traitors to the cause, unwilling to make the appropriate sacrifices for the sake of inclusion. This affects, in particular, those youth who do not conform to traditional sex roles or who insist on the right to bodily autonomy and sexual pleasure. Second, it encourages a vision of cultural pluralism that is only tolerant if certain distinctions are reined in or vanished. Hence the gay male football captain might come out and receive support from his peers, even as the queer in the drama club continues to be taunted.

But there is a larger, overarching problem with the drive toward normalization: it has a propensity to codify sexual and gender identities as stable categories with fixed meanings. These stable meanings often appeal to public ideas of normalcy, or the potential for gay and lesbian normalcy if victimization could just be curbed. And this stability calls for normalizing interventions, such as role models and curricular inclusion to build tolerance and self-esteem.

In his *The Trouble with Normal*, Michael Warner (1999) considers the etymological link of "normal" to standards (or standardized?) as operative in the present:

> When people want to be normal they might be partly under the influence of an association of the term that has become somewhat archaic in English, in which normal means certified, approved, as meeting a set of normative standards. This is why teachers' colleges are called normal schools. In French the association remains strong, and when one speaks of normalization, one refers to the whole process of training, testing, and authorizing people as full members of society. The deep sense of judgment and higher authority embedded in the idea of the normal may owe something to this sense of the term, even for Americans who don't associate it with the word. (56)

Normal, then, takes on an evaluative cast linked to standards for taste, behavior, and affiliations. And its relation to schooling and the development of the young is no accident. Yet as young people, queer or not, craft their identities, or engage in what Wexler (1992) calls the process of "becoming somebody," they play with norms, conforming to, challenging, and altering them. As Wexler (1992), like many sociologists and anthropologists of education, pointed out about the young people in schools he studied:

> They were not struggling to become nobody, some high postmodernist definition of a decentered self. They wanted to be somebody, a real and presentable self, and one anchored in the verifying eyes of the friends whom they came to school to meet. . . . Becoming somebody was an organizationally patterned process of production that used cultural resources deeply ingrained in more pervasive societal structures of inequality and difference. (7)

The complex dynamics of society, institution, and individual that Wexler describes cannot be addressed by conventional, liberal goals of tolerance, understanding, self-esteem, equity, and inclusion for queer youth that define such projects as "safe schools," providing accurate and positive curricular representations, or constructing "role models" for queer youth. The contributors to this volume aptly demonstrate how such goals are insufficient in addressing the ways heteronormalizing processes adversely affect all young people, regardless of their sexual and gender identifications.

The contemporary LGBT movement in the United States has a particular stake in distancing itself from queer youth or putting forth sanitized versions of queer youth who are dependent on adult care and support. For many years, the mainstream national LGBT community distanced itself strategically from issues involving children, youth, and schools. None of the national advocacy groups made a priority of youth issues. In fact, a separate national organization needed to form, the Gay, Lesbian and Straight Education Network, to address issues related to public education. Perhaps, because of social stigma that linked gays and child molestation, as Blount and Anahita demonstrate in this volume, a strategic distancing took place for many years. About a dozen years ago, at least in the United States, it became impossible to continue with such distancing, and hence the movement had to consider ways to address youth issues without looking like self-interested predators. A public understanding of queer youth as vital, empowered, strong, and sexual would be difficult to square with the conservative times and would not garner either empathy or votes. But, perhaps drawing on a tactic that worked so well in the 1980s in the AIDS fight—an ambivalent representation of queer people as victims, and hence deserving of public support—authentic incidents and representations of experience with oppression and violence were molded into the acceptable public face of queer youth. Over a brief period of time, what the public could know about queer youth—as with what the public could know about African American youth—became focused on pathology: they are "at-risk" kids for HIV, substance abuse, alcoholism, depression and suicide, homelessness, violence, sexually transmitted diseases, dropping out of school, and school achievement failure. A narrative trope that does exist and continues to be a partial, though sad and outrageous, reality becomes the entire portrait of this rich and complex population.

How might we reframe young people as creative participants in institutional and non-institutional spaces? And how might we challenge universalizing representations of queer youth in popular and scholarly discourse that focus on support and intervention, and consider instead young people's creativity in the negotiation of their sexual subjectivities, identities, and practices in various contexts? Young people's actions are not representations or enactments of a preconstituted, fixed group, but contingent invocations of identity in which they enunciate desires for affiliation, community, recognition, safety, and danger at the same time that they may articulate responses to exclusion and marginalization.

Queer Youth

In 1988, Michelle Fine wrote what has become a much-cited essay on "the missing discourse of desire" related to adolescent female sexuality in school-based sex education classes. Fine's analysis of dominant discourses identified sexuality as violence, sexuality as victimization, and sexuality as individual morality. Missing, she noted, were discourses of desire, sexual subjectivity, and agency. The official curriculum flattened young women into objects rather than subjects of sexuality. In somewhat parallel fashion, the complexity of queer youths' subjectivity, agency, sexuality, and cultural practices is flattened by a dominant framing of them in terms of danger and victimization. If adults tacitly acknowledge queer youths' desire, subjecthood, or creativity, they do not frequently actively address these elements of their lives or consider them as something from which adults might learn. Queer youth agency, whether linked to sexual desire or activity, or to projects of crafting the self and relations to others, is relegated to the domain of the unthinkable.

Who benefits from this flattening? And does this flattening assist in the positive transformation of social conditions that result in the oppression of youth or does it, in fact, intensify existing conditions?

Who gains from images of queer teens as confused, skittish, reckless, superficial, simple, and victimized? And who loses?

To suggest that educators, youth workers, and researchers need to acknowledge these complexities may sound like an additive approach to offering a "fuller" representation of queer youth, one that gets things right. Our goal here is not to get things right, particularly once and for all. But we do believe that adding to understandings of queer youth by analyzing the uses and effects of dominant discourses and by offering complex analyses of "queer" and "straight" youths' lives can help adults rethink their relations to young people, and can provide another perspective on queer youth's relations to the world. As feminist projects have taught us, the goal of adding is ultimately one of transforming. Thus, to understand queer young people in terms that include pleasure, subversion, and insubordination is to challenge the meanings of other terms that have long defined the categories they inhabit, terms that Rofes (in this volume) succinctly refers to as the "Martyr-Target-Victim" syndrome.

The authors in this volume take up questions of pleasure and agency in the lives of young people as they draw on competing discourses to create new identities, practices, and ideologies. What do young people do with stereotypes that they may or may not identify with? How do they put to use institutional and non-institutional spaces? What relations do they create to school rituals such as proms? What meanings do they create in the context of such programs as Gay-Straight Alliances, youth organizations, or safe schools? What meanings do these programs leave out or make impossible? How do depictions of LGBT youth relate to other pathologizing images tied to race, socioeconomic class, and urbanicity? How might educators and youth workers develop programs that support young people's negotiations of sexual and gender identity, community and ideologies in cultures that alternately deny their existence, construct them as deviant, or commodify them? What are the implications of transformed understandings of young people's sexual and gender identifications for educators, counselors, youth development workers, and activists?

About the Chapters

This book complements and extends existing analyses of and alternatives to the narratives of risk and persecution that frame much antihomophobic educational work. This text also breaks radically with traditional constructs of adolescents and adolescence, stepping off of contemporary critiques of childhood and adolescence appearing in cultural studies, social work, and critical theory. Such an approach opens up new possibilities for interpreting youth cultures and the relationship between youth agency, resistance, and community formation. Finally, the historical, ethnographic, psychoanalytic, critical, interpretive, and Foucauldian analyses that this text brings together offer multiple vantage points for reconceptualizing adolescent sexual subjectivities and institutional and cultural practices.

The contributors to part I of the volume, Rethinking Adults and Youth, rethink discourses that would frame queer youth by offering readings that challenge the common sense of adult-youth relations and adult interventions for youth. In the first chapter, Susan Talburt interrogates the fraught knowledges of LGBT young people in her study of the intelligibility and narrativization of queer youth. Through a reading of the film *But I'm a Cheerleader,* Talburt considers how young people's understandings of themselves and others are necessarily constrained by the interventions and perceptions that adults produce in relation to queer youth. In particular, her focus is on how young people are constructed in relationship to two devalued binary positions, "heterosexual/homosexual and adult/youth." For Talburt, this devaluing of queer youth creates another binary of (1) narratives of risk and danger and (2) narratives of the well-adjusted, out, and proud gay youth. Focusing primarily on the structure of the latter, Talburt problematizes the "success story" of queer youth and demonstrates how such stories produce queer young people in narrowly defined ways.

While Talburt's focus is on the problematics of pride, Eric Rofes explores the problematics associated with the mass production of contemporary images of LGBT youth in the United States that depict them as "at-risk." Naming this evocative characterization as the "Martyr-Target-Victim" model, Rofes considers how this model may be central to the ways in which some queer students see themselves (and are asked to see themselves). Rofes also examines some of the implications of his students' insistence that agency plays absolutely no role in the development of their gender and sexual identities. Finally, this chapter traces the ties that bind funding of services for adolescents (including LGBT adolescents) and pathology.

The third chapter in the book offers a valuable historical perspective on the "Historical Regulation of Sexuality and Gender" in the United States in the twentieth century. In this study, Jackie M. Blount and Sine Anahita analyze the interrelated experiences of LGBT students and school workers to consider how "Policies intended to affect one have had profound, though sometimes unanticipated consequences for the other." For Blount and Anahita, these consequences, anticipated and unanticipated, are important because they point to the malleability, over time, of what constitutes acceptable performances of gender and sexuality in school settings. Moreover, their study informs the ensuing chapters in this collection by providing a historical challenge to the "enduring truth" of LGBT young people's suicidality.

In a similar vein to Rofes' earlier chapter, Valerie Harwood is also critical of the trend to "psychopathologize queer youth." However, Harwood's focus is on the relationship between this process of pathologization and the ways in which discourses of psychopathology construct the notion of "non-normative" sexual and/or gender identities as psychopathological. In developing this critique, Harwood draws on the work of Michel Foucault to develop a genealogical strategy involving "four angles of scrutiny." This strategy, a valuable methodological tool, enables her to "Subject to Scrutiny" discourses that posit queer young people as psychopathological or as at imminent risk of psychopathology.

The final chapter in part I takes a psychoanalytic turn in order to posit questions regarding how the education of adolescents is necessarily influenced by the pervasive worries and anxieties of adults relating to their own adolescence. In undertaking this interrogation, Jen Gilbert focuses on language to consider the place of adolescence in adult narratives of growing up, and, on the grammars, vernaculars, and silences that structure and produce theories of "adolescence" and "the adolescent." The role of narrative is also central to Gilbert's discussion of sexuality education. She highlights the difficulties and pleasures of narrating our sexual selves within the institutional and curricular spaces of schooling while also rallying against the banality of contemporary sexuality education within schools.

As indicated by the title Rethinking Youth Practices, the second part of this volume focuses more specifically on young people themselves and on the myriad ways they negotiate agency, pleasure, and insubordination. Mary Louise Rasmussen's study of the production of "safe spaces" and "queer spaces" within and around high school settings in the United States introduces this section. Drawing on Foucault's notions of dividing practices and heterotopias (1982, 1986) in her analysis of the production of "safe spaces," "queer spaces," and lesbian prom kings, Rasmussen's focus is on young people's relationship to spaces that construct and are constructed by the politics of identity.

The complex interrelationships between identity, sexuality, citizenship, democracy, and youth are the focus of Andrea Coleman, Mary Ehrenworth, and Nancy Lesko's contribution to the volume. Utilizing the award-winning documentary film *Scout's Honor* (2001), about Scouting for All's founder, Steve Cozza, the authors focus on the film as an exercise in civic education, asking questions such as, "How does the film narrate Steve Cozza's political activism against the homophobic policy of the Boy Scouts of America? How does the film help construct the realm of the political? What effects does the portrait of Steve as a young, 'natural' superhero have for queer activism? What alternative stories, images, desires, or memories are available to queer this narrative of natural youth activists?" In asking such questions, Coleman, Ehrenworth, and Lesko prompt readers to reconsider "the ways 'we' understand queer youth activists' relationship to the political world and to themselves."

In the following chapter, Mollie Blackburn analyzes the ways young Black people who attend a queer youth center in Philadelphia make use of what they term "Gaybonics" for pleasure and subversion within and outside schools. In particular, Blackburn is interested in how these young people construct and deploy this "Borderland Discourse" "to elicit pleasure and to subvert oppression." Blackburn's chapter looks beyond homophobia to consider how these young people, so often represented as victims, exercise agency. She enables readers to see the complex interactions whereby these young people work with and against each other, and perceived outsiders, in order to protect themselves and create a discourse community where they police the boundaries.

While the analysis of *Scout's Honor* seeks to complicate Cozza's role as a superhero for queer activism, and Blackburn's chapter focuses on youth of color in a Philadelphia youth center, Deborah Youdell takes us across the Atlantic to England to tell us the story of a "bent" ballet dancer. In telling this story, Youdell offers what she terms "a self-consciously optimistic reading of the possibilities for queer inside school." Using data generated from a school ethnography and drawing on Judith Butler's (1997) notion of performative politics, Youdell considers how queer youth "might be not only recognized, but also taken as legitimate in school contexts" despite the domination of heteronormative and homophobic discourses. The methodological and analytical tools Youdell employs offer educators and researchers some innovative strategies for understanding and reforming existing and future practices relating to sexualities and schooling.

Lingering on the topic of subversive masculinities, David McInnes considers schooling in Australia and begins some theorizing of the sissy boy experience. McInnes notes that the experience of sissy boys is a relatively untheorized arena in queer theory and in education. In keeping with the spirit of this volume, McInnes uses the sissy boy to provide a salient critique "that extends beyond liberal notions of inclusion, tolerance, difference or diversity to more disruptive and lively engagements with gender as a cultural formation." In addition, McInnes provides a useful discussion of the differences he perceives between "homophobic discourses" and "discourse of homophobia" in order to argue against the tendency to obfuscate the significance of sissy boys' gender nonconformity. Ultimately, McInnes' goal is to "keep the formation of gender in view and uneasy, and provide the potential to work pedagogically in ways that resist reinscribing values around the performance of gender by young men and boys."

It is noteworthy that in a book that contextualizes itself as part of and a response to discourses of LGBT politics and communities, analyses and representations of bisexual and of transgender youth are lacking an explicit presence. Equally noteworthy is a preponderance of concern across a number of the essays with masculinity, as in bent ballet dancers, sissy boys, prom kings, and straight activist scouts. While we do offer a cheerleader, missing are femmes and young lipstick lesbians or even the homoerotics of the Girl Scouts. What is foregrounded and what is absent in this collection may be, in part, a reflection of particular cultural and political anxieties, such as proliferating cultural disquiet about suitable expressions of masculinity.

The chapters on non-normative male and female masculinities indicate the complexities of heteronormative politics within and outside educational settings; they also point to the problems of extrapolating the experiences of particular queer youth as somehow pertinent to all queer youth. Transgender, intersex, bisexual, gay, and lesbian identified young people will have common *and* very individual experiences of pleasure, subversion, and insubordination. Our hope is that the essays in this volume will encourage new analyses that take up "what's missing" in new and surprising ways.

While the volume's focus is principally on queer youth, the contributors contextualize these young people in relation to broader adolescent and institutional cultures and practices. This contextualization contributes to knowledge of the complex production of adolescent sexual and gender identifications and expands current understandings of how these identifications are continuously negotiated by people within and outside school communities. Overall, the chapters in this volume fulfill our desire to provide a more nuanced understanding of queer youth, while simultaneously disrupting the bifurcations that tend to reinforce their perceived vulnerability.

References

Bawer, Bruce. 1993. *A Place at the Table: The Gay Individual in American Society.* New York: Poseidon Press.

Butler, Judith. 1997. *Excitable Speech: A Politics of the Performative.* London: Routledge.

D'Emilio, John. 2002. *The World Turned: Essays on Gay History, Politics, and Culture.* Durham, NC: Duke University Press.

D'Emilio, John, and Estelle B. Freedman. 1997. *Intimate Matters: A History of Sexuality in America.* 2nd ed. Chicago: University of Chicago Press.

Fine, Michelle. 1988. "Sexuality, Schooling, and Adolescent Females: The Missing Discourse of Desire." *Harvard Educational Review* 58, no. 1: 29–53.

Foucault, Michel. 1982. "The Subject and Power." Pp. 208–226 in *Michel Foucault: Beyond Structuralism and Hermeneutics,* ed. Hubert. L. Dreyfus and Paul Rabinow. New York: Harvester Wheatsheaf.

———.1986. "Of Other Spaces." *Diacritics.* Spring: 22–27.

Irvine, Janice M. 2002. *Talk about Sex: The Battles over Sex Education in the United States.* Berkeley: University of California Press.

Kumashiro, Kevin. 2002. *Troubling Education: Queer Activism and Antioppressive Pedagogy.* New York and London: RoutledgeFalmer.

Lesko, Nancy. 2001. *Act Your Age! A Cultural Construction of Adolescence.* New York: Routledge.

Roman, Leslie. 1996. "Spectacle in the Dark: Youth as Transgression, Display, and Repression." *Educational Theory* 46, no. 1: 1–22.

Spargo, Tamsin. 1999. *Foucault and Queer Theory.* New York: Icon Books.

Vaid, Urvashi. 1995. *Virtual Equality.* New York: Anchor Books.

Warner, Michael. 1999. *The Trouble with Normal: Sex, Politics, and the Ethics of Queer Life.* Cambridge, MA: Harvard University Press.

Wexler, Philip. 1992. *Becoming Somebody: Toward a Social Psychology of School.* London: Falmer Press.

Part I

Rethinking Adults and Youth

Chapter One

Intelligibility and Narrating Queer Youth

Susan Talburt

William Haver (1998) has written that educators "have very nearly agreed that the pedagogical enterprise is about the production of subjects" (349). Although there is little agreement about what sorts of subjects education aims to produce, he says, "pedagogy is the work of *Bildung*, a coming to subjectivity as jubilant and relieved self-recognition" (350). Whether educators understand the subject as developing according to a natural ontology or according to culture, the education of subjects is defined by a project to "elaborate the 'systems of the world,' to make sense, and to transmit the sense that it makes" (350). This development of subjects entails the production of knowledge and self-knowledge, or what I will call "intelligibility." As children move through adolescence to adulthood, society expects that they will acquire knowledge of self and other (the world and their place in it will become intelligible to them) and that maturing youth will become intelligible to others, knowable as such and such. In this chapter, I explore this problem of intelligibility—not how we can attain it, but what it attains—as it relates to queer youth. The fraught knowledges that contribute to the construction of queer youth have implications for the interventions adults would create for them and for how queer youth come to know and understand themselves.

I trace the ways adults' recuperation of queer youth draws on the intersections of narratives of adolescent development and gay and lesbian cultural politics to produce particular narratives of queer youth. Historically, queer youth, who dwell in two devalued positions relative to the binary categories heterosexual/homosexual and adult/youth (not to mention other hierarchies of race and gender), have been unthinkable except in pathologizing terms. Activists and scholars, however, have combated models of homosexuality as deviance and disease in a number of fields. Yet, in their efforts to counter images of pathological queer youth by shifting pathology from intrinsic to the individual to an effect of oppression, antihomophobic discourses have constructed queer youth through a logic that creates a binary of (1) narratives of risk and danger and (2) narratives of the well-adjusted, out, and proud gay youth. Although these narratives depend on each other for their existence, I focus on the success story, a relatively tacit ideal that is implicit in adult talk of queer youth. My purpose is to denaturalize explicit and implicit norms adults have created as a step toward rethinking educational and institutional interventions aimed at queer youth. My basic premise is that dominant narratives about queer youth make youth intelligible—to others and to themselves in narrowly defined ways. These narratives constitute a production of subject positions in which adults administer a group with problems and needs—and participate in inventing those whom we would help.

Throughout this chapter, my focus is on the narrative character of the knowledge adults have created in defining the means and ends of building the young. My emphasis on intelligibility as a narrative endpoint leads me to use the term "subject" in a Foucauldian (1982) sense, suggesting "subject to someone else by control and dependence, and tied to his own identity by a conscience or self-knowledge" (212). And my thinking about narrative is informed by Roof's (1996) contention that its

> shapes, assumptions, and operations manifest a complex, naturalized process of organization, relation, and connection. . . . As a pervasive sense of the necessary shape of events and their perception and as the process by which characters, causes, and effects combine into patterns recognized as sensical, narrative is the informing logic by which individuality, identity, and ideology merge into a cooperative and apparently unified vision of the truths of existence. (xv)

She points out that we have come to expect narrative to produce something, "insight, a child, another story, the story itself, knowledge, identity" (Roof 1996, 6). And this productive nature of narrative itself, as well as what it produces, appear to be natural rather than effects of history and discourse. As I consider constructions of queer youth, I draw on several narrative forms—film, social science, and personal narrative—to create my own narrative about the shaping of adults' investments in supporting a certain type of queer youth development.

I begin with discussion of a film whose tongue-in-cheek developmentalism at once points to and problematizes adult interventions and naturalizes a certain type of narrative of queer adolescents: the 1999 *But I'm a Cheerleader*, directed by Jamie Babbit. I do so both to question and to sketch a portrait of the narrative positions, means, and ends adults construct for queer youth. I choose this film particularly due to its attention to gender and sexuality as developmental—and developable—narratives and to the ways adult discourses of adolescent sexuality can shape young people's self-identities and subjectivities. Indeed, Megan, the protagonist, is produced as a subject who moves from *behaving* differently to *being* different as she becomes intelligible to herself.

But This Is a Happy Ending

In *But I'm a Cheerleader*, Megan, a 17-year-old wholesome, Christian cheerleader, bored kissing her boyfriend, begins to wonder if she might be attracted to girls. But her wondering is not provoked by her own sense of her desires. Rather, such signifiers as her vegetarianism, Melissa Etheridge poster, and taste for Georgia O'Keefe's flowers confirm family and friends' suspicions. After they set up an intervention led by counselor RuPaul, clad in a t-shirt proclaiming "Straight is Great," Megan's parents place her in a rehabilitation camp, True Directions. The camp offers a five-step program where she can name the "root cause" of her homosexuality, learn gender-appropriate behaviors and desires, and return to her natural heterosexuality. At True Directions, signifiers are everything: girls wear bright pink and boys an electric cobalt blue.

After being inducted into the schedule and rules of the girls' dormitory, Megan is coerced by the camp's director into confessing her homosexuality and passes the program's first step, "Admitting You're a Homosexual." Megan and the other young people then move to the second step, "Rediscovering Your Gender Identity," in which they explore the "roots" of their homosexuality. Megan's peers name such causes as "being born in France," "going to an all-girl boarding school," "having a mother who got married in pants," and "participating in too many locker room showers with the varsity team." Megan is initially unsure how to participate in this construction of knowledge about the self, particularly since she does not identify with an identity for which she needs to name a cause. However, Megan soon learns how these discourses work. In the third step, "Family Therapy," she names her "root" as the year she may have learned inappropriate gender roles when her father was unemployed and her mother worked to support the family. After Family Therapy, Graham, another female teen at the camp, tells her, "This is bullshit, Megan. It doesn't work. You are who you are. The only trick is not getting caught." Little by little Megan finds herself attracted to Graham and soon a romance is blossoming. The romance is cemented when Lloyd and Larry, two ex-ex-gays, help the youth sneak out to Cocksuckers, a local gay bar. As they drive to the bar, the men explain that their goal is to offer balanced perspectives so the youth can make their own choices: "In the end it's. . . . whether you want to be who you are or keep it hidden." That night the girls kiss for the first time.

Once they pass the fourth step, "Demystifying the Opposite Sex," in which they are instructed in how to interact with and please men, Graham and Megan have sex and are reported for doing so. Threatened with expulsion and fearful of being disinherited by her parents, Graham makes a deal with the director and stays at True Directions. Megan, however, leaves with her suitcases and pom-poms and arrives at Lloyd and Larry's house, where she tells them, "I can't go back. I thought you could teach me to be a lesbian, what they wear, where they live, you know." In their house covered in rainbow paint, rainbow towels, and rainbow candles, they tell her, "Megan, we can't help you with that. There's not one way to be a lesbian. You just have to continue to be who you are." She goes out to Cocksuckers with a boy who has also failed True Directions' program and taken refuge at their house.

After considering her options, the distraught Megan appears at True Directions' graduation ceremony with the hopes of winning Graham back. When Graham hesitates to join her, Megan dons her cheerleading outfit and chants for all to hear,

> 1-2-3-4, I won't take "no" anymore,
>
> 5-6-7-8, I want you to be my mate,
>
> 1-2-3-4, You're the one that I adore,
>
> 5-6-7-8, Don't run from me because this is fate.

Graham realizes her mistake and follows Megan. They kiss and ride off in the back of Lloyd and Larry's truck. As the credits roll, viewers see Megan's father at a different therapeutic event with its own steps, a PFLAG meeting, at which he declares, "My daughter is a homosexual."

The film ends happily, with Megan's True Direction and true love winning out over the false direction friends and family sought for her.

While *Cheerleader* offers a "happy ending," it depicts the role that adult authority and cultural and institutional structures can play in defining the terms by which young people understand self and society and act on their understandings. Inserted into homosocial contexts and interpellated as deviant and in need of cure or protection from self, Megan comes to occupy a lesbian subject position. She crafts a lesbian subjectivity based on what is available to her, which are essentially essentialist emancipatory discourses that would limit her choices to "being who she is" or hiding it. Her resistance to rehabilitation and her identification with queer cultural practices and signifiers position her as comprehensible within the terms of identity constructed by the gay and lesbian movement's "gay is good" counterdiscourse to pathology as she follows her True Direction as the newly well-adjusted (and coupled) young lesbian on a rainbow path to happiness.

Particularly interesting is the way *But I'm a Cheerleader*'s narrative structure addresses viewers, who are positioned from the first scene as having more knowledge than the protagonist has. The film opens with Megan's football player boyfriend clumsily kissing her as she conjures images of her female peers' cheerleading bodies. Like viewers, her family and friends construct knowledge of Megan, which will become her self-knowledge. This movement from ignorance to knowledge is integral to the narrative, which offers the pleasure of closure and certainty through what Haver (1998) would call her "jubilant and relieved self-recognition" (349).

The film's playfulness with colors in the gender-segregated world of True Directions dramatizes the absurdity of teaching fixed gender roles. Knowing viewers laugh as the constructed nature of gender is highlighted in scenes that depict lessons in which the girls clean carpet stains and the boys learn to chop wood, repair cars, and watch football games. Yet, as Megan's interest in Graham is produced through the close, even eroticized, female contact of the program's steps, the film asks viewers to hope for a narrative ending in which Megan will follow her True Sexual Direction. Where gender is a fiction, sexuality is a fact. Despite the stunning visual contrast between the pink and blue world of True Directions and the rainbow world offered by Larry, Lloyd, and Cocksuckers, which could have the effect of caricaturing both heterosexual and homosexual essentialisms, or "truths," the rainbow world is aligned with goodness, rightness, and a struggle against oppression of an authentic self. In this happy coming-out movie, true community enables true identity.[1]

But I'm a Cheerleader depicts the role of intelligibility in enabling adult interventions into the lives of youth, including the signifiers that lead family and friends to stage the intervention that would protect heterosexuality, and the dependence of True Directions' steps on self-knowledge. In what follows, I touch on ways pathologizing discourses are pertinent to the evolution of antihomophobic narratives of queer adolescence. But I focus primarily on how adults frame the recuperation of the happy, well-adjusted, and normal queer protagonist. In order to contextualize the pleasing nature of narratives of the truth of sexuality, I backtrack to consider adolescence generally as a construct that frames antihomophobic constructions of queer adolescents.

The Dangerous Middle of Adolescence[2]

Adolescence itself is an idea overloaded with meanings, a site of society's anxieties and hopes for developing subjects and its future. As Cindy Patton (1996) has pointed out, science and society jointly imagine adolescence as a central trope of change in which individual biological and psychological growth occur simultaneously. And these individual changes are "analogized to the 'progress' of civilization itself" (44). However, adolescence does not constitute a smooth narrative of progress between childhood innocence and adult maturity, but a difficult, liminal process of becoming. She says, "These narrative tropes of development, the beginning and the ending, constitute a binary opposition joined through a transitional middle" (44). As a dangerous passage, this "transitional middle" must be monitored with an eye to the end of adulthood.

Taking up a distinctly narrative view of adolescence, Nancy Lesko (2001) links adults' concerns with individual progress and deviance to general anxieties about social progress and degeneration. As she describes, late-nineteenth-century worries about racial and national decline led psychologists, educators, and reformers to create developmental norms and evaluations for adolescents for purposes of "naming, studying, diagnosing, predicting, and administering an identifiable adolescent population" (69). Integral to the construction of modern adolescence in the United States was the psychologist G. Stanley Hall, who led the child study movement in the 1880s and 1890s. Child study involved administering questionnaires and gathering reports of children's play, ideas, and physical development. Hall interpreted these catalogues of children's "natural" interests through an evolutionary framework to explain a natural order of development that would serve as a scientific basis for educational methods (Ross 1972). Hall upheld the theory of recapitulation, the idea that "ontogeny recapitulates phylogeny," or that individual development follows the historical development of the race. As individuals recapitulated the evolution of their races, their development moved from primitive, childlike, emotional savage to civilized, reasoning, and autonomous adult (Lesko 2001). Yet because adolescence was a time of gaining mastery over primitive instincts, it was particularly important for adults to monitor and guide adolescents for the sake of individual and social progress. A developmental narrative that depends on making youth intelligible continues in the present.[3] In fact, the emphasis of contemporary research on adolescence on "turmoil, instability, and abnormality" (Ayman-Nolley and Taira 2000, 42) sets a stage for identifying problems that necessitate interventions. In Megan's case, the intervention included naming the "root cause" of her sexual deviance in a search for a cure or the antihomophobic response of helping her name herself lesbian.

Lesko's discussion emphasizes the ways adults position youth as essentially passive actors in a narrative of adult design. This future-oriented narrative watches for abnormalities that might inhibit proper progress: "[S]ince the end of the story matters, and adults know what the correct and happy ending is (increasing maturity and responsibility, school achievement, full-time employment, marriage and children, property ownership, in that order), only deviations or pitfalls along the prescribed plot merit attention" (132). This predictable narrative with a predictable end, like recapitulation's narrative of orderly evolutionary development that can be monitored and guided, has an affective dimension. Lesko comments,

> [T]o put adolescence into this narrative framework is to consider the "readers" of the stories, as well. We consumers of adolescent narratives are bound emotionally to the story. We are happy, satisfied, and comforted by narratives of fulfillment (conventional adolescent development); we are disturbed by precocity and risk. We may blame families, bad schools, uncaring governments, lack of economic opportunities, and crazy kids, all of which may be in part accurate. But what is generally absent from view is the narrative structure and conventions of the discourse on adolescence, in which we are emotionally and professionally invested (in both the problems and the solutions). (132)

And, indeed, from an antihomophobic perspective, *Cheerleader* offers a narrative of fulfillment. But to understand the implications of such a narrative, one might ask if, as Lesko argues, adolescence can be considered a "*technology* to produce certain kinds of persons within particular social arrangements" (50), what is produced with the creation of the queer adolescent? What subject positions and narrative endings are privileged when "sympathetic" adults seek to understand, define, and administer queer youth? How do adults combine ideas of "queer" and "adolescent"?

Adults and Narratives of Queer Youth

Over a decade ago, Eric Rofes (1989) wrote of schools' failure to address the educational needs of gay and lesbian youth, saying, "This across-the-board denial of the existence of gay and lesbian youth has been allowed to take place because their voices have been silenced and because [gay and lesbian] adults have not effectively taken up their cause" (446). Rofes sought an explanation for this omission beyond avoidance of accusations of "recruiting" youth. He conjectured, "Many adult gay men and women have not come to terms with their own youth and have not faced the pain of those years of repression, stigma, and harassment. Working with young people would force them to confront difficult, unresolved feelings" (446). Some years later, Irvine (1997) noted that in interviews she conducted, "Activists often resisted school-based initiatives out of a reluctance to revisit the pain of their own adolescence" (573). Taken in relation to Lesko's discussion of adults' investments in adolescent development generally, adult memories of adolescence offer an entry point for considering how adults frame narratives of queer youth.

Gordon (1999) situates adolescence as a founding point of adult gay identity:

> Turning back to adolescence is a seemingly mandatory gesture in any narrative of gay or lesbian identity. In its classic form, the "coming-out" narrative, this return typically involves a retrospective exegesis, from the perspective of the "out" adult gay or lesbian subject, in which virtually every aspect of his or her adolescent life can be understood in terms of its relation to the eventual realization of a homosexual identity. (1)

This narrative is constructed from the perspective of the "end," or a present of "outness," and creates a "middle" in which queer "adolescent subjectivity *is* intelligible but . . . its intelligibility is grounded in a narrativistic mode of knowledge" (6). And that intelligibility depends on what Gordon terms "the emancipatory metaphorics" (2) of the coming out narrative, in which a positive present is contrasted to a negative past. In this way, the temporality of queer adults' narratives uncritically positions queer adolescence as the scene of pain and abjection, "the reward for which is postponed until adulthood" (19).

Retrospective victory narratives that essentialize queer adolescence as an inevitable pain that can be reversed in adulthood may contribute to adults' thinking about queer youth in terms of preventing their victimization and working for certain types of "empowerment." In this sense, a narrative such as *Cheerleader* offers pleasure to those who remember an oppressive adolescence or search for narratives of progress. Roof (1996) suggests that identifications with characters in a narrative

> are produced . . . by a self-placement in a narrative economy that is partially determined by the dynamics of that narrative. For example, because narratives focus on protagonists, whether or not we are like specific protagonists, we can and do identify with them because of their position in the narrative dynamic that invests *power and effect in the protagonist.* (153; emphasis mine)

But the victory narrative, in which we seek resistance, salvation, or a positive end, is not individual but linked to a narrative of a community that has helped to secure individual and collective identity, address needs, and gain rights. Gordon, for example, notes a slippage "between historical and individual narrative temporalities, so that the past and the present are predicated with respect to both a periodized gay and lesbian history (pre- and post-Stonewall or, perhaps now, pre- and post-queer) and a bifurcated life story (closetedness and outness)" (12). There is a way, then, in which individual narratives, which circulate to partake of larger collective narratives, recapitulate (to return to Lesko and Hall) the queer community's narratives of its own development. Conversely, collective narratives draw on developmental metaphors. Consider Silin's (1995) description of gay men's post-AIDS stories as a

> developmental narrative of a community coming of age: The 1950s are seen as the infancy of the gay movement, the 1960s its childhood, the 1970s its adolescence, and the 1980s its adulthood. The culture of the 1970s, a reaction to years of life in the closet and relegation to sissidom, is interpreted as a time of youthful rebellion, sexual experimentation, and immaturity that was destined to play itself out. We have been appropriately chastened by a disease that has taught us the real lessons of sex and drugs. (24)

This movement between individual and collective narratives is pleasurable in that subjects use them to construct an individual sense of self, an intelligibility, and a place in a community, linking them to a whole that marks progress. Jeffrey Weeks (1999) contends that narratives

> indicate both changing perceptions and changing possibilities. New stories about sexual and intimate life emerge when there is a new audience ready to hear them in communities of meaning and understanding, and when newly vocal groups can have their experiences validated in and through them. This in turn gives rise to new demands for recognition and validations as the new narratives circulate. The radical oppositional identities, such as lesbian, gay, bisexual, transgendered or "queer," that have flourished in such abundance since the 1960s, can from this perspective be seen as equivalent to fictions: elaborate narrative forms which give shape and meaning to individual lives, and link us to a larger collective story, which tells of oppression, survival, resistance, transgression and claims to full citizenship. Without them we would have no basis to explain our individual needs and desires, nor a sense of collective belonging that provides *the agency and means of change*. (14; emphasis mine)

Weeks' own narrative of progress positions narratives of exclusion and resistance as both artifact and method of social change. Similar to Roof's discussion of readers' or viewers' identifications with protagonists in a narrative as structured by a search for agency, Weeks positions the collective belonging produced through narratives of identity as constitutive of agency. On one hand, I am partial to Weeks' thinking that narrative can encourage a proliferation of diverse identities and practices. However, he does not acknowledge the repetitious nature of coming-out narratives due, perhaps, to ways in which, like recapitulation theory, they are structured by a logic that valorizes certain difficult passages and certain types of progress.

The naturalization of a past of abjection and a present of recuperation through individual and collective narratives leads me to suggest that implicit in queer adults' framing of queer youth are investments in happy endings that would unite gay youth and political progress. A particularly interesting example of queer youth advocates' assumptions of adults' painful adolescence and desires for recuperation lies in the mode of address of a recent fundraising letter from YouthPride, a community center for queer youth in Atlanta, where I live. A brochure offered these words on its cover: "We've all been there." Inside, side-by-side with a description of YouthPride's programs and activities and a fundraising pitch, were the words of one young man: "YouthPride has, in fact, instilled in me a sense of pride that I might never have realized if I had not been given the opportunity to come to it. It has inspired me to be who I am." In another brochure, a young person offered testimony: "YouthPride is one of the only places I feel I can grow and learn and feel better about who I am." This brochure was accompanied by a letter from the Director of Giving, who offered another quote from one of YouthPride's participants:

> Since my first experience at YouthPride in April of last year, I have "come out" to my friends and family, I have started a gay-straight alliance at my high school, become more aware of who I am, and have had numerous opportunities to help the LGBTQ community. All of these achievements were made possible with the support I was given by the staff at YouthPride. (November 15, 2002)

YouthPride's material interpellates readers as former youth-in-need through its seemingly obvious message that "We've all been there." It reminds us that we're not "there" anymore—we're here, in another place in the narrative, adults with community and resources that will contribute to helping YouthPride create youth who will complete individual and collective narratives of pride, authenticity, and community activism. We all partake of the narrative of happy outcomes, or else we most likely would not be on YouthPride's mailing list.

These popular narratives have counterparts in social scientific discourse that has sought to make queer youth intelligible in order to create interventions for them. Social science's developmental narrative of queer youth recapitulates narratives of the gay community's evolution, from pre-Stonewall isolation and furtive communities to increasing group coalescence to pride.

Narrative Convergences

In her study of safe-sex education in the late 1980s, Cindy Patton (1996) identified two views of adolescence in circulation, "storm and stress," and theories of youth as subculture. "Storm and stress" portrayed white heterosexual youth as "normally abnormal," passing through stages ending in (hetero)sexually responsible adulthood. Gay teenagers, on the other hand, "were treated as a subculture anxiously linked both to heterosexual peers and to adult homosexuals" (37) who would enter a distinct adult subculture. Although Patton's distinction suggests differing narrative means and ends for queer and straight youth, their positions have become intertwined as adults have sought to create a sort of "normal abnormality" for queer youth development.

After a protracted silence on the part of those who would advocate for rather than pathologize queer youth, researchers, educators, and youth development workers began to speak of their plight. The prevailing image invoked was the suffering, isolated, and suicidal young person who was ostracized by society. The 1989 U.S. Department of Health and Human Services' *Report of the Secretary's Task Force on Youth Suicide,* which reported that gay and lesbian youth commit some 30 percent of teen suicides, served as the cornerstone of this discursive incitement. Queer youth suicide became a refrain, such that article after article, essay after essay, and report after report portrayed youth as at risk through statistics on queer youth suicide, drug and alcohol abuse, sexually transmitted diseases, homelessness, dropping out, depression, verbal and physical assaults, and so on (e.g., Edwards 1997; Harris 1997; Jennings 1999; Khayatt 1994; O'Conor 1995; Sedgwick 1993; Uribe 1994; Uribe and Harbeck 1991). Even with cautions such as Harbeck's (1995), that "With this extreme and sole focus on teen suicide we may be trading one negative stereotype for another" (127), writers have persisted in using these statistics and narratives of victimization to justify specific counseling services, youth programs, and calls for educational equity through arguments that harassed gay and lesbian students are denied equal access to opportunities to learn.[4]

The discourse of risk and stigma attached itself to the identification of specific problems gay youth face in achieving positive developmental outcomes. Advocates drew on universal narratives that elaborate all teenagers' needs to accomplish "certain developmental tasks" (Uribe, 1994, 168), such as establishing a stable identity, building self-esteem, adapting to an adult sexual role, separating from family, and forming peer relationships (Peters 1997, 53; Uribe 1994, 168). Queer youth were said to share in these "tasks," but with a twist, due to the difficulties of "adjustment to a socially stigmatized role in isolation without adequate, honest information about themselves or others who are like them" (Uribe and Harbeck 1991, 13). By this logic, gay and lesbian youth can partake of the "normal abnormality" of their heterosexual peers, separating, relating, and forming unitary identities, except that they have special subcultural needs for information and community.

These subcultural needs, which reiterate dominant gay and lesbian narratives of community development, have become foundational to social scientific narratives of queer youth. For example, Gilbert Herdt's (1989) anthropological narrative of gay adolescence is predicated on subcultural experiences associated with coming out, which he likens to "a rite of passage" (21) similar to those of "tribal initiates" among "traditional peoples" (21). Coming out is structured like a life crisis event, which follows a pattern of separation from society as a whole, isolation in a "liminal" period, and "assimilation" back into society (21). This transition is accompanied by rituals "to adjust people's behavior to new and appropriate rights and duties, knowledge and identities, as these refashion social relationships with others" (21). Yet much of this narrative passage is distinguished by negative feelings and isolation, as queer youth do not come out into a clearly defined space "in which they can move and be recognized as esteemed social actors" (22). However, Herdt offers a narrative of post-Stonewall progress in the form of increasingly accessible media, self-help groups, and gay and lesbian cultures that offer queer youth resources.

Two influential gay identity development models, those of Vivienne Cass (1984) and Richard Troiden (1989), reiterate narratives of isolation and community. Cass introduces her model as part of a movement of research "away from the earlier emphasis on etiology, treatment programs, and psychological adjustment, to focus instead on the homosexual situation as experienced by homosexuals themselves" (143). She outlines six stages in the acquisition of a homosexual identity, each needing resolution before movement to the next: *identity confusion* (perceptions that one's behaviors may be homosexual, feelings of shame and/or lowered self-esteem); *identity comparison* (feelings of difference and alienation as one says, "I may be homosexual"); *identity tolerance* (increasing commitment to a homosexual self-image and seeking company of homosexuals); *identity acceptance* (increasing contact with homosexual subculture and selective disclosure to others); *identity pride* (anger at heterosexuals and loyalty to homosexuals as a group); *identity synthesis* (a balance in which homosexuality is one aspect of one's sense of self as one integrates public and private identity) (147–153).

Troiden's four-stage model of homosexual identity formation bears a striking resemblance to Cass'. As he introduces his model, Troiden is careful to point to historical and sociocultural variations, to disavow step-by-step linearity, and to clarify that his is an "ideal type" based on how "committed homosexuals" recall having constructed their homosexual identities. His stages include childhood *sensitization* (feelings of difference from same-sex peers, particularly in terms of gender norms); adolescent *identity confusion* (similar to Cass', and exacerbated by stigma and inaccurate knowledge about homosexuals); *identity assumption* (coming to define the self as homosexual and to present oneself as such to other homosexuals, a process aided by positive contacts with homosexuals); and *commitment* (adopting homosexuality as a way of life, marked by self-acceptance of homosexual identity and role). Troiden contends that "homosexual identity is emergent: never fully determined in a fixed or absolute sense, but always subject to modification and further change" (68). Nonetheless, his model fixes differences and experiences, problems and solutions. Cast as a narrative, Troiden tells a story that opens with experiences of (gender) difference and stigma, moves to a middle of needing knowledge and contact with like others, and ends with a narrative resolution and *commitment* to an intelligible identity and role.[5] Based as they are on adult recollections, these models resonate with Gordon's theorization of queer adult narratives of adolescence, both in their movement from stigma to pride and from isolation to community. But is this a natural narrative order or one that has become naturalized?

Probyn (1996) has written of childhood as "at once the most personal of possessions and the most public of concerns" (98), increasingly central to inquiry in such fields as psychology, political theory, psychiatry, and psychoanalysis. Similar to Gordon, she points to individual narratives, in which "childhood is a staple of the coming-out story, a point at which many recollect the realization of their queerness. Individual and common, story after story recounts the feeling of somehow not belonging, of not fitting in, until the move is made to belong to another community and another kind of family" (98–99). Yet she questions this search for an intelligible narrative progression from child to adolescent to adult, suggesting an ideology of a search for origins underlying popular and social scientific discourse alike. For example, Probyn notes that "the 'folk beliefs' about gender and sexuality that are quantified in psychological research reappear as key narrative elements through which gay and lesbian identity is recited" (108). Indeed, in interviews with adult lesbians about their childhood play with Barbie, Erica Rand's (1995) participants constructed autobiographical narratives that depicted "political coming-to-consciousness tales or narratives of identity formation" (7). What she calls these "dyke destiny stories" (105) narrated "a sequential progression from gender outlaw at the Barbie age to sexual outlaw sometime later" (106). In other words, narratives sought causality for sexuality according to tropes of gender inversion (Sedgwick 1990). Rand notes that femme stories were obscured, as their gender conformity did not inform later sexual deviance or offer a narrative of resistance to Barbie norms. This closeting of "straight" stories, in which the past does not stand as answer to the present, suggests an intertwining of "dominant ideologies, narratives, and narrative styles" (Rand 1995, 130) that reiterates early searches for a cause or signs of (homo)sexuality and fixes queerness as intelligible. In this sense, narrative is productive in that it seems to imitate life as it actually shapes ideas of what life is.

At first glance, it appears that antihomophobic and emancipatory personal and social scientific narratives function as counterdiscourses to pathologizing knowledges that identify the subject for purposes of control. Yet these narratives are complicit with the regulation of sexuality by drawing on the terms of a dominant discourse that searches for causality and intelligibility. For example, *But I'm A Cheerleader* appears to undermine the search for causality as it satirizes True Directions' rehabilitative step of "Rediscovering Your Gender Identity," particularly since the protagonist is conventionally "feminine" (a cheerleader). Yet, the film upholds ideologies of gender inversion in its depiction of the boys' horror at the prospect of watching football games and their incompetence repairing cars. And the intelligibility True Directions seeks in its first step, "Admitting You're a Homosexual," leads to a deviation from the program's steps to alternative steps that look very much like those of Cass and Troiden's post-Stonewall identity development models, as Megan assumes a "committed" homosexual identity. The film, like other narratives, casts "the recognition of identity as the victorious product of a struggle with the self" (Roof 1996, xxxv). Intelligibility, rewritten as affirming, is the happy narrative end, even as the premises of intelligibility remain unquestioned. What does the emphasis in these converging narratives on the production of the "out" and "committed" queer subject mean for understandings of the lives of queer youth in and out of schools and for interventions adults would design for them?

Intelligible and Unintelligible Ends

Although risk and danger continue to be the prevailing discourses invoked to justify interventions on behalf of queer youth, the out and resistant youth exists as an invisible, unnamed figure, a goal to be reached. In a review of empirical studies on gay youth in England during the 1980s, Plummer (1989) named four mechanisms that sustain heteronormativity: the hidden curriculum, the absence of lesbian and gay role models, the organization of peer relations around heterosexuality, and overt homophobia (202). Yet Plummer pointed out that "gay youth do not passively accept this suffering and condemnation, but instead make very active paths to construct a gay identity, to enter a gay world, to work for acceptance, and even challenge the heterosexual assumption" (209). He offered as examples of youth agency, coming out to family members, telling select peers, and involvement in gay youth organizations and clubs—all consonant with the logic of gay and lesbian cultural politics. I do not wish to argue that access to resources in gay and lesbian communities or coming out are negative. Certainly, both have been and continue to be significant and enabling to many. And, as resources, they are always open to new uses. But might such a list of enabling activities, one that resonates neatly with individual and social scientific narratives of development, limit our understandings of queer youth? Does research look for queer youth agency on terms defined by adult understandings? And do the interventions adults would design encourage a repetition of the logic of coming out, or gaining voice and visibility, that has defined gay and lesbian cultural politics? My concern is that narratives of empowerment, haunted by their opposite of isolation, pain, and risk, may impose certain subject positions and forms of intelligibility on queer youth and exclude those who do not conform to their logic.

Assumptions based on a prevailing narrative that individual and collective outness entail progress do not inquire into the meanings of outness for all queer youth. As Epstein, O'Flynn, and Telford (2000–2001) caution, without understanding "which bits of their queer identity are privileged in their outness, the consequences of being 'out' for their own identities and the identities of others, and the limitations of being 'out' as well as the 'freedoms' it brings, it is difficult to reify 'outness' as desirable for young queer students. Possibly, all it achieves is a perpetuation of the same-other binary" (151). It may also reify, or fix, resistance as possible only through a fixing of self.

I do not intend to dismiss the accomplishments of advocates for queer youth and youth themselves in disrupting silencing, harassment, and homophobic practices in public schools or through community-building outside of schools, including safe schools initiatives in Massachusetts and Washington, the national proliferation of Gay-Straight Alliances, the Harvey Milk School or Project 10, non-profit youth centers such as YouthPride, or organizations such as the Gay, Lesbian Straight Educators Network. In a conservative political context, these projects constitute an important angle from which to open dialogue and create resources. Yet the common sense of the narratives on which this angle is based appears to leave other narratives and approaches uninvestigated.

Present projects involving youth take part in the mainstreaming of dominant gay politics over the past decade, which has involved a turn away from a politics of freedom and social change and toward inclusion, rights, and legitimation (D'Emilio and Freedman 1997; Vaid, 1995). Although these need not be incompatible goals, legitimation has depended on visibility of a normalized gay person in order to work for mainstream integration. The intelligibility of queer youth has constituted one tactic in the search for inclusion, one that may be both productive and counterproductive, offering youth resources while simultaneously ceding potential for cultural transformation by circumscribing queer youth identities and practices.

As part of a narrative of progress, mainstream politics' logic of visibility defines school interventions in terms of encouraging teachers to come out (as part of the role model discourse), offering positive curricular representations of gays and lesbians, and supporting the development of GSAs. These practices of inclusion speak a language policy can understand and follow a narrative structure that gay and lesbian politics can understand: representational visibility through teachers' bodies and accurate curricular images will move students from ignorance to knowledge, which will lead to tolerance of queer youth and enhanced self-esteem for queer youth. And, not surprisingly, this logic dovetails neatly with narratives of gay identity development, in which young people need information and contact with like others to achieve their natural developmental trajectories of identity pride, synthesis, and commitment. In fact, this representational logic allows young people to identify with and insert themselves into individual narratives. Roof (1996) points out, "In Horatio Alger fashion the role model is testimony to the ability of an oppressed minority character to occupy the position of protagonist in the victory narrative; his or her very presence is proof that the story can belong to anyone" (151). For both "target" audiences (straight and gay), knowledge and intelligibility are at stake. Yet there is no promise that visibility will not continue to function within the logic that produces heterosexuality and homosexuality as identities rather than calling attention to and challenging the power relations through which identities are produced. Indeed, visibility often "leads to identity rather than to any deconstructive consciousness of the category *gay*" (Roof 1996, 146).

It is possible to put resources, role models, curricular representations, or safe spaces to creative uses. However, educators and youth workers should not unequivocally support these changes as solutions or even necessary steps to "progress." While these resources may be enabling for some, even many, I am concerned that their means and ends are based on singular narratives that repeat dominant narratives and exclude others. Even as adults ostensibly seek to cultivate the creativity of queer youth, seemingly natural narratives with happy endings create a structuring of possibilities, in which "the exercise of power consists in guiding the possibility of conduct and putting in order the possible outcome" (Foucault 1982, 221). These regulating narratives of queer youth contribute to constructing what Foucault (1982) referred to broadly as "government," which is less about political structures or the state than it is about the ways subjects act "freely" within a field of possibilities that orients them toward appropriate paths.

These paths appear in *Cheerleader* as Megan, to return to Herdt's (1989) anthropological formulation, adjusts her "behavior to new and appropriate rights and duties, knowledge and identities, as these refashion social relationships" (21). Her adjustment can be understood through Foucault's (1982) project of "creat[ing] a history of the different modes by which, in our culture, human beings are made subjects" (208). His three modes of objectification point to the place in which narratives of queer adolescence have gotten stuck. The first is objectification, or "the modes of inquiry which try to give themselves the status of sciences" (208) as they turn subjects into objects of inquiry. The second is "dividing practices," in which subjects are categorized, divided from others: the sane and the insane, the heterosexual and the homosexual. And the third is "the way a human being turns him- or herself into a subject. For example, . . . how men have learned to recognize themselves as subjects of sexuality" (208). Dominant antihomophobic narratives have mistaken their emancipatory uses of the first two practices as means of progress. They use reverse discourses to depathologize queerness but not to challenge the premises underlying the production of queer as an identity. The third, subjectification, then, logically turns to intelligibility as a means of crafting self as subject in positive rather than negative terms, as in the fulfillment of Megan's roles. But if we attend closely to Foucault's ideas of "technologies of the self," or the practices, discourses, and techniques through which individuals construct the self, we would emphasize the cultivation of freedoms and forms of relation over truths and knowledges. Foucault (1989b) sought to cultivate an art rather than a science of life, and stressed the creation of new relationships to self and other: "Another thing to distrust is the tendency to relate the question of homosexuality to the problem of 'Who am I?' and 'What is the secret of my desire?' Perhaps it would be better to ask oneself, 'What relations, through homosexuality, can be established, invented, multiplied and modulated?'" (1989a, 308). If adults were to shift their attention from intelligibility and toward a Foucauldian ethics of the self, research about youth and adult-youth relations might look different.

Rather than containing youth in adult narratives, how might we avoid repeating identities? How can we encourage practices that do not depend on the intelligibility that dominant (adult) narratives presume to be necessary? How might adults come to see the identities we and youth adopt as creative rather than as evolving copies? Of course we must acknowledge the power of adults and institutions to define needs and solutions while denying the ways youth themselves may be creating cultures or identities. And of course adults must listen carefully to and learn from queer youth as we seek to work with them, questioning our overt and implicit agendas for young people in order to respond to them in the present. Yet there is a more urgent need for adults to queer our relations with young people. This will mean taking on and living out different narratives. As we do so, we might remember that queer can mark individual and collective identity even as it questions the grounds of that identity by crafting "relationships of differentiation, of creation, of innovation" (Foucault 1989b, 385).

Susanne Luhmann (1998) has theorized a queer pedagogy that "interferes with the repetition of both heterosexual and lesbian/gay normalization" (141). She argues that rather than teaching identities and intelligible subjects, adults should consider relations with young people and pedagogical forms that "resist the desire for authority and stable knowledge" (147). Such a pedagogy is consonant with a queer narrative that does not depend on its subject matter for its queerness. A queer narrative acts through its own relation to narrative itself, complicating and questioning narrative's productive ends of identity and knowledge. A loss of narrative mastery—ceasing to produce intelligible subjects—could shift our emphasis in relations with young people "from the satisfying end to a more indeterminate middle" (Roof 1996, 129). This queer narrative would understand that the end, too, is indeterminate. A narrative that defies intelligibility is consonant with Foucault's (1989a) call for inventiveness in relation to coming out: "We must make the intelligible appear against a backdrop of emptiness, and deny its necessity. We must think that what exists is far from filling all possible spaces" (312).

Part of that queer narrative entails letting go of a narrative of adolescent-becoming and adult-being that situates the present as accomplished fact rather than as part of continual processes of becoming. This queering implicates adults' relations to self and to young people. Rather than mastering the past of adolescence as a ground for, cause of, or answer to the present or future of adulthood, if we consider both youth and adulthood as contingencies and relations, we might see them and development in general as pertaining to the realm of possibilities rather than to the realm of truth (Probyn 1996). Roof (1996) suggests that such queering could be attained through practices of "countermemory" where myths of origin and causality are replaced by the elaboration of detail such that standard ideologies "are exploded from within, overfull of the detail that prevents easy ideological reassimilation" (178). A narrative queering of a straight line from past to present acknowledges desires to understand a past, present, and future, but also acknowledges desires for creativity and for being different from what we are.

Notes

1. My reading of *But I'm a Cheerleader* is admittedly partial to imagining an audience that takes pleasure in the truth of sexuality. A queer reading of the film might construe many of its elements—gender, sexuality, "gay is good," and heteronormativity—as equally hyperbolic, and thus as parodies of struggles over "truth." My thanks to Mary Louise Rasmussen for pressing me to think about this point.
2. Portions of this section are reprinted by permission from *Theory into Practice* 43, no. 2 (spring 2004). Copyright 2004 by the Ohio State University College of Education.
3. It should be noted that schools are narratively organized by adult regulation of "the development of 'the child' into adulthood in finely divided stages" (Epstein and Johnson 1998, 120) that monitor the gendered and sexed body (for example, through uniforms, dress codes, or rules about who is allowed to wear make-up and when).
4. See especially Macgillivray (2000) on the need to combat antigay violence by "making all people, but especially educators, aware of the horror stories that many GLBTQ students live through" (321). A portion of this and the following paragraph are reprinted by permission from *Theory into Practice* 43, no. 2 (spring 2004). Copyright 2004 by the Ohio State University College of Education.
5. The preceding portion of this paragraph is reprinted by permission from Susan Talburt, "Construction of LGBT Youth: Opening Up Subject Positions," *Theory into Practice* 43, no. 2 (spring 2004). Copyright 2004 by the College of Education, The Ohio State University. All rights reserved.

References

Ayman-Nolley, Saba, and Lora L. Taira. 2000. "Obsession with the Dark Side of Adolescence: A Decade of Psychological Studies." *Journal of Youth Studies* 3, no. 1: 35–48.

Barry, Richard. 2000. "Sheltered 'Children': The Self-creation of a Safe Space by Gay, Lesbian, and Bisexual Students." Pp. 84–99 in *Construction Sites: Excavating Race, Class, and Gender among Urban Youth*, ed. Lois Weis and Michelle Fine. New York: Teachers College Press.

Cass, Vivienne C. 1984. "Homosexual Identity Formation: Testing a Theoretical Model." *The Journal of Sex Research* 20, no. 2: 143–167.

D'Emilio, John, and Estelle B. Freedman. 1997. *Intimate Matters: A History of Sexuality in America*. 2nd ed. Chicago: University of Chicago Press.

Edwards, Ann T. 1997. "Let's Stop Ignoring Our Gay and Lesbian Youth." *Educational Leadership* 54, no. 7: 68–70.

Epstein, Debbie, and Richard Johnson. 1998. *Schooling Sexualities*. Buckingham, UK: Open University Press.

Epstein, Debbie, Sarah O'Flynn, and David Telford. 2000–2001. "'Othering' Education: Sexualities, Silences, and Schooling." *Review of Research in Education* 25: 127–179.

Foucault, Michel. 1982. "The Subject and Power." Pp. 208–226 in *Michel Foucault: Beyond Structuralism and Hermeneutics*, ed. Hubert L. Dreyfus and Paul Rabinow. Chicago: University of Chicago Press.

———. 1989a. "Friendship as a Way of Life." Pp. 308–312 in *Foucault Live: Interviews 1961–1984*, ed. Sylvere Lotringer and trans. John Johnston. New York: Semiotext(e).

———. 1989b. "Sex, Power, and the Politics of Identity." In *Foucault Live: Interviews 1961–1984*, ed. Sylvere Lotringer and trans. Lysa Hochruth and John Johnston. New York: Semiotext(e).

Gordon, Angus. 1999. "Turning Back: Adolescence, Narrative, and Queer Theory." *Gay and Lesbian Quarterly* 5, no. 1: 1–24.

Harbeck, Karen M. 1995. "Addressing the Needs of Lesbian, Gay, and Bisexual Youth and Their Advocates." Pp. 125–133 in *The Gay Teen: Educational Practice and Theory for Lesbian, Gay, and Bisexual Adolescents*, ed. Gerald Unks. New York: Routledge.

Harris, Mary B., ed. 1997. *School Experiences of Gay and Lesbian Youth: The Invisible Minority*. New York: The Harrington Park Press.

Haver, William. 1998. "Of Mad Men Who Practice Invention to the Brink of Intelligibility." Pp. 349–364 in *Queer Theory in Education*, ed. William F. Pinar. Mahwah, NJ: Lawrence Erlbaum.

Herdt, Gilbert. 1989. "Introduction: Gay and Lesbian Youth, Emergent Identities, and Cultural Scenes at Home and Abroad." *Journal of Homosexuality* 17, nos. 1–2: 1–42.

Irvine, Janice M. 1997. "One Generation Post-Stonewall: Political Contests over Lesbian and Gay School Reform." Pp. 572–588 in *A Queer World*:

The Center for Lesbian and Gay Studies Reader, ed. Martin Duberman. New York: New York University Press.

Jennings, Kevin. 1999. "Silence Is the Voice of Complicity: Addressing Homophobia in Schools." *Independent School* 58, no. 2: 54–59.

Khayatt, Didi. 1994. "Surviving School as a Lesbian Student." *Gender and Education* 6, no. 1: 47–61.

Lesko, Nancy. 2001. *Act Your Age! A Cultural Construction of Adolescence*. New York: Routledge.

Luhmann, Susanne. 1998. "Queering/Querying Pedagogy? Or, Pedagogy Is a Pretty Queer Thing." Pp. 141–155 in *Queer Theory in Education*, ed. William F. Pinar. Mahwah, NJ: Lawrence Erlbaum.

Macgillivray, Ian K. 2000. "Educational Equity for Gay, Lesbian, Bisexual, Transgendered, and Queer/Questioning Students: The Demands of Democracy and Social Justice for America's Schools." *Education and Urban Society* 32, no. 3: 303–323.

O'Conor, Andi. 1995. "Breaking the Silence: Writing about Gay, Lesbian, and Bisexual Teenagers." Pp. 13–15 in *The Gay Teen: Educational Practice and Theory for Lesbian, Gay, and Bisexual Adolescents*, ed. Gerald Unks. New York: Routledge.

Patton, Cindy. 1996. *Fatal Advice: How Safe-Sex Education Went Wrong*. Durham: Duke University Press.

Peters, Andrew J. 1997. "Themes in Group Work with Lesbian and Gay Adolescents." *Social Work with Groups* 20, no. 2: 51–69

Plummer, Ken. 1989. "Lesbian and Gay Youth in England." *Journal of Homosexuality* 17, nos. 3–4: 195–223.

Probyn, Elspeth. 1996. *Outside Belongings*. New York and London: Routledge.

Rand, Erica. 1995. *Barbie's Queer Accessories*. Durham and London: Duke University Press.

Rofes, Eric. 1989. "Opening up the Classroom Closet: Responding to the Educational Needs of Gay and Lesbian Youth." *Harvard Educational Review* 59, no. 4: 444–453.

Roof, Judith. 1996. *Come As You Are: Sexuality and Narrative*. New York: Columbia University Press.

Ross, Dorothy. 1972. *G. Stanley Hall: The Psychologist as Prophet*. Chicago: The University of Chicago Press.

Sedgwick, Eve Kosofsky. 1990. *Epistemology of the Closet*. Berkeley: University of California Press.

———. 1993. *Tendencies*. Durham: Duke University Press.

Silin, Jonathan G. 1995. *Sex, Death, and the Education of Children: Our Passion for Ignorance in the Age of AIDS*. New York: Teachers College Press.

Snider, Kathryn. 1996. "Race and Sexual Orientation: The (Im)possibility of These Intersections in Educational Policy." *Harvard Educational Review* 66, no. 2: 294–302.

Talburt, Susan. 2004. "Constructions of LGBT Youth: Opening up Subject Positions," *Theory into Practice* 43, no. 2: 116–121.

Troiden, Richard R. 1989. "The Formation of Homosexual Identities." *Journal of Homosexuality* 17, nos. 1–2: 43–73.

Uribe, Virginia. 1994. "The Silent Minority: Rethinking Our Commitment to Gay and Lesbian Youth." *Theory into Practice* 33 (3): 167–172.

Uribe, Virginia, and Karen M. Harbeck. 1991. "Addressing the Needs of Lesbian, Gay, and Bisexual Youth: The Origins of Project 10 and School-based Intervention." *Journal of Homosexuality* 22, nos. 3–4: 9–28.

Vaid, Urvashi. 1995. *Virtual Equality.* New York: Anchor Books.

Weeks, Jeffrey. 1999. "Myths and Fictions in Modern Sexualities." Pp. 11–24 in *A Dangerous Knowing: Sexuality, Pedagogy, and Popular Culture*, ed. Debbie Epstein and James T. Sears. London: Cassell.

C h a p t e r   T w o

Martyr-Target-Victim

Interrogating Narratives of Persecution and Suffering among Queer Youth

Eric Rofes

Are We Truly All Matthew Shepard?

This chapter offers a critical look at teaching—my teaching. It traces some of the valuable lessons I've learned during the first three years of designing, preparing, and teaching a new course in a new field. It also captures a dramatic shift in my thinking about lesbian, gay, bisexual, and transgender (LGBT) youth, teachers, and parents, and the appearance of a series of new questions that have emerged for me through the teaching of this course.

This chapter explores the sociopolitical dynamics involved in the mass production of contemporary images of LGBT youth in the United States that depict these youth as at-risk for a range of behaviors and diseases. After situating the images, narratives, and representations of queer youth as emerging from an attempt to develop a unit on queer youth within a larger course on LGBT issues in K-12 schools, the chapter focuses on a reading of a key text used in the class that presents a narrow portrait of LGBT youth and their relationships to schools. The chapter then examines what is centered in this text—which typifies most of the books, videotapes, and popular movies focused on queer youth—and what is decentered, marginalized, or vanished. The author argues that the dominant image emerging of LGBT youth characterizes them narrowly in a "Martyr-Target-Victim" model.

The chapter then puts forward a problematic case study from the third year of teaching this class, in which a paper was assigned to students intended to probe the possible role of agency in the production of students' gender and sexual identities. One of the key elements emerging from this case study was the insistence by students—especially students identified as "lesbian," "gay," or "queer—that agency played absolutely no role in the development of their gender and sexual identities ("I was born this way"), and that, by giving the assignment and probing the issue of agency, the instructor was "blaming" students for persecution they had suffered. What emerges from this case study is the realization that "Martyr-Target-Victim" narrative may be central to the ways in which some queer students see themselves (and are asked to see themselves), and may serve to intensify the contemporary cultural drive to understand sexual orientation and gender identity as caused by biology or genetics.

Finally, this chapter raises a number of issues related to ramifications of the ways in which LGBT youth are depicted in the public sphere, including the relationship such images might have to the broader historic pathologizing of homosexuality in the United States; ways in which race, socioeconomic class, and urbanicity may be tied to such images; and the link between the funding of services for adolescents (including LGBT adolescents) and pathology.

A few recent incidents may be useful to the framing of this chapter:

- I recently attended a workshop for local educators focused on making schools safe for LGBT youth. The teacher leading the session identified herself as heterosexual during the opening introductions, and began the program by announcing: "Let me make it perfectly clear why we are all here today." Then, assuming a tone of voice escalating with dramatic passion, she read a list of "statistics" about LGBT youth that focused on their risk for depression and suicide, substance abuse, alcoholism, dropping out of school, tobacco use, homelessness, and HIV infection.

- The mailbox at my home is regularly filled with solicitations from various organizations working to advance LGBT rights and services for people with HIV/AIDS. During one recent month, I received 27 letters from a range of local and national organizations. Seven of these letters utilized the "plight" of queer youth as a trope to motivate the reader to send money—and four of these groups were not explicitly youth-focused programs. The youth depicted in these solicitations struggled alternately with bullying, suicide, HIV/AIDS, antigay violence, and homelessness.

- At a meeting of national leaders of LGBT organizations, two of the directors of groups serving queer youth organized a presentation that began with a powerful attack on *Queer as Folk*, the Showtime series focused on gay men in their teens and 20s living in Pittsburgh, Pennsylvania. The leaders derided the producers and writers of the show for the "awful" image they put forward of young gay men because the show features gay youth involved in the club scene, drug use, and sexual promiscuity. They argued that the show did not offer proper "role models" for queer youth, and instead put forward a portrait that depicted them as sex-obsessed, reckless, and defiant. They then went on to offer their thumbnail portraits of LGBT youth, focusing on "good kids" who are "victims of discrimination, persecution, and abuse by students, teachers, and parents."
- As I was completing work on an early draft of this chapter, the American public was treated to not one, but two major television spectacles focused on the death of Matthew Shepard, the Laramie, Wyoming, gay male youth who had been tied to a fence post in a remote area and killed by antigay toughs just three years earlier. Three different nongay students I teach in an elementary education credential program sent me emails about these highly publicized television dramas. One stated, "'This helped me understand what it must be like to be a gay teenager.'"

This final anecdote reminds me of what a lesbian student said in a class on contemporary education issues that I taught the year of Shepard's murder. During a discussion exploring the question of whether the perpetrators of the crime and the citizens of Laramie, Wyoming, were typical of people throughout the United States and whether what happened in Laramie could happen in our college town, one of my most articulate students spoke up. A leader in the university's LGBT student group and a person with a flare for the dramatic, Nina turned the question around and asked whether Matthew Shepard and the choices he made that evening were similar to or different from those that she—and other queer students—would make. She argued that actions such as hanging out in a small-town bar and taking a ride with strangers whose sexual identities were unknown were not unusual or foolish choices. As my students debated this matter, it became clear that Nina deeply identified with this tragic incident. At one point she banged her fist on her desk and insisted, "What he did, I have done. What he did, all queer youth have done. He was not stupid. He was not naïve. He was not unusual. We are all Matthew Shepard!"

This incident stuck in my memory because it was the moment I realized that one of the reasons Shepard's tragedy may have elicited such powerful emotions from many of my LGBT students is that, not only might they identify with his predicament, isolation, and vulnerability, but they might also identify with his martyrdom.

Teaching Queer Issues in an Education Department

This chapter focuses on a course I've taught three times during the past six years and the ways my thinking, teaching, and analysis concerning LGBT issues in schools has shifted, in large part due to feedback—often passionate or angry feedback—from my students, the influence of my deepening immersion in social theory, and conversations with colleagues. It captures changes in the ways in which I understand identity, community, and sexuality, and changes in my political perspective concerning popularized narratives of queer youth.

This course emerged out of my experience as a graduate student at UC Berkeley's Graduate School of Education in the late 1990s. I was enrolled in a small program titled "Social and Cultural Studies," which offered a radical critique of the institution of schooling and examined education and culture in deep and critical ways. The program's faculty had done a great deal of work on issues of race, ethnicity, and socioeconomic class and offered courses to undergraduates and graduate students focused in these areas. At the time I was admitted, I was told that they were looking to expand their work on issues related to gender and sexuality. Because of my work as an openly gay teacher and a community organizer on LGBT issues in schools, I was invited to develop a course titled "Experiencing Education: Gay and Lesbian Issues in Schools."

With the support of the faculty in my program, I taught this one-semester course for two years at Berkeley, attracting 28 students during the first year and 46 students during the second year. Most of the students were undergraduates, though a few graduate students were enrolled as well. When I was hired to teach at Humboldt State University (HSU), just south of the Oregon border and 300 miles north of the San Francisco Bay Area, I indicated my interest in teaching this course at my new university, and my department chair and dean both expressed support. I have managed to teach the course three times during my first five years at HSU, attracting 23, 25, and 42 students, this time a mix of undergraduates, credential candidates, and graduate students.

My experience developing the course has brought me surprising satisfaction and also surprising challenges. Perhaps my greatest satisfaction has involved the significant numbers of students who have enrolled in the course each time it has been offered and the overall enthusiasm of most of my students for the topics upon which we focused. I wondered initially whether the topic of gay issues and schooling was so specialized that I would be leading a small seminar of perhaps 8–12 students. I've always surveyed the students on the first day to learn their reasons for signing up for the class. While many simply need an extra three-unit course in their schedule or found the topic mildly interesting, I've been happy to find several students who had hungered for a deep immersion in this topic. One Ph.D. student and several M.A. students hoped to focus their dissertations or theses on gay issues in schools and found that the university's other educational offerings provided scant opportunity to learn about this field. Several students have attended because they had relatives—including parents—who were gay or lesbian and they felt this course might assist them in learning more about their relatives' experiences. Finally, many LGBT students took the course hoping to grapple with issues they had faced when they were in K-12 schools or issues that might confront them as they become schoolteachers.

Another satisfaction I found in the course involved the large numbers of heterosexually identified students who enrolled. While I have never surveyed my class formally concerning their sexual orientations, by the end of the course students have often shared their experiences and social location in explicit ways. I hadn't anticipated the large number of heterosexuals in the course and hence beefed up the readings and course work focused on the topic of "heterosexual allies."

During the pilot years of this course, I've also faced some surprising challenges. Perhaps the greatest challenges have been in three specific areas: (1) identifying texts and videotapes that discuss LGBT teachers, students, and parents in a broad, thoughtful, and critical manner; (2) developing teaching techniques that elicit a broad range of opinions from the students (because many are nervous about being considered homophobic, they often do not express their candid views at the full-class level); (3) addressing students' limited ways of thinking about sexual- and gender-identity development and the limited historical information they have about LGBT organizing and social formations.

This chapter focuses most intensely on point #1 and also a bit on point #3. I am currently preparing a paper on point #2, focused on what I've learned as a teacher that allows me to welcome into the classroom a broader range of perspectives than those the students derisively call "politically correct."

The Martyr-Target-Victim Construct

When I began teaching the course, I was excited to have the opportunity to utilize several new books focused on LGBT issues in schools. While some of these texts were scholarly and others journalistic, I felt privileged to have the opportunity to immerse myself and my students in what felt like a new, burgeoning field that had much to teach us about education, democracy, and social justice. My enthusiasm for the topics that we'd cover—ranging from teachers coming out at school to HIV education for gay youth to homophobia in girls' sports to children's books for the kids of LGBT parents—made my review of the literature an enjoyable experience. I spent a few weeks perusing materials, placing orders for books and videos, and preparing my syllabus.

I heard the first critical comment about the course materials during the sixth week, after I had shown a videotape on LGBT youth. This was the third videotape we'd seen, and, at the precise moment when the video focused upon a statement like "Lesbian and gay youth are three times more likely to commit suicide than their heterosexual counterparts," one of my students let out a snicker of sorts and I noted some tension in the room. I thought little of this, beyond noting it as something to discuss after the videotape was finished.

When I questioned the young man who snickered during the discussion, I got an earful. The snickering student raised a question to me, and to the entire class, about the function of the issue of suicide among queer youth. He argued that he was not convinced that this much-repeated statistic was accurate and that—as a young gay man—he felt insulted by its linkage to queer youth. I recall him insisting that he felt it was "homophobic" to characterize queer youth in this way. As the instructor who is simultaneously a gay activist, I recall feeling defensive but also trying to counter his arguments and address his concerns. I defended my use of the materials in the course.

This began an ongoing discussion of the use of the trope of "suicidal gay youth" that threaded throughout the course during the remainder of the semester. Students—including queer students—were not of one mind on this matter and we had much lively discussion about whether it was possible to identify an alternative framework from which to discuss queer youth (alternative to a pathologizing framework rooted in being seen as at-risk for suicide, drug abuse, and dropping out). The students also debated whether or not the texts and videos we utilized in the class reflected their real lives, or whether the written discourse on queer youth didn't characterize them in narrow and ultimately destructive ways. We had no easy answers.

My thinking was shaken up by this matter and I found myself working in earnest to identify curricular materials that looked at queer youth in schools from multiple perspectives, outside what I'd come to think of as the "Martyr-Target-Victim" syndrome. I wanted materials that took us beyond Matthew Shepard, Brandon Teena, and other LGBT youth who had become martyrs to the cause; texts that understood queer students not only as targets of bullying, sexual harassment, and classroom taunts; videos that captured teenagers as whole human beings, not narrow victims of their parents, teachers, or peers. I wasn't aiming to deny or obscure the role homophobia and heterosexism play in the lives of many LGBT students, but I grew to wonder what it meant that a specific cohort of youth were defined by their victimization. As I spoke with colleagues I came to understand that this was not a predicament faced by LGBT youth alone, but that many adolescent populations were pathologized in narrow ways, especially African American urban youth (Fordham 1996; McDermott 1987; Polite and Davis 1999; Porter 1998). Immersing myself in the literature on adolescents, I came to understand that adolescence itself was a socially constructed stage of life that had itself been branded with characteristics ranging from "self-centered" and "unpredictable" to "risk-taking" and "rebellious" and that this branding process had powerful social, political, and economic underpinnings (Aries 1965; Frankenburg 1992; Kincaid 1998; Luker 1996; Moran 2000). These realizations served to motivate me to find materials that provided a rich portrait of queer youth in schools and that discussed both the challenges and the joys they faced.

This proved difficult. By the end of the semester, one student had used a highlighter to identify the readings and videotapes on my syllabus that she felt captured a nonpathologized vision of LGBT youth: there were three items identified. She rightfully pointed out that the reader that I had spent weeks preparing contained only stories that focused on the persecution of queer youth. "Where is the joy?!!" she wrote on the syllabus before presenting it to me. "Don't these people ever have fun?"

Examining the Text

One of the primary books I utilized with the class that first year was *The Gay Teen: Educational Practice and Theory for Lesbian, Gay, and Bisexual Adolescents,* edited by Gerald Unks (1995). This book appears to be typical of the depictions of queer youth that were featured in the scholarly and journalistic essays in my reader. A superficial review of the text might lead one to think that the book might infuse a useful dose of theory into a course on LGBT issues in schools, and hence not produce a large number of "Martyr-Target-Victim" narratives to which my students might object. Because the book is an edited nonfiction collection from multiple authors, at first glance one might think that the book would offer a diversity of the much-needed perspectives my students talked about.

By utilizing the book and dialoguing with my students, I found myself asking a number of perplexing questions that had not dawned on me earlier and that I am still in the process of answering: What are the politics of narrowly focusing a book titled *The Gay Teen* on homophobia and heterosexism? Is it appropriate to define the experiences of LGBT youth entirely or mainly by their experience with discrimination and persecution? Or is this only part of the picture? Looking at students facing other forms of institutional oppression, I wondered whether a book titled *The Black Teen* should capture its subject primarily through the lens of racism, or whether *The Female Teen* should interpret young women entirely through the lens of sexism? When one places the word "Gay" adjacent to the word "Teen," do we simply take a long history of pathologizing, demonizing, and blaming adolescents (Aries 1965; Moran 2000) and link it up to a parallel history that concentrates on the victimization of homosexuals? What are the politics of placing the problems that a population confronts center-stage in a text that might more suitably capture a rich portrait of the group?

These questions emerge because the essays in the collection collude to present a powerfully tragic portrait of queer youth. While preparing this chapter, I devoted two days to closely reading, reviewing, and coding the texts of all 17 essays in the volume and placing each chapter's overall depiction of queer youth in one of three categories: (1) balanced/ mixed experiences; (2) Martyr-Target-Victim framework; (3) not applicable. Only two chapters were ranked as "balanced / mixed experience," chapters focused on "Black-Gay or Gay-Black?: Choosing Identities and Identifying Choices" (Sears 1995), and "'Gay/Straight' Alliances: Transforming Pain to Pride" (Blumenfeld 1995). Ten chapters were categorized as "Martyr-Target-Victim," and, for five of the essays, this analysis was not applicable. These were primarily theory-focused chapters that did not focus closely on the lives of queer youth.

A brief walk through the text captures some of these problematic dynamics. The opening chapter, by the book's editor, begins the book in a manner that might trigger the anger of some of my students. This essay sees queer youth primarily through their struggles against homophobia. Entitled "Thinking About the Gay Teen," the piece—and the volume—begins:

> Homosexuals are arguably the most hated group of people in the United States. While other minorities have gained a modicum of protection and acceptance, homosexuals remain essentially outside the pale. In their public lives, few Americans any longer use words such as "nigger," "kike," "gook," or "wop." Yet "faggot," "fairy," "homo," and "queer" are used by many without hesitation. Picking on persons because of their ethnicity, class, religion, gender, or race is essentially taboo behavior, but adults and children alike are given license to torment and harm people because of their sexuality. The civil liberties of most minorities are fairly secure; those of homosexuals are tenuous at best, and nonexistent at worst. In spite of mighty gains by other minorities, homosexuals stand alone, outside, despised, and ripe for discrimination. (3)

Putting aside the accuracy and racial politics of these assertions, one might question the objectives motivating the author's use of this opening for a book on LGBT teenagers. The first part of the essay clearly focuses on establishing gay youth as victims, highlighting specific types of persecution experienced by queer youth, the lack of support systems available, and the roles schools play in maintaining heterosexism and homophobia, which are explicated and defined. The essay next focuses on the manifestation of discrimination on the basis of gender and sexual orientation in the culture of high schools. We hear that, "Lacking any significant support system, it is not surprising that the homosexual adolescent may achieve poorly, drop out of school, engage in substance abuse, run away from home, or attempt suicide" (7). Hence the chapter, and the book, begin by building an argument focused on the persecution of queer youth and the toll such victimization takes on these students' health and school achievement.

The author next shifts to a discussion of suicidality and gay youth, beginning the section,

> The occurrence of suicide among adolescent homosexuals is possibly the most widely publicized data about them. That this is the case is perhaps

the cruelest irony in the chronicle of the woes of gay teens. How unfortunate it is that they must make the *ultimate* statement about their condition in order to get a significant cohort of the public to pay attention to them. (7)

The author's uncritical acceptance of much-debated statistics on gay youth and suicide (Remafedi 1994: Savin-Williams 1999) and the linkage of such tragic acts to an intentionality related to the need for public attention are problematic. To his credit, the author then raises questions about the accuracy of these statistics, citing critics' questioning the methodologies behind this research and the focus on pathology rather than strengths:

Perhaps more importantly, this historic emphasis on the psychosocial problems faced by lesbian and gay youth has frequently obscured any systematic consideration of their particular talents. Certainly, most lesbian and gay youth do survive adolescence. They move willfully into adulthood by virtue of an extraordinarily powerful and creative resilience. (8)

Yet rather than move into an exploration of the potential talents of queer youth, their strategies for survival, and their lives outside of the persecution framework, the author returns to a focus on suicide, the need for "gay-friendly" curricula, and the conflicts such curricula might ignite. He finishes the chapter arguing for the "student's right to know" about homosexuality and the obligation of schools to provide "reliable knowledge."

The other chapters in the book include a similar emphasis on the suffering of LGBT students and almost consistently place these youth in the position of victims or, at best, survivors. We learn little about the lives of queer students except for their problems. The chapter that follows this initial piece begins with the suicide mantra, insisting, "One in three [lesbian and gay youth] have reported committing at least one self-destructive act. Nearly half repeatedly attempt suicide." (O'Connor 1995, 13). Chapter four is launched by a focus on the attacks on a gay-positive curriculum in New York City and the "homophobic barrage from a multiethnic chorus, informed with religious zealotry" (Lipkin 1995, 37). Chapter seven, written by this author and titled, "Making Our Schools Safe for Sissies," focuses on the abuse and humiliation experienced by a young gay boy (Rofes 1995). One entire piece focuses on "Gay Teens in Literature," and serves as a tour through the "not-so-covert negative messages" in fiction for gay youth (Brogan 1995).

While there are two chapters that offer a bit of balance to the repeated framing of queer students as victims (one, authored by Jim Sears [1995], focuses on an African American gay male youth whose joy appears to emerge from his Black identity rather than through his gay identity; the other, by Warren Blumenfeld [1995], focuses on the organizing work of gay/straight alliances). The overall framework for the book is clearly locked into the "Martyr-Target-Victim" paradigm.

While *The Gay Teen* was the book I used in my course during its first year, as I surveyed other books focused on LGBT students, hoping to find a much broader portrait, I found similar problems with the focus on a narrative of victimology. I had chosen the Unks text over others because it was specifically focused on schools. Many of the other volumes focused on queer youth only included incidental material focused on schools, and many of these shared Unks' Martyr-Target-Victim focus. Linnea Due's *Joining the Tribe: Growing Up Gay and Lesbian in the '90s* (1995), while offering some of the most astute analyses of homophobia and the shifting experiences of queer youth and occasional moments of joy and levity when the author allowed youth to speak for themselves, remains dominated by an overarching frame focused on the difficulties faced by the teens. In fact, Due makes a compelling argument that the increased presence of gay issues in the public sphere has removed a layer of protective disguise that had previously protected these youth. Likewise in *Children of Horizons* (1993), by Gilbert Herdt and Andrew Boxer, a study of a gay youth program in Chicago, the authors offer a rich and nuanced look at the historical and social context in which queer youth are emerging; at the same time, the book relies upon a traditional narrative of persecution and victimization to explain the youth's motivation for entering a gay community depicted as open and embracing. The books I liked the best focused, unfortunately, on students in another country (Epstein 1994; Epstein and Johnson 1998), or students in one specific region of the country far different from where my students hailed (Sears 1991). Two books that I liked appeared after the first time I taught the course, but seemed designed primarily as handbooks for queer youth coming out, rather than as portraits of young people in their schools (Bass and Kaufman 1996; Pollack and Schwartz 1995).

During my second year of teaching the course, I thought I had broadened my syllabus to include more articles, essays, and newspaper clippings focused on what I considered to be positive aspects of being a queer youth, though I still utilized the original text. Yet I was well aware that some of the materials I thought to be essential to the course included a focus on suicide, HIV risk, and substance abuse among queer youth. It felt appropriate to include some of the risks faced by queer students, but also balance them with some of the positive experiences. When the new cohort of students also was not satisfied with the materials, I asked them to create a list of youth-oriented topics that they'd prefer to see in a course on gay issues in schools. Rather than gripe and complain, I challenged them to suggest features that they felt would create a richer, more textured portrait of queer youth, and one that sounded real to them. I was sincerely interested in learning what more I could add to the mix. Their topics included the following:

- Falling in love
- Romance
- The Ones Who Are Happy
- Fun
- Sex
- Laughter
- Healthy Gay Teens
- Good Things
- Good Students Who Don't Drop Out
- Music
- Dancing
- Art
- People With Supportive Parents
- Normal Queer Youth

At the same time, I still was not fully clear about what my students felt that I needed to add to my syllabus and what source materials or texts might be available.

Student Perspectives on the Origins of Sexual Orientation

Three years ago, when I taught the class for the third time, I was teaching the course at a new school and was aware that the student population was different from the one at my previous university. I had moved from being a graduate student instructor leading the class at an elite public institution (UC Berkeley) to being an assistant professor leading the class at a non-elite public institution (Humboldt State University [HSU] is part of the California State University system). Hence my students were more likely to be the first in their families to attend college and a larger percentage appeared to be from working-class or poor backgrounds. The distinction was also heightened by the fact that a larger portion of my current students were raised in rural parts of the state, as HSU is the sole four-year university servicing six large rural counties in the northwest corner of California. I wondered, with a student population hailing from lower socioeconomic backgrounds and less urban/suburban areas than I'd previously experienced, whether they would experience a course on LGBT issues in schools in a different way?

While I have not noticed a great deal of difference between my students at these two universities, especially in their academic skills, preparation, and knowledge, I did notice that my new students often maintained distinctly different social analyses than my Berkeley students. Part of this I attributed to the different racial and class backgrounds of my students, but I believe part may be linked to the differences between urban cultures and those of isolated rural areas. I thought a great deal about these distinctions when this cohort of students, for the first time, didn't seem to feel that there were significant problems with the "Martyr-Target-Victim" narratives running through the literature and videotapes on queer youth. Had I finally succeeded in diversifying the syllabus successfully? Or did these students hold perspectives distinct from my students in the same class when I taught it at Berkeley?

I'd made at least one other significant change in the course when I began teaching it at HSU. I added an assignment that was intended to grapple with questions related to agency in the construction of students' own gender and sexual identities. Over the past decade, I'd become increasingly convinced by a series of readings (Greenberg 1990; Kitzinger 1988; Scarce 1999; Terry 1999) that what we've come to discuss as the "social construction" of various identities needed to be grounded in people's real lives. It sometimes felt as if the ways in which I discussed gender as performance or sexual identity as fluid resonated only on a theoretical level with my students. When we discussed issues ranging from butch/femme dynamics to the origins of homosexuality to whether lesbian mothers will produce more LGBT children than heterosexual parents, it seemed as if my students maintained a traditional biologized understanding of both gender and sexual identity (Brookey 2002). I was eager to explore this through an assignment.

The second assignment in the course, distributed after seven weeks of classes and significant background reading on these topics, focused on identifying "an experience, incident, moment, or activity during your first 18 years where you believe you may have exhibited a form of agency in the ways in which you enacted your gender or sexual identity." I asked students to consider "times you may have resisted or acceded to expectations by parents, peers, or external sources" and to "choose a moment that suggests the possibility of an active strategic role on the part of children and teens related to the ways in which they create themselves as gendered and sexual beings." The students had three weeks to write a three- to five-page paper on this topic.

I did not find many questions when I first presented the assignment but, the following week, when I touched base with my students about their initial thoughts, I was met with some serious resistance to the assignment. Several students were confused by the assignment and were not sure what I was precisely asking for them to accomplish in the paper. I offered a number of examples of incidents they might create the paper around, ranging from the decision to take a same-sex partner to a junior prom, to the moment a girl decided to try out for the (boys') football team; what students said when their parents first caught them playing with clothing of the other sex to the moment they noticed they were eroticizing a person who was "wrong" for them for some reason; the choice of a boy to wear clothing because it looked "tough" or "masculine," or the moment when a girl decided to quit the field hockey team because it was time to stop being a tomboy. I was attempting to offer a broad range of topics related to conformity and resistance and not privilege one over the other.

After sharing the examples, I was met with one of those teaching moments when a teacher realizes he or she is speaking a language the students do not understand. This required me to take a few minutes to engage in a feedback process with my students about their questions and concerns. It was here that my students' objections were finally expressed.

One gay male student insisted that there was never an element of choice in the creation of his gender or sexual identity. He asked whether I was saying that people "choose to be gay." I attempted to deflect his comments by turning the question back on him. "I was born this way," he insisted firmly. "Ever since I was a small child I was different, and I was persecuted for being different. Why would I choose to be persecuted?"

A heterosexual woman also raised concerns, arguing, "I don't think children even think about these issues at all. They're not aware of terms like 'social construction' and they don't have the ability to consciously decide to act masculine or feminine. They just *are*."

I found myself facing a barrage of concerns, with the majority of the class approaching the assignment in, at best, a dubious manner. A few students who seemed to understand the core of the assignment provided examples from their own lives of ways they thought would be appropriate in fulfilling the assignment. I hoped this would enlighten the others about the intent of the assignment, but the resistance didn't budge. I asked the students to mull over the assignment before our next session and got on with the lesson of the day, but, after class, when I reflected on the discussion, it seemed to me that the assignment itself was less of an issue than my opening up the possibility that gender and sexual identity may include an element of agency. Some of my students seemed to experience this suggestion as unsupportive or undermining. I wanted to learn more about their perspectives here.

When the assignments were turned in two weeks later, I reviewed them eagerly that same evening. Most of my students had identified autobiographical incidents on which to explore the topic. Several students took directly from my examples and wrote about the times they did something that violated the gender norms inculcated by their parents. One woman wrote about climbing a tree in a dress as a young girl. Another wrote about playing sports with the boys. One young man wrote about his high school decision to style himself as a "jock."

A few students wrote very powerful essays about being persecuted because they did not meet expectations for gender performance. One young man who framed his essay with a message to me stating "I am only completing this assignment because I have to in order to get a good grade in this class, but I do not agree with the assumptions behind it," wrote of his painful experiences being bullied in junior high school and his decision to join the tennis team in order to be seen as more acceptably masculine. Another wrote of being mocked by a teacher because he was gentle and lisped, and his determination to alter his speech patterns and gestures in response. One female student wrote about reaching physical maturity at a young age and trying to flatten her chest because of feelings of discomfort with looking like a woman when she was only eleven years old.

When I read the narratives of pain in some of my students' papers, I was seized with mixed feelings about this assignment. What had I done? In an attempt to explore the role of agency, I seemed to have forced my students to dredge up intense memories of suffering from their pasts. Was I naïve in expecting superficial anecdotes with dispassionate analysis? Did the assignment itself read to students as an invitation—or a demand—for deep disclosure? What were the ethical issues involved here and did I owe my students an apology?

When the papers were returned, I gave the students the chance to share them in small groups of three to four students, but I made it clear that students could choose not to share them with their peers. Most read their papers but several did not. I then opened up a discussion about both the assignment and the issue of agency as perhaps implicated in the construction of identities. I took away two key learnings from this discussion and from the experience of giving this particular assignment.

First, most of the students who spoke during the discussion found consideration of agency to be meaningless to them. They found the assignment, to use one man's phrase, "a waste of time." They felt this way because they did not believe this was a meaningful or helpful way to understand the identity formation process of children and adolescents. While some were familiar with social construction theories from their women's studies or queer studies courses, they believed it applied to adults rather than children. They very much believed that biology or genetics were the engines behind who they are today.

Second, they experienced the assignment as an accusation or, in one woman's words, as "blaming the victim." Some of the students argued that by simply opening up the question of agency or choice, they were being told that they were responsible for the pain in their childhood and adolescent lives. When I tried to suggest that their lives were a lot more than pain and that there may have been elements of agency in both the bad times and the good times, these same students were not satisfied. They experienced me as an adult, an academic, whose reality was fully removed from the real worlds they inhabited

This was a very difficult experience for me as a teacher and one about which I continue to ponder. My students at the new university appeared in large part to embrace naturalized explanations for sexual and gender identity and, at the same time, feel greater identification with the "Martyr-Target-Victim" characterization of queer youth than students at my previous university. I wondered how these two might be related and whether the idea that homosexuality might be inborn might be conceptually linked to the narrative of victimization central to cultural discussions of queer youth. I also found myself wondering about the ways in which socioeconomic class and urbanicity affected young people's understandings about gender and sexual identity.

Discussion:
Continuously Rethinking the Course

I remain committed to teaching this course, but continue to confront a series of daunting issues that make the preparation of a syllabus and the design of specific assignments and lessons problematic. Perhaps more important, I've become aware of the ways in which the characterization of LGBT youth as martyrs, targets, and victims may serve to keep in place specific social and cultural dynamics that actually merit resistance. For example, I have considered various ways in which this particular depiction of the lives of queer youth—and the hegemonic narratives of depression, substance abuse, homelessness, and suicide— might serve to:

- Create a teenage population of queer youth who see themselves within the victim framework, rather than focus upon their survival strategies or methods of subverting status quo understandings of sex and gender. Given that homosexuality itself has long been pathologized, this seems especially problematic (Scarce 1999; Terry 1999).
- Discourage the coming out of young people who either do not want to contend with victimization or do not want to see themselves—or have others see them—as martyrs, targets, or victims.
- Distract attention from more important issues about sexuality and gender that the lives of LGBT youth might suggest, including the role of pleasure and sex in young people's lives and the ways in which our culture's social, economic, and legal regulations work to constrain and regulate a population that trans-historically and cross-culturally has enjoyed nearly full participation in civic life (Aries 1965; Moran 2000).

The issues raised in this chapter also lead me to wonder whether the repeated public use of martyr-target-victim images, narratives, visuals, and historic incidents works to narrow who and what we think of as LGBT youth—and who allows themselves to identify as LGBT youth. While nonprofit organizations might tug at the heartstrings of donors by utilizing this particular construct, does it also serve as a major deterrent to the entrance of many other young people into identities and communities of queer youth? Certainly winning funding for services to queer youth, in the current American system of human services funding, demands a focus on the ways in which such funding might ameliorate issues of homelessness, substance abuse, suicide, or HIV infection in this population. Yet does such a focus lead to the creation of a different type of barrier that keeps out portions of the precise population these agencies are trying to reach? Do young people with same-sex desires who shape themselves in gender-conforming ways or do not abuse drugs, alcohol, or sex, feel as if they would not fit into contemporary queer youth programs?

I believe that the vast numbers of young people who experience same-sex desires never find their way into queer youth groups, campus gay student organizations, or the sample populations of surveys and studies of queer youth. And I believe this is closely linked in two ways to

the Martyr-Target-Victim image. First, many queer youth might experience the image as a deterrent to coming out and instead decide to
compartmentalize their identities or remain fully closeted in order to
maximize their chances of experiencing their high school or college
years as a positive experience. Second, this creates only a partial
portrait of queer youth—a population that might include a disproportionate number of young people who have suffered greatly, exhibit
specific behaviors linked to persecution, and share in the Martyr-
Target-Victim paradigm.

Another significant problem linked to the current literature on
LGBT youth is that the canon suggests that these teenagers identify
primarily with their sexual identity rather than with their racial, ethnic,
or religious identities. This matter also might create two distinct
dynamics. First, young people whose primary identities are as Native
American or African American or Italian American might organize
their identities with an ethnic or racial focus because of the familial and
social support and pleasure they find in their original cultures. This joy,
with a few exceptions (Sears 1991; Heron 1993; Montiero and Fuqua
1995; Bass and Kaufman 1996; Kumashiro 2001), is often absent from
the pages of texts on queer youth, which focus instead on the suffering
they find as they enter LGBT cultures. Second, by absenting themselves
from formal identification and involvement with LGBT youth organizations, we may find ourselves conducting research on primarily those
young people who do not have strong racial, ethnic, or religious ties.
Hence many of the school-based programs for LGBT youth find
themselves working with primarily white and middle-class populations, even when the schools are quite diverse (Kumashiro 2001;
McCready 2001).

Finally, some recent shifts in discussions of LGBT youth suggest
some new possibilities and also some new risks of reinscribing the
Martyr-Target-Victim narrative on queer youth. Discussions of young
people have focused in recent years on the concept of "resilience"
examining ways in which children and youth raised under difficult
circumstances are still able to thrive and succeed (Anthony and Cohler
1987; Fraser 1997; Warschaw and Barlow 1995). This concept has
recently begun circulating among researchers and service providers
focused on LGBT youth (Russell, Driscoll, and Truong 2002; Savin-
Williams 1999).

While this shift offers real possibilities—the exploration of skills and
attributes gained under adversity, a focus on survival strategies that are
applicable throughout life, the creation of a survivor trope to partially
balance the victim trope—it also continues to rely upon the original

deficit model of queer youth by defining these young people by their relationship to victimization and suffering. Hence while we might welcome the focus on resilience, it would be wrong to think this represents a radical shift in our framework for looking at LGBT youth.

As I prepare to teach this course again next year, I am heartened that I have discovered that a number of new texts have appeared in the field (Owens 1998; Sonnie 2000) and hope these materials might represent a second stage of discourse focused on the lives of LGBT youth. I am also aware that new books have appeared that are aimed to clinically assist queer youth (Besner and Spungin 1995; Ryan and Futterman 1998), and I am glad these books are titled and marketed as clinical sourcebooks. What I seek for my course are new and nonclinical ways of conceptualizing and articulating the broad range of life experiences of queer youth in school—including the persecuted sissy or tomboy, but also the average students, football stars, valedictorians, drama club students, and others. Finding ways to support a broad mix of students in finding their voices and sharing their stories through diverse narratives and frameworks seems critically important. Part of this involves providing these students with access to various social institutions, including the media, but part of this also involves supporting young people's leadership and full participation in civil society, including public schools and the queer public sphere.

We also need studies that look critically at research methodologies and make an attempt to identify clearly the strengths and limitations of the sample population. Several recent studies are beginning to suggest that earlier data on suicide, for example, might have oversampled the at-risk portion of queer youth and undersampled the remaining population (Russell, Driscoll, and Truong 2002; Savin-Williams 2001). Finally, we need to create cultural products—books, videotapes, films, journalism—that capture queer youth's lives in schools beyond their relationship to homophobia and heterosexism and beyond the ways in which they find attending school to be difficult or painful. We need these for all adolescents, but we especially need such materials for queer adolescents.

References

Anthony, E. James, and Bertram J. Cohler, eds. 1987. *The Invulnerable Child.* New York: Guilford Press.

Aries, Philippe. 1965. *Centuries of Childhood: A Social History of Family Life.* New York: Random House.

Bass, Ellen, and Kate Kaufman. 1996. *Free Your Mind: The Book for Gay, Lesbian, and Bisexual Youth—and Their Allies*. New York: HarperCollins.

Besner, Hilda F., and Charlotte I. Spungin. 1995. *Gay and Lesbian Students: Understanding Their Needs*. Washington, DC: Taylor and Francis.

Blumenfeld, Warren. 1995. "'Gay/Straight' Alliances: Transforming Pain to Pride." Pp. 211–224 in *The Gay Teen: Educational Practice and Theory for Lesbian, Gay, and Bisexual Adolescents*, ed. Gerald Unks. New York: Routledge.

Brogan, James. 1995. "Gay Teens in Literature." Pp. 67–78 in *The Gay Teen: Educational Practice and Theory for Lesbian, Gay, and Bisexual Adolescents*, ed. Gerald Unks. New York: Routledge.

Brookey, Robert Alan. 2002. *Reinventing the Male Homosexual: The Rhetoric and Power of the Gay Gene*. Bloomington: University of Indiana Press.

Due, Linnea. 1995. *Joining the Tribe: Growing Up Gay and Lesbian in the '90s*. New York. Doubleday.

Epstein, Debbie. 1994. *Challenging Lesbian and Gay Inequalities in Education*. Buckingham, UK: Open University Press.

Epstein, Debbie, and Richard Johnson. 1998. *Schooling Sexualities*. Buckingham, UK: Open University Press.

Fordham, Signithia. 1996. *Blacked Out: Dilemmas of Race, Identity, and Success at Capital High*. Chicago: The University of Chicago Press.

Frankenburg, Ruth. 1992. "Contribution to Conference on the Consent of Disturbed and Disturbing Young People." London: Institute of Education, University of London.

Fraser, Mark W, ed. 1997. *Risk and Resilience in Childhood: An Ecological Perspective*. Washington, DC: NASW Press.

Greenberg, David F. 1990. *The Construction of Homosexuality*. Chicago: The University of Chicago Press.

Herdt, Gilbert, and Andrew Boxer. 1993. *Children of Horizons: How Gay and Lesbian Teens are Leading a New Way Out of the Closet*. Boston: Beacon Press.

Heron, Ann, ed. 1993. *One Teenager in 10: Writings by Gay and Lesbian Youth*. Boston: Alyson Publications.

Kincaid, James. 1998. *Erotic Innocence: The Culture of Child Molesting*. Durham: Duke University Press.

Kitzinger, Celia. 1988. *Social Construction of Lesbianism*. Thousand Oaks, Calif.: Sage.

Kumashiro, Kevin. 2001. *Troubling Intersections of Race and Sexuality: Queer Students of Color and Anti-Oppressive Education*. Lanham, MD: Rowman and Littlefield.

Lipkin, Arthur. 1995. "The Case for a Gay and Lesbian Curriculum." Pp. 31–52 in *The Gay Teen: Educational Practice and Theory for Lesbian, Gay, and Bisexual Adolescents*, ed. Gerald Unks. New York: Routledge.

Luker, Kristin. 1996. *Dubious Conceptions: The Politics of Teenage Pregnancy*. Cambridge, MA: Harvard University Press.

McCready, Lance. 2001. "When Fitting In Isn't an Option, or, Why Black Queer Males at a California High School Stay Away from Project 10." Pp. 37–53 in *Troubling Intersections of Race and Sexuality: Queer Students of Color and Anti-Oppressive Education*, ed. Kevin Kumashiro. Lanham, MD: Rowman and Littlefield.

McDermott, Ray, 1987. "Achieving School Failure: An Anthropological Approach to Literacy and Social Stratification." Pp. 82–118 in George Spindler, ed., *Education and Cultural Process: Anthropological Approaches*. Prospect Heights, IL: Waveland.

Montiero, Kenneth, and Vincent Fuqua. 1995. "African-American Gay Youth: One Form of Manhood." Pp. 159–188 in *The Gay Teen: Educational Practice and Theory for Lesbian, Gay, and Bisexual Adolescents*, ed. Gerald Unks. New York: Routledge.

Moran, Jeffrey P. 2000. *Teaching Sex: The Shaping of Adolescence in the 20th Century*. Cambridge, MA: Harvard University Press.

O'Connor, Andi. 1995. "'Breaking the Silence. Writing About Gay, Lesbian, and Bisexual Teenagers." Pp. 13–16 in *The Gay Teen: Educational Practice and Theory for Lesbian, Gay, and Bisexual Adolescents*, ed. Gerald Unks. New York: Routledge.

Owens, Robert E. 1998. *Queer Kids: The Challenge and Promise for Lesbian, Gay, and Bisexual Youth*. Binghamton, NY: Haworth.

Polite, Vernon C., and James Earl Davis. 1999. *African American Males in School and Society: Practices and Policies for Effective Education*. New York: Teaches College Press.

Pollack, Rachel, and Cheryl Schwartz. 1995. *The Journey Out: A Guide for and about Lesbian, Gay, and Bisexual Teenagers*. New York: Viking.

Porter, Michael. 1998. *Kill Them Before They Grow: The Misdiagnosis of African American Boys in America's Classrooms*. Washington, DC: African American Images.

Remafedi, Gary, ed. 1994. *Death by Denial: Studies of Suicide in Gay and Lesbian Teenagers*. Boston: Alyson Publications.

Rofes, Eric. 1995. "Making Our Schools Safe for Sissies." Pp. 79–84 in *The Gay Teen: Educational Practice and Theory for Lesbian, Gay, and Bisexual Adolescents*, ed. Gerald Unks. New York: Routledge.

Russell, Stephen T., Anne K. Driscoll, and Nhan Truong. 2002. "Adolescent Same-Sex Romantic Attractions and Relationships: Implications for Substance Use and Abuse." *American Journal of Public Health* 92 , no. 2: 198–202.

Ryan, Caitlin, and Donna Futterman. 1998. *Lesbian and Gay Youth: Care and Counseling*. New York: Columbia University Press.

Savin-Williams, Ritch C. 1999. *"And Then I Became Gay": Young Men's Stories*. New York: Routledge.

———. 2001. *Mom, Dad, I'm Gay: How Families Negotiate Coming Out*. Washington, DC: American Psychological Association.

Scarce, Michael. 1999. *Smearing the Queer: Medical Bias in the Health Care of Gay Men.* Binghamton, NY: Harrington Park Press.

Sears, James. 1991. *Growing Up Gay in the South: Race, Gender and Journeys of the Spirit.* New York: Harrington Park Press.

———. 1995. "Black-Gay or Gay-Black: Choosing Identities and Identifying Choices." Pp. 135–148 in *The Gay Teen: Educational Practice and Theory for Lesbian, Gay, and Bisexual Adolescents*, ed. Gerald Unks. New York: Routledge.

Sonnie, Amy, ed. 2000. *Revolutionary Voices.* Los Angeles: Alyson Publications.

Terry, Jennifer. 1999. *An American Obsession: Science, Medicine, and the Place of Homosexuality in Modern Society.* Chicago: University of Chicago Press.

Unks, Gerald, ed. 1995. *The Gay Teen: Educational Practice and Theory for Lesbian, Gay, and Bisexual Adolescents.* New York: Routledge.

———. 1995. "Thinking About the Gay Teen." Pp. 3–12 in *The Gay Teen: Educational Practice and Theory for Lesbian, Gay, and Bisexual Adolescents*, ed. Gerald Unks. New York: Routledge.

Warschaw, Tessa Albert, and Dee Barlow. 1995. *Resiliency: How To Bounce Back Faster, Stronger, Smarter.* New York: Master Media Ltd.

Chapter Three

The Historical Regulation of Sexuality and Gender of Students and Teachers

An Intertwined Legacy

Jackie M. Blount and Sine Anahita

Introduction

During one sweltering July afternoon in New Orleans, thousands of delegates attending the 1988 National Education Association (NEA) Representative Assembly braced for fireworks as the speaker introduced a much-anticipated and highly controversial resolution. If passed, Resolution C-11 would commit the vast resources of the two-million member association to supporting sensitive counseling for lesbian, gay, and bisexual students. In contrast with then-pervasive school counseling practices that emphasized becoming heterosexual and gender-conforming, C-11 would support programs that helped lesbian, gay, and bisexual students accept and adjust to their sexual orientation. During representative assemblies in the early 1980s, NEA members had weighed similarly contentious resolutions concerning newly emerging issues related to AIDS, such as mandatory testing and the right of AIDS- and HIV-positive students and staff to remain in schools. Before AIDS, however, discussion of issues related to sexual orientation rarely reached floor debate of these annual meetings (National Education Association 1986, 332–341; 1987, 212–221). Clearly, the pandemic had provoked normally reticent delegates to confront sexual orientation squarely.

As discussion of C-11 opened, the NEA Secretary-Treasurer spoke first as an individual, recounting having worked "with a student who had survived an extended coma as a result of an attempted suicide due to her depression over social oppression she was experiencing because of her own sexual orientation." With supportive counseling, instead of that which promoted self-hatred, she might "have had the option to build a strong self-concept based on a sense of self-esteem and dignity, no matter her sexual preference." The Secretary-Treasurer continued, "As I watched her in a state of convulsion for over 70 hours sitting by her bedside, I vowed I would never again be silent on this issue." Immediately, a delegate from Oklahoma countered that the resolution should be voted down because, "We are going to see this used against the membership so they can't be as successful as they'd like to be and need to be." After debate continued for several tense minutes, the President of the North Carolina delegation summarized the reasons to support the resolution: "C-11 is about children, it is about giving all children a sense of self-esteem, it is about children who are being denied equal access to education, who are at a greater risk for suicide, who face isolation, rejection, and verbal and physical abuse, who comprise a disproportionately large percentage of homeless youth, who often resort to dropping out and running away. . . . These students need our support, our counsel, and our love. Let's not fail them today." With debate over, a close voice vote followed. Then President Mary Hatwood Futrell announced that the resolution passed. Immediately, yells and groans from angry delegates filled the hall, necessitating a standing count. However, after a lengthy process of counting and recounting each of the thousands of delegates, Futrell finally declared that the resolution passed (National Education Association 1988, 227–233).[1]

Despite deep divisions in delegates' sentiments on this resolution, its passage meant that the financial and human resources of the large association would flow to organizations committed to improving resources for youth struggling with their sexual orientation. Virginia Uribe, founder of Project 10 for LGBT students in Los Angeles, soon would receive NEA funding to develop counseling materials for national distribution.[2] If such programs encountered legal problems, the NEA theoretically could lend its legal support. Support providers everywhere would be able to cite the NEA vote as evidence that their own efforts on behalf of LGBT youth not only were justifiable, but also in the mainstream of teacher opinion. Indeed, approval of C-11 signaled a palpable shift in sentiment regarding LGBT youth. Evidence of this shift soon would mount.

In 1989, only months after the NEA passed C-11, the U.S. Department of Health and Human Services published a landmark study on youth suicide. In the enormous, four-volume report, one relatively brief chapter, "Gay Male and Lesbian Youth Suicide," captured the spirit of

the NEA resolution by describing links between adolescent LGBT
identity and heightened risk of suicide. However, because the incoming
George H. W. Bush administration deemed the chapter on LGBT youth
to be politically offensive, the entire report languished in boxes for two
years—until LGBT activism, national media attention, and the taint of
scandal forced its release (National Gay and Lesbian Task Force 1989;
Maugen 1991).[3] The chapter opened dramatically:

> A majority of suicide attempts by homosexuals occur during their youth,
> and gay youth are 2 to 3 times more likely to attempt suicide than other
> young people. They may comprise up to 30 percent of completed youth
> suicides annually. . . . The root of the problem of gay youth suicide is a
> society that discriminates against and stigmatizes homosexuals while
> failing to recognize that a substantial number of its youth has a gay or
> lesbian orientation. . . . Schools need to include information about
> homosexuality in their curriculum and protect gay youth from abuse by
> peers to ensure they receive an equal education. Helping professionals
> need to accept and support a homosexual orientation in youth. Social
> services need to be developed that are sensitive to and reflective of the
> needs of gay and lesbian youth. (Gibson 1989, 110)

With this shattering report's eventual release in 1991, headlines around
the country echoed its alarming findings about suicide among LGBT
youth. Suddenly, LGBT youth existed. Furthermore, reporters depicted
them almost entirely as imperiled, victimized, and in need of adult
intervention.

This was a significant national media debut for an entire class of
adolescents. Before this time, LGBT youth hardly figured in public
discourse. Instead, concern about LGBT issues in schools focused
exclusively on the employment of LGBT school workers. As the post-
Stonewall gay liberation movement gained strength during the early
and mid-1970s, a few lesbian and gay teachers took tentative steps out
of the closet—only to trigger a virulent backlash movement from the
likes of Anita Bryant and her "Save Our Children" campaign in Florida
in 1977 and John Briggs's Proposition 6 effort in California in 1978.
These high-profile political battles placed lesbian and gay *school
workers* at the heart of religious and political conservatives' agendas
(Blount, 2004). The possibility that LGBT *youth* existed hardly graced
discussions—except to the extent that critics depicted lesbian and gay
teachers as corrupting the "normal" sexual and gender development of
their charges. Despite this overwhelming silence on the topic of LGBT
youth, a few individuals around the country labored diligently to serve
the unique needs of these students. In Los Angeles, San Francisco,

Boston, and other urban settings, visionary educators and activists organized programs for queer youth. Some offered advice on safe sex; most provided a safe space where LGBT adolescents could gather with supportive peers and mentors; and all offered information, informal counseling, and other resources that otherwise were unavailable. Other than these scattered, though significant efforts, few devoted attention to queer youth.

With the 1991 release of the report on LGBT youth suicide, attention shifted decisively from school workers and toward LGBT youth. For example, gay/straight student alliances began popping up in high schools, first in the northeast, then in urban areas in other regions, and finally in suburban and rural districts throughout the country.[4] Also, the Massachusetts Legislature in 1993 passed a landmark law forbidding harassment and discrimination against LGBT students, a measure backed up with nearly a half-million dollars in funding for the first year.[5] Who could be faulted for wanting to assist youth identified as so at-risk—especially in the era of AIDS? With such potentially deadly consequences lurking especially for young gay and bisexual males, focusing on the needs of queer youth had become an urgently pressing issue. On the other hand, activism on behalf of LGBT school workers remained politically dangerous. Despite much research to the contrary, religious and political conservatives continually accused LGBT school workers of molesting, recruiting, or otherwise corrupting youth.

Since this time, the harassment, rejection, invisibility, and discrimination experienced by LGBT youth have remained the primary concerns of persons interested in LGBT issues in schools. Some LGBT school workers have been able to come out in their workplaces to serve such youth, thus carving a niche acceptable to ambivalent colleagues and community members. More likely to incur ire, though, are the LGBT school workers who labor for their *own* employment rights.

This situation offers one illustration of how conditions for LGBT students and school workers have intertwined during the twentieth century. Neither quite in parallel nor in opposition, conditions for one group have shifted in response to those for the other, which in turn have provoked yet more changes—and so on. As we will argue in this chapter, the school experiences of queer students are closely linked to those of queer school workers. Policies intended to affect one have had profound, though sometimes unanticipated consequences for the other. To better understand conditions for queer students in schools, then, it is important to examine the conditions for queer school workers, too. Public fears or illusions about LGBT students and school workers have impacted school policies, procedures, and, even more important, school cultures.

A historical analysis can deepen our understanding of this longstanding, interwoven relationship. It can reveal how public notions of adolescent sexuality, expectations that teachers will model acceptable sexuality and gender roles, and fears of same-sex desire and/or gender transgression have changed over time. And finally, a historical approach recasts the still-prevailing stereotype of suicidal LGBT adolescents so that it can be seen as part of a historical moment, rather than as an enduring truth. In this chapter, we explore some of the interconnections between the experiences of LGBT school workers and students by examining three time periods during the past 100 years: the late nineteenth through early twentieth centuries, the early Cold War years, and the 1990s. These eras, each quite different in cultural contexts, highlight some of the significant changes in ethos regarding same-sex desire and gender non-conformity over the twentieth century—and how they have played out in schools in the United States.

Late Nineteenth through Early Twentieth Centuries

The decades around the turn of the century brought a number of significant changes in notions of acceptable sexuality and gender. The rapid growth of urban areas, increasing availability of employment opportunities for middle-class women, widespread access to birth control information and technology, and the strengthening women's suffrage movement together ushered in a time of greater sexual freedoms for many. Thriving male homosexual communities appeared in large cities around the country (Boyd 2003; Chauncey 1994). Unprecedented numbers of educated women chose to remain unmarried for much, if not all, of their lives, some opting to live with other women in committed romantic and/or sexual relationships (Donovan 1938, 228; Faderman 1999). Marriage and childbearing rates among young women declined noticeably while divorce rates headed upward. And women who wished to marry could afford to be choosy in selecting partners. Indeed, romance became increasingly important to many.

Anxieties often accompanied these sweeping shifts, as social institutions sought to rein in excesses or to prevent the realization of worst fears. David Wallace Adams describes how, in the late 1800s, the education reformers who ran boarding schools for Native American students saw as one of their primary objectives "to reconstruct students' attitudes toward gender roles and sexual mores" (Adams 1995, 173). Also, parents and benefactors demanded that elite private boarding schools monitor students ever more closely to ensure that their charges developed correct gender characteristics—and more important, that they keep students from acquiring sexual vices. Of particular concern was reportedly rampant sexual activity between older and younger boys at such institutions (Honey 1977; Smith-Rosenberg 1978). In the late 1800s, soon after enactment of the British law criminalizing male homosexual behavior, the much-publicized trial and imprisonment of Oscar Wilde fueled a rapidly growing awareness of same-sex desire on both sides of the Atlantic. Some even regarded homosexuality as the vice of the owning class because elite boarding schools supposedly nurtured it. One American expert on health described boys' boarding schools as "the most infected . . . first, because their boys are highly organized, and as such experience proportionally greater pleasure and injury; and secondly, this vice pre-eminently is catching especially as they commingle thus freely with each other." He summarized: "This sending children to school, however select, is a most grievous evil; because, as children are imitative creatures, all the bad habits of all the scholars are adopted by all the others. Schools are complete nuisances, propagating vice; nor can the evil be remedied till parents educate their own children" (Smith-Rosenberg 1978, S233). Evidence suggests that such reformers focused on masturbation, which they sometimes employed as code for homosexuality. They argued that masturbation and homosexuality were linked because male students frequently taught others the "solitary vice"—and some then became sexual partners (Bullough and Voght, 1973). In 1920, the Harvard president convened a secret court to investigate a supposed homosexual network operating on campus. Students who testified indicated that they had developed homosexual habits in their boarding schools before coming to Harvard and that such practices were widespread (Paley 2002). The reputation of male boarding schools in the United States for producing students with "homosexual habits" spread to the point that one writer in 1908 explained: "A special observer of youthful homosexuality in America has stated that the practices of uranian boys [those who seek intimacy with other males] in schools are . . . 'nowhere quite so general' as in the United States" (Stevenson [1908] 1983).

During these years, male boarding schools instituted a variety of changes designed to curb students' enthusiasm for these activities. Some kept lights on and doors open in students' quarters. Others scheduled intense physical and other activities continuously throughout the day to leave boys supposedly too exhausted for sexual activity. Schoolmasters also sought to eliminate any closed or hidden quarters on campus where such dalliances might occur. Most forbade boys from hugging or other physical displays of affection, encouraging them instead to direct their passions toward fulfilling the broader mission of the school (Honey 1977).

Meanwhile, the men who taught in these boarding schools faced increased scrutiny as well. Some of them undoubtedly desired others of the same sex, but either kept their sexual activities entirely apart from their duties or sublimated their desires into their work. These men had attended such boarding schools themselves and so were well acquainted with sexual practices among students. In the end, they complied with parents' wishes and cracked down on boy's activities.

Female boarding schools bore such scrutiny, too. By many accounts, girls commonly developed crushes on much-admired older students or teachers. Physical displays of affection were part of the social fabric of such schools, enjoyed as much by students as female faculty (Faderman 1991; Vicinus 1984). However, as suffrage-era successes of the broader women's movement accumulated, scrutiny of life within all-female institutions increased. Havelock Ellis, the pioneering sexologist, argued in his 1895 volume *Sexual Inversion of Women* that girls' boarding schools and women's colleges fostered "ardent attachments" between students. In these contexts, "kissing and . . . sleeping with the friend" were common, and one or both girls might experience "sexual emotion." Although females were supposed to keep a proper distance from males, they were permitted to enjoy "a considerable degree of physical intimacy" among themselves. This acceptance of physical intimacy between females, he contended, masked evidence of "homosexuality." In response, headmistresses shunned hugging, kissing, and other demonstrative behaviors among their students as unhealthy. They essentially became instrumental in thwarting budding romantic relationships among their charges (Ellis [1895] 1983). Martha Vicinus has argued compellingly that the women who worked in female boarding schools also often encouraged students to channel their passionate love for other females into higher causes. They might direct young women to aspire to greater religious virtue, to the betterment of the school, or to improving conditions for all women—rather than giving in to the temptation of romantic and/or sexual relationships (Vicinus 1984, 605, 611).

Some of the women who taught in female boarding schools maintained romantic, and possibly sexual, relationships with other women. A few lived together and generally were known as companions, whether this was spoken publicly or not. At the time, two women living together did not necessarily raise suspicion because there were many publicly acceptable reasons they might do so, including safety, companionship, sharing economic resources, and splitting household chores (Faderman 1999). Lillian Faderman's work on lesbians in the late-nineteenth- and early-twentieth-century United States documents the role played by the early sexologists on "pathologizing" middle-class and working-class romantic friendships and love between women. The sexologists were instrumental in changing the "scientific" understanding of lesbianism from being a sin, to being a result of congenital abnormality inherited from parents without the proper gender characteristics (40). As a result of the popularizing of the sexologists' work, by the dawn of the twentieth century, Faderman reports that many of the women who previously engaged in same-sex love and desire cultivated a public image of femininity and even celibacy so as to conceal and keep secret their private lives (53).

Calls for coeducation quietly rose from some quarters as a possible solution to these seeming problems at single-sex boarding schools. Feminists long had contended that girls deserved education of equal quality to that provided for males, which often meant allowing females to enroll in male institutions. Psychologists, educators, and others argued, though, that girls would get used to being around males and could more effectively channel their romantic energies toward them if they attended school together (Long [1919] 1983). Otherwise, as one writer expressed it, boarding schools prevented students from finding a "normal" sexual outlet (Waller 1932, 110).

Although public schools typically were coeducational from the start, mainly as a means of reducing costs, they faced their own challenges regarding the proper gender and sexual development of students. During these years, unmarried women accounted for the overwhelming majority of teachers, especially in urban areas (Barnes 1912; Folger and Nam 1967, 81). The few male teachers who remained wanted to recruit greater numbers of men into the work. For example, after pay cuts, the male teachers in New York organized to increase their pay as one means of enticing more men, but these pleas largely fell on unresponsive ears, especially as women eagerly stepped forward to teach for those lowered wages. However, when male teachers linked their plight to that of their male students, charging that the overwhelming numbers of women teachers made boys effeminate, the *New York Times* reported their efforts.[6]

Before long, unmarried women teachers took the blame not just for supposedly causing boys to become effeminate, but also for inducing female students to remain in school, to excel, and in many cases, to enter the profession of teaching themselves. In this strange manner, such women were thought to reproduce themselves, influencing their female students to avoid marriage and motherhood. After enactment of women's suffrage, criticisms of unmarried teachers became more menacing. Detractors insinuated that such women harbored sexual maladies, constituted a "third sex," or, more boldly, were lesbians. Some studies of the time indicated that, in fact, a number of unmarried women teachers did desire other women sexually (Davis 1929, 247, 263). School officials wished to distance themselves from the growing stigma attached to spinster teachers. By mid-century, school districts around the country began hiring large numbers of married women teachers—to the near exclusion of unmarried women (Blount, 2004).

Unmarried women teachers, then, became problematic when it seemed that large numbers of female students might follow their lead in remaining unmarried, pursuing careers, and living independently. Because of the perceived effect of unmarried teachers on female students, hiring practices shifted spectacularly. In contrast, teachers in same-sex boarding schools initially were not seen as culprits in causing their students to engage in same-sex emotional and/or sexual relationships. Students were thought ready and eager to participate in such relationships on their own. However, teachers were held to account for deterring such activity. As such, they monitored students much more closely—while simultaneously avoiding the taint of sexual deviance themselves.

Early Cold War

During the interwar years, sexologists and psychiatrists institutionalized their power to define and stigmatize lesbians, warning, in particular, of the dangers spinster teachers posed to youth (Oram [1989] 1993). These same professionals also projected the increasing cultural anxieties about sexuality onto schoolgirls, and pathologized schoolgirl "crushes" and all-girl schools as producing young women who eschewed marriage, motherhood, and the institution of heterosexuality itself (Oram and Turnbull 2001). The increasing concern with marriage and heterosexuality in opposition to spinster teachers and the taint of lesbianism also affected feminist ideology about marriage and sexuality. In Britain, for example, the earlier Suffragists valorized spinsterhood as a strategy women teachers could use in order to protect themselves from subservience in heterosexual marriage. By the mid-1930s, younger feminist teachers who were members of the National Union of Women Teachers (NUWT) responded to sexologists' attacks on unmarried teachers by assuring critics that the only impulse spinster teachers had toward their students was *maternal*, not sexual (Oram [1989] 1993). These younger teachers were responding to the increasing pressure of the heterosexual imperative that swept over the Western world during the interwar period.

The years immediately following WWII brought unprecedented awareness of the sexual diversity of the United States. During the war, a number of recognizable homosexual communities had emerged in urban military centers around the country as critical masses of soldiers, military industrial workers, and others who desired persons of the same sex gathered to drink, for entertainment, and to seek the company of others like themselves (D'Emilio 1998). Then in 1948 and 1953, Alfred C. Kinsey and his team of researchers published their landmark volumes on male and then female sexual behavior, in turn bringing the topic of sexuality into popular conversation. One of the most surprising findings of these reports concerned the unexpectedly high incidence of same-sex behavior among men and, to a lesser extent, among women. Though many celebrated these and other findings, detractors soon held sway. Some charged that Kinsey's team *promoted*, rather than *described* sexual practices (Kinsey, Pomeroy, and Martin 1948; Kinsey, et al. 1953; Morantz 1977). During the deeply polarized Cold War years, homosexuals quickly became as feared and despised as communists. Not surprisingly, Senator Joseph McCarthy's much-reported congressional investigations into the extent of communist infiltration of federal agencies soon gave way to investigations of homosexuality in those same bureaus (U.S. Senate repr. 1975). The stiff penalties attached to homosexuality and/or to transgressing one's designated gender compelled many to go to the extreme of exaggerating their heterosexuality and gender conformity.

Schools soon became surprisingly active institutions in battling the supposed "homosexual threat" during the 1950s and 1960s. Warned that homosexual teachers existed everywhere and, furthermore, sought to recruit students into the life, school officials began screening the ranks carefully to avoid hiring teachers who seemed sexually suspect (D'Emilio 1998, 44; Major 1950). Because gender nonconformity was widely regarded as evidence of homosexuality, hiring officials watched for signs of effeminacy in men and masculinity in women. In Britain, girls' schools were advised to hire only those women who were physically attractive (J. Newsom [1948] in Oram and Turnbull 2001). The idea behind this was that female teachers who were unmarried should look as if they could have married, in order to reinforce heterosexual marriage as the ideal for students. Marital status itself offered another clue. School officials typically preferred hiring married women rather than those who were not married. One school official in Kentucky remarked, "The attractive woman who finds it easy to marry and establish a home is the kind of woman that the schools need and cannot secure or retain under regulations against marriage. . . . Married women tend to have a saner view on sex, and are less likely to become 'queer'" (Chamberlain and Meece 1937, 57). Men needed to be either married or likely to wed in the near future. A mechanism suggested by one scholar required hiring officials to ask male teaching candidates if they liked boys, then watching to see if respondents expressed too much enthusiasm (Waller 1932, 147–149). Florida went several steps further by launching broad investigations of homosexuals in the state's teaching force, enlisting the state superintendent in the effort to remove the teaching credentials of discovered suspects. California passed statutes requiring law enforcement officers to notify school officials whenever teachers were arrested on so-called morals charges (Harbeck 1997, 179–207).

School officials did not end their efforts with teachers. They watched high school students closely as well. The early Cold War years brought record high school enrollments all over the country. At the same time, commercial interests began catering to this new demographic group, as "teen-agers" everywhere created and reveled in their own fashions, rituals, music, and culture. A growing national obsession with juvenile delinquency, however, revealed deep adult anxieties about adolescent sexuality. In turn, communities pressed schools into service to minimize the problems of so-called juvenile delinquency—which included not just the usual categories of intransigence such as theft, drinking, and loitering, but also transgressing conventional gender bounds and engaging in same-sex sexual activities (Wattenberg 1966).

Schools employed a number of tactics to accomplish these ends. First, high school curricula during these years included gender-segregated tracks, with girls taking such female-associated course sequences as clerical skills and domestic arts, and boys taking male-associated coursework such as industrial training or advanced math and science courses. These tracks also effectively segregated students by social/economic class because working-class students were encouraged to enroll in programs emphasizing manual trades. Through curricula such as these, students prepared for careers deemed gender-appropriate—as well as connected with their social/economic class. Second, teachers of life adjustment courses sought to impart social skills to their students—as well as normative gender and sexuality. Hundreds of films available for such courses offered pointers on matters such as choosing suitable heterosexual partners, dating etiquette, avoiding entanglements with homosexuals, and responsible manhood (Smith 1999).[7] Third, a broad variety of extracurricular activities and school rituals reinforced notions of acceptable sexuality and gender. Increasingly popular proms and other school dances compelled students to conform to and celebrate heterosexual norms. Even highly competitive women's sports such as basketball changed rules so that athletes appeared less aggressive and more gender compliant (Grundy 2000). Fourth, school staff were advised to monitor female students' hairstyles and the way they walked for possible evidence of homosexuality. Schools were advised not to hide from the "problems of homosexuality" should students be spotted who were nonconforming in these ways (H. Richardson [1969] in Oram and Turnbull, 2001, 154). Finally, as described earlier, school officials closely monitored the gender conformity of teachers, ever-watchful for signs that might betray homosexuality. Not only were homosexual teachers feared as possible seducers of the young, but also, because teachers had come to be regarded as important role models for youth, any displays of gender impropriety theoretically influenced students to the same. At this point, little is known about how these trends played out in racially segregated schools during the 1950s and 1960s. The degree to which gender-conformity and sexuality were monitored in traditionally African American, Mexican American, and Native American schools requires further study.

Essentially, two main anxieties compelled these changes: adult fears of adolescent sexuality in general and societal fears of homosexuality in particular. Some changes addressed both fears at once, such as hiring obviously gender-conforming and seemingly heterosexual teachers to serve as role models for students and who apparently would not recruit them into homosexuality. There is little evidence ultimately about the effectiveness of these strategies. Only scattered and unsubstantiated anecdotal evidence ever existed for homosexual teacher "recruitment" among students (Major 1950; Merrow 1977; Schrag 1977). Lesbian and gay teachers usually eluded detection and most took great pains to avoid any appearance of impropriety. Little research existed to show that the sexuality or gender expression of teachers influenced adolescent students. Students who desired others of the same sex typically found community outside of school, especially in more populous areas where clusters of such youth might gather. A few who were revealed at school usually were referred to counselors determined to impress on them the importance of becoming heterosexual (Kriegman 1969). The failures of this approach now are legendary. In the end, school officials behaved as though a critically important link existed between the gender/sexuality of teachers and students—even though evidence was tenuous at best.

Into the Present

In the wake of the 1969 Stonewall Rebellion, LGBT persons around the country began organizing to resist the oppressions they long had experienced in relative silence. A grassroots gay liberation movement energized activists everywhere, particularly in large urban areas such as New York, Los Angeles, and San Francisco, which established Stonewall-inspired parades each summer to commemorate the landmark event. Some LGBT school workers joined in this larger movement by establishing their own organizations, by marching in gay pride parades as "out" teachers, or by challenging discriminatory employment practices by waging legal battles.

With the increased visibility of LGBT school workers, though, came a potent backlash movement that inflamed fears about the consequences of employing such school workers. During the 1970s and 1980s, public concern about LGBT issues in schools centered on school workers—and whether or not such persons should teach while openly claiming LGBT identities. Anita Bryant's "Save Our Children" campaign in 1977 successfully overturned the Miami-Dade nondiscrimination ordinance that included sexual orientation. Bryant and her supporters did so by evoking the specter of "militant homosexuals" preying on students and causing them in turn to become homosexual. California Senator John Brigg's Proposition 6, introduced in 1978, targeted for dismissal school workers who openly identified themselves as LGBT— or *any* school worker who supported the rights of LGBT persons. Though voters rejected Proposition 6, politicians in Oklahoma and other states subsequently attempted to pass similar measures in the 1980s (Blount 2004; Harbeck 1997).

By the early 1990s, the NEA had passed the resolution for supportive counseling for LGBT youth. The government report containing the hard-hitting data on LGBT youth suicide had been released to the public. These developments unfolded against the backdrop of the ongoing AIDS epidemic and the groundswell of LGBT activism that it had inspired. In 1993, a march on Washington, D.C., with a display of the AIDS quilt, drew one million LGBT persons and allies. And by the mid-1990s, lesbian and gay persons and characters appeared regularly in national media, albeit in often highly stereotypical roles. Truly, LGBT issues had moved from the periphery to the mainstream—and everywhere individuals, families, schools, and communities grappled with their significance.

In a momentous turn of events, since the 1990s students who identify as LGBT or allies have begun taking matters into their own hands, organizing student groups and strategizing to win their rights. Kevin Jennings and the Gay, Lesbian Straight Education Network (GLSEN) that he helped found, have played a central role in helping high school students around the country establish hundreds of gay/straight alliances. These student-run groups offer social support, educate their school communities about LGBT issues, and generally aspire to improve the climate for all LGBT persons and allies in schools. Both LGBT and ally teachers work with these groups, linking with the larger organization and a network of supportive colleagues (Woog 1995, 299–305; Jennings 1994). In Massachusetts, students around the state, many active in their gay/straight alliances, organized a highly successful campaign to get the legislature to pass a law protecting the rights of LGBT youth and, furthermore, provide financial commitment to back that up.[8] A number of other LGBT students have sponsored alternative proms, brought their partners and allies to traditional dances, and organized nationwide events such as the annual "Day of Silence," which educates communities about conditions for LGBT persons in schools. In short, LGBT youth and their allies have demonstrated impressive agency in winning improved places in schools and refusing to accept the stereotype of the victimized "gay teen."

This trend toward empowerment of LGBT and allied youth, however, caps a century in which adults have tried various means of restricting students' sexual and gender expression. When word of widespread sexual activity among students in boarding schools circulated, teachers and school administrators were expected to control these youthful indiscretions and to instill values disdainful of emotional and physical displays of affection. In public schools, teachers were thought to influence the proper gender and sexual development of students, so school officials eventually sought married women and men teachers, once nonmarried women came to be regarded as suspect, if not sexually perilous. At mid-century, homosexuals generally were viewed as so dangerously enticing that students could not be exposed to them for fear of corruption. What youth could resist? Schools responded, of course, by trying to remove all homosexuals from the proximity of students. And then in the late 1980s, as the NEA weighed Resolution C-11, students who identified as LGBT were deemed helpless and in need of adult intervention. Though programs that grew out of this view were quite well-intentioned and certainly necessary for the welfare of many students, the category of "suicidal gay youth" was drawn with such sharp lines that the image has lingered in the public mind since. As such, the category masks the richness, diversity, and agency that so many LGBT youth exhibit.

• Recent social science research illustrates the continued focus on the stereotyped at-risk LGBT adolescent. Sullivan and Wodarski (2002) reviewed risk factors for queer youth, including substance abuse, depression, and suicide. They concluded that a pressing need exists for professional intervention in the lives of gay and lesbian youth. Noell and Ochs (2001) interviewed 532 homeless adolescents in Oregon and concluded that suicide ideation among lesbian and gay youth is a topic of great concern. The authors generalized their findings among home-less youth, who are more likely to be depressed, to queer youth in general.•Hershberger, Pilkington, and D'Augelli (1997) studied na-tional survey data to identify predictors of suicide attempts in LGBT youth. They concluded that coming out is strongly correlated with suicide attempts, and further, that youth who come out earlier or who know they are LGBT at a relatively young age are at special risk for psychological problems. Studies such as these inform educational policy. In reviewing similar research conducted earlier, Muehrer (1995) concluded that no national or statewide data on LGBT youth suicide existed. As such, studies that claim high suicide rates among such youth are methodologically problematic in that they have nonrepresentative samples, no nongay control groups, and measures that are not valid/reliable.

However, activist students who claim LGBT and queer identities and who work to secure their rights challenge adults' prior assumptions about their likelihood of attempting suicide. Such youth claim the right to be sexual beings who can make their own sexual choices. They refuse to be seen as sexually innocent or nonsexual, views that strip them of part of their identity. They resist the theory that teachers bear an encompassing responsibility for their sexual or gender identities. Instead, they base their identities on matters that may lie beyond the reach of schools to control or influence. And they refute the stereotype of the helpless queer youth. Essentially, they insist that schools rethink efforts to influence, control, or regulate students' sexual and gender identities.

At the same time, though, LGBT teachers and other school workers do not yet universally feel free to claim their identities openly and be assured of retaining their jobs. Although fourteen states now have laws against discrimination on the basis of sexual orientation (four also including gender presentation), the remainder do not.[9] Though both the AFT and NEA are committed to defending teachers dismissed, harassed, or otherwise penalized on account of sexual orientation, many LGBT teachers keep as low a profile as possible to avoid either formal sanctions or informal social ones such as parental complaints. Many teachers are economically vulnerable and consequently choose to take few risks with the profession for which they have prepared. Matters are more difficult still for LGBT school administrators who serve at the pleasure of their school boards and who do not have the same backing of a supportive professional association as teachers unless they have retained their membership in either the AFT or NEA. In many ways, then, the impressive gains scored by LGBT youth now have outstripped those won by LGBT school workers—despite the fact that LGBT school workers have been bringing high-profile, precedent-setting lawsuits for over thirty years; have been organizing and agitating for their rights for almost as long; and enjoy the rights, benefits, and privileges of adulthood.

There are at least two key differences, however. First, students are *required* to attend school. Teachers have *chosen* to pursue their work. Arguably, because LGBT students must go to school, the task of assuring their rights presses more urgently. Second, though, is the ever-powerful and persistent view that LGBT adults seek to molest or corrupt youth. Though a great deal of research has proven conclusively that LGBT persons are less likely to molest young persons than heterosexual males given their proportion in the population, the molestation bugaboo still haunts the field (Merrow 1977; Schrag 1977). And even for detractors who concede that molestation is quite unlikely, the fear lingers that LGBT teachers somehow might influence youth to become homosexual or gender-nonconforming. As a result, teaching continues to lie in the zone of greatest vulnerability for the larger LGBT movement.

These ongoing doubts or fears about LGBT school workers share common features. Mainly they are grounded in a belief that youth are nonsexual or sexually innocent beings, and that they only become sexual when corrupted or exposed to dangerous adults. However, as most any young person today will concede easily, youth are sexual beings—and their sexuality must be acknowledged and respected. These doubts also are predicated on the seemingly contradictory notion that although youth are thought nonsexual or sexually innocent, their sexuality must be controlled or regulated closely by adults. Finally, they are based on a belief that LGBT adults want nothing more than to convert as many youth as possible to "the life." If anything, many LGBT adults over the past few decades have been reticent about developing friendships or mentoring relationships with youth for fear that they would be accused of corrupting minors.

The gay/straight alliances in high schools around the country, then, may well continue providing a powerful means by which not only students, but teachers and other school workers eventually will expand their rights and places in schools. These organizations allow LGBT and allied youth to interact meaningfully with LGBT and allied school workers—around LGBT issues in schools. LGBT students can and do encourage school workers to be out at work. LGBT school workers can and do help address harassment of students and other problems. By working cooperatively for the larger good of their schools, they make clear that policies or social practices directed at LGBT students do in fact affect LGBT school workers and vice versa. The intertwined relationship becomes explicit, tightly linked, and positive rather than subterranean, indirect, and vexing.

Notes

1. Blount served as a North Carolina delegate during this event.
2. Patricia Ward Biederman, "Will Continue Work with Homosexuals, School Advisor Says," *Los Angeles Times*, March 17, 1988, 1, 17; Dell Richards, "Gay Teens in L.A. Helped by Model School Program," *Bay Area Reporter*, November 24, 1988, 14; and Craig Wilson, "Teacher Takes Homophobia to Task," *USA Today*, February 12, 1991.
3. Susan Okie, "Sullivan Cold-Shoulders Suicide Report," *Washington Post*, January 13, 1990, A5.
4. Scott S. Greenberger, "Gay Alliance Taking Hold in Schools," *Boston Globe*, April 15, 2001, B5; James Brooke, "To Be Young, Gay and Going to High School in Utah," *New York Times*, February 28, 1996, B8, col. 1; and Dan Woog, "Gay-Straight Groups Grow," in *School's Out* (Boston: Alyson, 1995).
5. Karen Diegmueller, "Massachusetts Approves Bill Outlawing Bias against Gay Students," *Education Week*, December 15, 1993.
6. "Appeal for Men Teachers," *New York Times*, October 4, 1911, col. 7, 12. During the first decade of the twentieth century, the topic of the seeming effeminacy of male students provoked heated discussion among male educators. One observed that "a boy needs forceful, manly control. He should learn the grip and control of a man. If he is to become a manly man, he should hardly be deprived of the daily contact of a virile man. He also needs the strength of a man to control and direct his strong, boyish proclivities" ("Are There Too Many Women Teachers?" 1904). A member of a British research team in 1903 wrote that to "develop a virile man," there should be more male teachers in schools. Otherwise, "the boy in

America is not being brought up to punch another boy's head or to stand having his own punched in a healthy and proper manner. . . . There is a strange and indefinable feminine air coming over the men; a tendency towards a . . . sexless tone of thought" (Armstrong 1903, repr. 1969, 13).

7. For background on life adjustment curriculum, see Herbert Kliebard, *The Struggle for the American Curriculum, 1893–1958* (Boston: Routledge and Kegan Paul, 1986).

8. Sara Rimer, "Gay Rights Law for Students Advances in Massachusetts," *New York Times*, December 8, 1993, A18.

9. The National Gay and Lesbian Task Force maintains a current map of states with laws that protect against discrimination on account of sexual orientation and gender identity: http://www.ngltf.org/downloads/civilrightsmap.pdf.

References

Adams, David Wallace. 1995. *Education for Extinction: American Indians and the Boarding School Experience, 1875–1928*. Lawrence: University of Kansas Press.

"Are There Too Many Women Teachers?" *Educational Review* 28 (June 1904): 101.

Armstrong, Henry. 1903, repr. 1969. "Report." In *Reports of the Mosely Educational Commission to the United States*. London: Co-operative Printing Society, Limited, 1903; repr. New York: Arno Press and The New York Times.

Barnes, Earl. 1912. "The Feminizing of Culture." *Atlantic Monthly* (June), 770–773.

Bay Area Reporter, November 24, 1988.

Blount, Jackie. 2004. *Fit to Teach: Same-Sex Desire, Gender, and School Work in the Twentieth Century*. Albany: State University of New York Press.

Boston Globe, April 15, 2001.

Boyd, Nan. 2003. *Wide Open Town: A History of Queer San Francisco to 1965*. Berkeley: University of California Press.

Bullough, Vern and Martha Voght. 1973. "Homosexuality and Its Confusion with the 'Secret Sin' in Pre-Freudian America." *Journal of the History of Medicine and Allied Sciences* 28, no. 2: 143–155.

Chamberlain, Leo, and Leonard Meece. March 1937. "Women and Men in the Teaching Profession." *Bulletin of the Bureau of School Service*. Lexington KY: University of Kentucky, 1–60.

Chauncey, George. 1994. *Gay New York: Gender, Urban Culture, and the Making of the Gay Male World, 1890–1940*. New York: Basic Books.

Davis, Katharine Bement. 1929; repr. 1972. *Factors in the Sex Life of Twenty-Two Hundred Women*. New York: Arno Press and the New York Times.

D'Emilio, John. 1998. *Sexual Politics, Sexual Communities: The Making of a Homosexual Minority in the United States, 1940–1970,* 2nd ed. Chicago: University of Chicago Press.

Donovan, Frances. 1938. *The School Ma'am.* New York: Frederick A. Stokes Co.

Education Week, December 15, 1993.

Ellis, Havelock. repr. 1983. "Sexual Inversion of Women." Pp. 269–273 in *Gay/Lesbian Almanac: A New Documentary,* ed. Jonathan Ned Katz. New York: Harper and Row.

Faderman, Lillian. 1991. *Odd Girls and Twilight Lovers: A History of Lesbian Life in Twentieth-Century America.* New York: Penguin.

———. 1999. *To Believe in Women: What Lesbians Have Done for America—A History.* Boston: Houghton Mifflin.

Folger, John K. and Charles B. Nam. 1967. *Education of the American Population: A 1960 Census Monograph.* Washington, D.C.: U.S. Government Printing Office.

Gibson, Paul. 1989. "Gay Male and Lesbian Youth Suicide." In *Report of the Secretary's Task Force on Youth Suicide,* vol. 3. Washington, D.C.: U.S. Department of Health and Human Services.

Grundy, Pamela. 2000. "From Amazons to Glamazons: The Rise and Fall of North Carolina Women's Basketball, 1920–1960." *Journal of American History* 87, no. 1: 112–146.

Harbeck, Karen. 1997. *Gay and Lesbian Educators: Personal Freedoms, Public Constraints.* Maulden, MA: Amethyst.

Hershberger, Scott L., Neil W. Pilkington, and Anthony R. D'Augelli. 1997. "Predictors of Suicide Attempts among Gay, Lesbian, and Bisexual Youth." *Journal of Adolescent Research* 12, no. 4: 477–497.

Honey, J. R. de S. 1977. *Tom Brown's Universe: The Development of the English Public School in the Nineteenth Century.* New York: Quadrangle.

Jennings, Kevin. 1994. "I Remember." Pp. 19–28 in *One Teacher in 10: Gay and Lesbian Educators Tell Their Stories,* ed. Kevin Jennings. Los Angeles: Alyson.

Kinsey, Alfred C., Wardell B. Pomeroy, and Clyde E. Martin. 1948. *Sexual Behavior in the Human Male.* Philadelphia: W. B. Saunders Company.

Kinsey, Alfred C., Wardell B. Pomeroy, Clyde E. Martin, and Paul H. Gebhard. 1953. *Sexual Behavior in the Human Female.* Philadelphia: W. B. Saunders Company.

Kliebard, Herbert. 1986. *The Struggle for the American Curriculum, 1893–1958.* Boston: Routledge and Kegan Paul.

Kriegman, George. 1969. "Homosexuality and the Educator." *Journal of School Health* 39, no. 5: 306–310.

Long, Constance. 1983. "A Sign of the Times for Those Who Can Read Portents." Pp. 385–387 in *Gay/Lesbian Almanac: A New Documentary,* ed. Jonathan Ned Katz. New York: Harper and Row, Publishers.

Los Angeles Times, March 17, 1988.

Maguen, Shira. 1991. "Teen Suicide: The Government's Cover-Up and America's Lost Children." *The Advocate* (September), 40–47.

Major, Ralph H. 1950. "New Moral Menace to Our Youth." *Coronet* (September): 101–08.

Merrow, John. 1977. "Gay Sex in the Schools." *Parents' Magazine* 52, 9: 66, 100, 104, 106.

Morantz, Regina Markell. 1977. "The Scientist as Sex Crusader: Alfred C. Kinsey and American Culture." *American Quarterly* 29: 563–589.

Muehrer, Peter. 1995. "Suicide and Sexual Orientation: A Critical Summary of Recent Research and Directions for Future Research." *Suicide and Life-Threatening Behavior* 25: 72–81.

National Education Association. 1986. *Proceedings of the Sixty-Fifth Representative Assembly*. Washington, D.C.: National Education Association.

———. 1987. *Proceedings of the Sixty-Sixth Representative Assembly*. Washington, D.C.: National Education Association.

———. 1988. *Proceedings of the Sixty-Seventh Representative Assembly*. Washington, D.C.: National Education Association.

National Gay and Lesbian Task Force. August 10, 1989. Press release: "Department of Health and Human Services Report Calls for Action Against Lesbian/Gay Youth Suicide." "Youth Suicide" folder, June Mazer Collection.

New York Times, October 4, 1911; and December 8, 1993.

Noell, John W., and Linda M. Ochs. 2001. "Relationship of Sexual Orientation to Substance Use, Suicide Ideation, Suicide Attempts, and Other Factors in a Population of Homeless Adolescents." *Journal of Adolescent Health* 219, no. 1: 31–36.

Oram, Alison. 1989, 1993. "'Embittered, Sexless or Homosexual': Attacks on Spinster Teachers 1918–1939." Pp. 99–118 in *Not a Passing Phase: Reclaiming Lesbians in History 1840–1985*, ed. Lesbian History Group. London. The Women's Press Ltd.

Oram, Alison, and Annmarie Turnbull. 2001. "Education." Pp. 129–154 in chapter 4 in *The Lesbian History Sourcebook: Love and Sex Between Women in Britain from 1780 to 1970*. London and New York: Routledge.

Paley, Amit. 2002. "The Secret Court of 1920." *The Harvard Crimson* (November 21).

Schrag, Peter. 1977. "Education Now." *Saturday Review* 5, no. 4: 53–54

Smith, Ken. 1999. *Mental Hygiene: Classroom Films, 1945–1970*. New York: Blast Books.

Smith-Rosenberg, Carroll. 1978. "Sex as Symbol in Victorian Purity: An Ethnohistorical Analysis of Jacksonian America." *The American Journal of Sociology* 84, Supplement: Turning Points: Historical and Sociological Essays on the Family: S212-S247.

Stevenson, Edward. 1908, repr. 1983. "The Intersexes." Pp. 326–32 (excerpt) in *Gay/Lesbian Almanac: A New Documentary*, ed. Jonathan Ned Katz. New York: Harper and Row, Publishers.

Sullivan, Michael, and John S. Wodarski. 2002. "Social Alienation in Gay Youth." *Journal of Human Behavior in the Social Environment 5*, no. 1: 1–17.

U. S. Senate, 81st Congress 2nd Session, Committee on Expenditures in the Executive Departments Document #241, 1875. repr. 1975. "Employment of Homosexuals and Other Sex Perverts in Government." Reprinted in *Government Versus Homosexual*, ed. Leslie Parr. New York: Arno Press, 1975.

Vicinus, Martha. 1984. "Distance and Desire: English Boarding School Friendships, 1870–1920." *Signs: Journal of Women in Culture and Society 9*, no. 4: 600–622.

Waller, Willard. 1932. *The Sociology of Teaching*. New York: John Wiley and Sons.

Washington Post, January 13, 1990.

Wattenberg, William, ed. 1966. *Social Deviancy Among Youth: The Sixty-Fifth Yearbook of the National Society for the Study of Education*. Chicago: University of Chicago Press.

Woog, Dan. 1995. *School's Out: The Impact of Gay and Lesbian Issues on America's Schools*. Boston: Alyson.

Chapter Four

Subject to Scrutiny

Taking Foucauldian Genealogies to Narratives of Youth Oppression

Valerie Harwood

Introduction

Minority sexual orientation and gender atypicality are early magnets *for maltreatment. . . . An implication is that lesbians and gay men may be more vulnerable than heterosexual women and men to the onset of psychiatric disorders at an early age because of early psychologically stressful experiences arising from stigmatisation.*

—Cochran 2001, 937; emphasis added

In the above quote Cochran (2001) claims that a relationship exists between "sexual orientation and gender atypicality" and the "onset of psychiatric disorders at an early age." Extending this further, Cochran maintains that this "relationship" is due to the "early psychologically stressful experiences arising from stigmatisation" (937). What is clearly problematic is the way in which this statement attempts to connect lesbians and gay men to psychiatric disorders.

A similar interest in making this connection is apparent in the article "Is Sexual Orientation Related to Mental Health Problems and Suicidality in Young People?" published in the *Archives of General Psychiatry*.[1] In this article Fergusson, Horwood, and Beautrais (1999) claim that conduct disorder is more prevalent in gay, lesbian, or bisexual (GLB[2]) youth than in heterosexual youth. This term "conduct disorder" refers to a mental disorder defined in the American Psychiatric Association's (APA) (1994) *Diagnostic and Statistical Manual of Mental Disorders (DSM-IV)*. Here it is described as being "characterized by a pattern of behavior that violates the basic rights of others or major age-appropriate societal norms or rules" (38).[3] The psychiatric and psychological literature largely portrays conduct disorder as a scientifically genuine mental disorder and offers limited, if any, critique of it as a construct (Harwood 2003). Indeed, rather than skepticism, it is invariably described as a legitimate child and youth disorder and is characterized in somewhat ominous ways. For example, Dumas, Prinz, Smith, and Laughlin report that "conduct disorder (CD) is a chronic disorder that is very difficult to change and often results in multiple adverse outcomes" (1999, 38).

Thus Fergusson et al.'s (1999) claim bears considerable foreboding for GLB youth. When read in the context of Cochran's assertion used to open this chapter, it seems to be a powerful and gloomy declaration about GLB youth. For example, if we uncritically entertained Fergusson et al.'s declaration and considered it in the light of the quote by Cochran, the conclusion could be drawn that this alleged prevalence of conduct disorder in GLB youth is reflective of their status as "early magnets for maltreatment" and their "vulnerability" for psychiatric disorders. Furthermore, following this reasoning it could be asserted that those GLB youth considered conduct disordered not only purportedly experience the "early onset of psychiatric disorders," they also meet with a psychiatrically prophesized future of "chronic adverse outcomes."

These claims, I suggest, are indicative of a shift whereby rather than a young person being labeled psychopathological *by virtue* of their sexual and/or gender non-normativity, they are instead deemed psychopathological *because* of what their sexual and/or gender non-normativity is likely to cause. This shift sustains a dangerous association whereby certain sexual and gender markers defined as non-normative are construed by proxy, psychopathological. This is significant given the removal of homosexuality from psychiatric classification in the American Psychiatric Association's (APA) *Diagnostic and Statistical Manual of Mental Disorders (DSM)* in 1973. What this shift suggests is that this removal is not the guarantee that it may seem. Thus in an uncanny twist through recourse to narratives of GLB youth oppression, certain young people in Fergusson et al.'s (1999) research can, via their sexual orientation, be linked to psychopathology.

This chapter thus sets out to critically analyze the emergence of psychopathologized queer youth and Fergusson et al.'s (1999) declaration that conduct disorder is more prevalent in GLB young people.[4] I employ the term psychopathologized queer youth to describe the practices that configure youth sexual and gender non-normativity as psychopathological. Drawing on Seidman's statement that "Queers are not united by a unitary identity but only by their opposition to disciplining, normalizing social forces" (1993, 133), the word queer is used in this chapter to signify the sexual and gender identities configured as non-normative by these discourses of psychopathology. The term "psychopathologized queer youth" is thus deployed in a critical sense to indicate the ways in which discourses of psychopathology construct the notion of non-normative sexual and/or gender identities as psychopathological.

In this analysis I draw closely on Foucauldian genealogy to scrutinize these discourses. To do this I work with a genealogical strategy that involves four angles of scrutiny. This strategy comprises the angles of emergence, contingency, discontinuity, and subjugated knowledges. The chapter begins with a brief outline of genealogy and the four angles of scrutiny. This then leads to the discussion of each of these angles in relation to the notion of psychopathologized queer youth. In pursuing this analysis I provide a critical examination of the discourses that posit queer[5] young people as psychopathological or as at imminent risk of psychopathology and argue that this claim must be subjected to scrutiny.

Genealogy and the Angles of Scrutiny

Genealogy offers what I consider to be a valuable perspective in the analysis of the discourses of psychopathologized queer youth.[6] This usefulness of genealogy is illustrated in the following statement: "for it really is against the effects of the power of a discourse that is considered to be scientific that the genealogy must wage its struggle" (Foucault 1980, 84). This struggle against the scientific is relevant for this genealogical analysis since claims to scientificity are crucial to supporting notions of psychopathologized queer youth. A similar critique of scientific discourses is taken up by McCallum (1997), who uses genealogical techniques to analyze the production of personality disorders. In so doing, McCallum argues that "Much of the existing certainty and truthfulness of the category of personality and personality disorder is disturbed by attempts to map out a genealogical analysis of its contemporary uses" (69).

A crucial feature of genealogy is its emphasis on the present. Here Foucault makes the point that "I set out from a problem expressed in the terms current today and I try to work out its genealogy. *Genealogy means that I begin my analysis from a question posed in the present*" (1988a, 262; emphasis added). This emphasis on the present is clarified by Ransom (1997), who explains genealogies as "historical studies whose purpose is to produce critical effects in the present" (79). In considering the history of the present, genealogy can draw attention to the constructed nature of this notion of psychopathologized queer youth. This is a valuable approach since it can offer a critique of the scientific discourses implicated in claims such as Cochran's (2001) and Fergusson et al.'s (1999).

The four angles of scrutiny are drawn from my interpretation of Foucauldian genealogy, and provide a suggestion of one approach to genealogy. These four angles are depicted in figure 4.1.

The angles comprise the following genealogical tools: emergences, contingency, discontinuity, and subjugated knowledges. Using these angles of scrutiny provides one way to think about applying genealogy. It is, however, by no means a prescription of how to do genealogy.[7] In the remainder of this chapter I discuss how each of these angles can be deployed to scrutinize the constitution of psychopathologized queer youth.

Angle One: Emergences

Accentuating emergences provides a way to draw attention to the manifestation of psychopathologized queer youth. The assertion by Fergusson et al. (1999) of the prevalence of conduct disorder in GLB youth produces a seemingly scientific explanation of the way in which sexual and/or gender non-normativity is linked to behavior disorders, and ipso facto, to psychopathology. The question must therefore be asked, How has this notion of psychopathologized queer youth emerged? To respond to this question I begin by analyzing Fergusson et al.'s (1999) claim regarding conduct disorder, and then move to consider other examples that assert the notion of psychopathologized queer youth.

Fergusson et al. (1999) report that 32.1 percent of the young people in their New Zealand longitudinal study who identified themselves as gay, lesbian, or bisexual (GLB) fitted the diagnostic criteria for conduct disorder. The "32.1" percentage certainly appears high when compared to those who identified themselves as heterosexual, of whom only 11 percent fitted the criteria for conduct disorder (Fergusson, Horwood,

Figure 4.1

Four angles of scrutiny

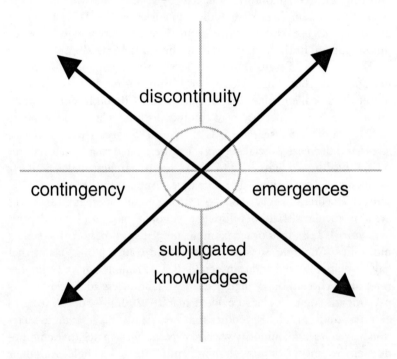

discontinuity

contingency   emergences

subjugated
knowledges

and Beautrais 1999). Yet this figure and the method for classifying "GLB" participants demands closer examination. According to Fergusson et al. (1999), "of the 1007 subjects questioned at age 21 years, 20 (2 percent) identified as GLB . . . [and] a further 8 subjects self-identified as heterosexual but disclosed that they had had sexual relationships with a same sex partner since the age of 16 years" (877).[8] They explain that "a classification of GLB orientation was constructed by including into the definition all of those who reported GLB orientation or those reporting having same-sex partners" (877). Drawing on these results, Fergusson et al. (1999) make the remarkable declaration that GLB young people "who disclose same-sex sexual contact are at clearly increased risks of psychiatric disorder and suicidal behaviors" (880).

This interpretation is made regardless of the issue that it is taken from a small sample of 28 "GLB" young people.

Notably this declaration is made by drawing on the *DSM-IV* (APA, 1994). The influence of this manual of mental disorders on researchers working with GLB youth is indicated by Anhalt and Morris (1998), who direct researchers to use the categories in the *DSM-IV*. They encourage its use, stating, "this manual is the most widely accepted among mental health professionals in the United States" (228).

The claim by Fergusson et al. (1999) about conduct disorder is extraordinary, but as indicated above, is by no means the only one made about the so-called behavioral problems of GLB youth. For instance, while not referring specifically to conduct disorder, Hart and Heimberg (2001) claim that research on GLB[9] youth "suggests that increased stress and decreased social support may be related to a higher risk for mental health problems . . ." (615). Other researchers make similarly problematic conclusions. For example, Anhalt and Morris (1998) write, "The literature . . . points to a strong possibility that GLB youths are at particular risk for developing psychopathology and maladaptive behaviors" (228). In another example, in their study of homeless sexual minorities, Cochran, Stewart, Ginzler, and Cauce (2002) claim that gay, lesbian, bisexual and transgender (GLBT) adolescents have higher rates of psychopathology than heterosexual homeless adolescents. This psychopathologizing is also evident in Elze (2002), who, referring to externalizing[10] problems, reports that her "study suggests an association between sexual minority youths' perceptions of a negative community environment for gay, lesbian, and bisexual people and their externalizing problems" (97).

In yet another example, Baumarind (1995) notes that "Hershberger and D'Augelli concluded from the literature that, even without victimization, nonheterosexual youths are particularly vulnerable to mental health problems, which they attributed largely to the stigmatisation of their oppression" (133). This statement seems to make psychopathologized queer youth a possibility with or *without* such issues as homelessness. Thus according to this line of argument, because the non-normative is non-normative, they are prey to oppression and associated stigmatization, and so are therefore vulnerable to mental health problems.

This idea of being prey to oppression and stigmatization is taken one step further and linked to fear by D'Augelli, Pilkington, and Hershberger (2002). Citing another study, D'Augelli et al. (2002) state, using a representative sample of Massachusetts high school students, and comparing lgb-identified youths with heterosexual youths, Garofalo, Wolf, Kessel, Palfrey, and DuRant (1998) found that one-quarter of the lgb youths said they had missed school in the last month because of fear, compared to 5 percent of the non-lgb youths. (149)

It is relevant to note that not attending school is an issue that is often associated with conduct disorder in the psychiatric literature. In the situation described above, LGB youth not attending school due to fear could be recast by scientific discourses as having behavior problems.

In the light of these alleged connections, consider the following statement from Rivers and Carragher (2003):

> The concept of abnormal development is one that researchers have not dismissed entirely, however, rather than pathologizing the development of lesbians and gay men, attempts have been made to understand the difficulties they face from a socio-cultural perspective. (374)

When Rivers and Carragher (2003) state "have not dismissed entirely, however," there is a sense of reappraisal. It seems to me that this reappraisal is one that continues to gaze at its object (namely the psychopathologized queer youth) but does so in a different light. Hence it appears that despite the removal of homosexuality from the *DSM* and the utilization of terms such as "socio-cultural," homosexuality as a psychopathologized object remains, albeit in a different guise.

This different guise is evident in the following postulation by Fergusson et al. (1999). They state that one of the reasons for what they argue is the high risk of mental disorder for GLB youth is "the possibility of 'reverse causality' in which young people prone to psychiatric disorder are more prone to experience homosexual attraction or contact" (Fergusson et al. 1999, 880). This statement quite explicitly links homosexuality to psychopathology. To take this point further, consider this comment by Bailey (1999):

> A second possibility is that homosexuality represents a deviation from normal development and is associated with other such deviations that may lead to mental illness. One need not believe that homosexuality is a psychopathologic trait (i.e., a behavioral or emotional trait that necessarily creates problems for the individual or society) to believe that evolution has worked to ensure heterosexuality in most cases and homosexuality may represent a developmental error. (884)

The above statement by Bailey would have us believe that homosexuality is a deviation and, as such, one that is linked to mental illness.[11] Bailey also invokes a scientific discourse of evolution to claim the dominance of heterosexuality, and thereby construes homosexuality as a "developmental error." These ideas appear to lay claim to a purported relationship between psychopathology and "homosexual attraction or contact." Likewise, for Fergusson et al. (1999) the proposition is made that psychiatric disorder can make young people more "prone" to nonheterosexual behavior.

These examples suggest a moment of emergence. Where once (and I acknowledge there remain[12]) discourses of homosexuality *as* mental illness spoke the truth about the homosexual; now discourses of psychopathology speak the truth about the vulnerabilities, propensities, possibilities, and hazards that *inhere* in the developing homosexual (or GLB, or nonheterosexual) youth. This term "inhere" conveys the way in which these psychopathological discourses construct these various hazards as characteristic of non-normative sexual and/or gender identity, and in so doing, fuse this hazard with psychopathology.

Angle Two: Contingency

Highlighting emergences draws attention to the way in which the notion of the psychopathologized queer youth is spoken into existence. What contingency offers is to draw attention to those practices upon which such emergences are reliant. This use of contingency is possible because as Foucault (1988b) states, "the things which seem most evident to us are always formed in the confluence of encounters and chances, during the course of a precarious and fragile history" (37). Thus the analysis of contingency places prominence on what may be contingent in the constitution of the psychopathologized queer youth.

For example, this emphasis can be deployed to highlight that which is contingent in the claims made by Fergusson et al. (1999) regarding the suggestion of a relationship between conduct disorder and GLB youth. In this way contingency can alert us to the "fragile history" of the notion of psychopathologized queer youth. Notably, it can be deployed to challenge the rationality of the psychiatric expertise that defines and speaks of such psychopathology. In Foucauldian terms we can thus imagine that, "what different forms of rationality offer as their necessary being, can perfectly well be shown to have a history; and the network of contingencies from which it emerges can be traced" (Foucault 1988b, 37). This perspective and the types of questions it may provoke suggest an altogether different interpretation of the scientific veracity of the claims that posit conduct disordered GLB youth. Instead of taking the notion of conduct disorder as a *given*, one is prompted to ask, On what factors is this conduct disordered GLB youth contingent? One possible contingency is the idea of the interiority of the young person. For example, it can be argued that interiority is required for the young person to experience what the literature argues to be the problem of internalized homophobia. According to some of the psychiatric literature, it seems that internalized homophobia is a contemporary feature of psychopathologized queer youth. This notion of internalized homophobia is asserted by Cochran (2001),

> lesbians and gay men, like heterosexual women and men, incorporate learned negative attitudes and beliefs about homosexuality in the process of growing up. The effect of this, which is labeled *internalized homophobia,* is psychological problems with self image and social functioning during adolescence and adulthood. (940, emphasis added)

Here it seems that for internalized homophobia to be produced, these "learned negative attitudes" need to be situated in the *interior* of the young person. Once located within this interior, this internalized homophobia has the effect, according to Cochran (2001), of causing psychological problems. This suggested relationship between internalized homophobia and psychopathology is also made explicit by Lock and Steiner (1999). These authors state that,

> The etiology of problems among sexual minority youth is unclear. What seems to be a risk factor are homophobic attitudes—internalized or experienced (Shidlo 1994). Data from this study support the notion that internalized homophobia insofar as it is measured by comfort with sexual orientation seems to be correlated with more psychosocial difficulties, and these difficulties overlap, not surprisingly, with some of those health domains (Mental Health Problems and General Health Problems) that were problems for GLB youth. (302)

As maintained in this quote, it could be contended that a youth's capacity for "internalization" and the likelihood of "internalized homophobia" form a key contingency in the construction of the notion of psychopathologized queer youth.[13] This notion of interiority is thus a principal assumption in the assertion of internalized homophobia, and as such a revealing contingency for the notion of psychopathologized queer youth.

Claims such as Fergusson et al.'s (1999) of the relationship between conduct disorder and GLB youth are also contingent on a notion of youth and adolescence. For example, there is need for this contingency in order for statements such as Elze's to be made, "gay, lesbian, and bisexual adolescents share risk factors with other vulnerable adolescents, but also face psychosocial challenges unique to their experience as members of a stigmatized group . . ." (2002, 96). What appears to be important to these claims is not only that these psychopathologized queer young people are considered non-normative in terms of sexuality and/or gender, but also that they are *young*. Much of the psychopathology literature discussed in this chapter singles out age and developmental processes as key factors in the development difficulties in GLB youth. For example this is evident in the quote by Cochran used to open this chapter. Here the emphasis is placed on "early psychologically stressful experiences arising from stigmatisation" (Cochran 2001, 937). Similarly, Fergusson et al. (1999) state that regarding their research study,

> there was some evidence to suggest small tendencies for the GLB group to have experienced more troubled childhoods, with this group having greater exposure to parental change including separation and/or divorce and remarriage and higher exposure to parents with a history of criminal offence. (879)

Again attention is drawn to troubled childhood experiences, to difficulties with parents, and, in particular, to parental histories of criminal offenses. It is interesting to note that this latter detail is probably a significant point to highlight for researchers such as Fergusson et al. (1999) who are seeking to make claims about GLB youth and conduct disorder. This is because conduct disorder is frequently claimed to be associated with delinquency (for a critical discussion see Harwood 2003). Similarly, there are also various claims about causation, including that by Pincus, who states, "physical and sexual abuse, familial explosiveness and violence, familial and maternal depression, and suicide distinguished those with conduct disorder from those without conduct disorder" (1999, 547). Thus by making such comments about childhood troubles these authors draw on both the discourses of conduct disorder *and* on the discourses that situate childhood as fragile and vulnerable. In so doing Fergusson et al. (1999) can attempt to establish authority for their study.

Turning to another example, in the quote cited previously, Bailey (1999, 884) conveys the opinion that homosexuality "represents a developmental error," a deviation that "may lead to mental illness." It seems that this notion of psychopathologized queer youth derives much of its force through its reliance on the idea that "stressful experiences" occur at "early" points in the GLB young person's life. It thereby relies on both the contingency of discourses of developmentalism and notions of the fragility of the child/youth. Furthermore, this so-called fragility of youth is also likely to be situated as prey to its own interiority. Consequently the discourses of the psychopathologized queer youth can situate the vulnerability of youth as also susceptible to the peril of internalized homophobia.

By taking the Foucauldian (Foucault 1972, 49) inspired statement that a discourse of psychopathologized queer youth "produces the objects of which it speaks," we could make the argument that the dangers of "early stigmatisation" and fragility are involved in the production of psychopathologized youth. Similarly, the peril of the interior and its susceptibility to homophobia could also be involved in this production. As an object, therefore, the notion of psychopathologized queer youth shares an intimate relationship with the practices of psychopathology that "speaks it into existence." I suggest that if we understand this relationship as mutually dependent we can come closer to grasping the contingencies upon which the notion of the psychopathologized queer youth depends—and consequently, how it is produced.

It is more than likely that there are other contingencies in the production of the notion of psychopathologized queer youth. However, by considering two, namely the interior that makes internalized homophobia possible and the notion of early and young, it can be seen that the constitution of such notions is dependent on arguably problematic assumptions. Endeavoring to trace such contingencies therefore provides a cogent form of critical analysis that can be applied to the important task of scrutinizing these discourses.

Angle Three: Discontinuity

As discussed above, a genealogical perspective concerns itself with questions from the present and then considers these in terms of a history of the present. To perform this genealogical history of the present demands thinking very differently about history,

> if the genealogist refuses to extend his [sic] faith in metaphysics, if he listens to history, he finds that there is "something altogether different" behind things: not a timeless and essential secret, but the secret that they

have no essence or that their essence was fabricated in a piecemeal fashion from alien forms. (Foucault 1977, 142)

This idea of listening for "something altogether different" draws attention to the discontinuity "behind things," and, in the case examined in this chapter, to the discontinuity of conduct disorder and psychopathologized queer youth. It lends itself to conceiving that this mental disorder "has no essence" and that the purported essence "was fabricated in a piecemeal fashion from alien forms" (Foucault 1977, 142).

Following from this perspective, it can be argued that it is the seeming continuity of conduct disorder that gives researchers such as Fergusson et al. (1999) the authority to speak about certain young people and their propensity for psychopathology. Thus we need to ask, What is it that is discontinuous in conduct disorder? One apparent continuity that can be examined is the definition of conduct disorder. This definition is posited as having continuity (as might be suspected, since this adds weight to its legitimacy), yet upon closer analysis, it appears to be more discontinuous than continuous.

One of the ways that the continuity of conduct disorder is posited is by asserting that changes in definition are results of what researchers such as Lahey and Loebar (1997, 52) call the evolvement of its definition. The idea of evolving invokes notions of scientific improvement, and a deepening knowledge of its object, namely the conduct disordered youth. Yet as I will argue, such claims appear to buckle under genealogical scrutiny. This can be demonstrated by considering the changes made to the *DSM* definition of conduct disorder, and, in particular, the treatment of the notion of running away.

"Running away" is a phenomenon that is mentioned across several editions of the *DSM*, including *DSM-II, DSM-III, DSM-III-Revised (DSM-III-R)*, and *DSM-IV*.[14] This continued attention would appear to suggest that running away is significant in terms of defining behavioral disorders. However, genealogical analysis that draws on discontinuity can provide a different perspective. The attention to running away may seem an odd—or at best, a dated—view of children. However, a compelling association is frequently made between GLB young people and running away, and between conduct problems and the child runaway.

For example, Anhalt and Morris (1998) in the section of their article on GLB adolescents and history of conduct problems begin by noting the prevalence of running away. Describing research by Remafedi (1987), they write, "In his sample of young gay and bisexual men, Remafedi (1987) found that (a) 48 percent of participants had run away from home at least once in their lifetime, (b) 43 percent of youth who ran away at least once reported doing so for sexuality-related conflicts" (Anhalt and Morris 1998, 224). In their article they immediately follow this discussion of GLB youth and running away by turning to discuss delinquency and conduct problems. Drawing on the same study by Remafedi (1987), Rotheram-Borus, Rosario, Rossem, Reid, and Roy (1995) in their discussion of gay and bisexual male adolescents state, "Conduct problems were reflected in the high rates of running away from home (48 percent) and reports of delinquent acts that led to contact with the criminal justice system (48 percent)" (75). Again we see an emphasis on running away, and, in this instance, on "delinquent acts."

What is interesting from a genealogical point of view is how the *DSM-II* (APA 1968) "Runaway Reaction of Childhood" evolved into the *DSM-III* (APA 1980) category titled "Conduct Disorder, Undersocialized, Nonaggressive." The *DSM-II* category states that

> Individuals with this disorder characteristically escape from threatening situations by running away from home for a day or more without permission. Typically they are immature and timid, and feel rejected at home, inadequate, and friendless. They often steal furtively. (APA 1968, 50)

The discontinuity in this evolvement is apparent when we compare the above category to that contained in the subsequent edition, *DSM-III* (APA 1980). The definition in this edition has several features that suddenly appear, including: substance abuse, violating the rights of others, serious lying, extending "oneself for others when no immediate advantage is likely," "avoidance of blame and informing." Yet by contrast, the earlier version, *DSM-II,* contains none of these features.

This concern with running away is also incorporated in the next edition of the manual, *DSM-III-R* (APA 1987). In this edition running away is included among a list of the thirteen items that comprise the diagnostic criteria for conduct disorder. Interestingly, here the specific diagnostic description for running away is, "has run away from home overnight at least twice while living in parental or parental surrogate home (*or once without returning*)" (APA 1987, 55; emphasis added). In the next edition, *DSM-IV* (1994), running away is slotted into the diagnostic criteria for conduct disorder under the category "Serious Violations of Rules." This criterion stipulates, "has run away from home overnight at least twice while living in parental or parental surrogate home (*or once without returning for a lengthy period*)" (APA 1994, 90; emphasis added). It appears that between the two versions of the *DSM* there is a discontinuity in the length of time that is deemed worthy of being a criterion for conduct disorder. For the 1987 version, *DSM III*, "once without returning" was deemed sufficient. By contrast, the 1994 version *DSM IV* has the added stipulation "or once without returning for a lengthy period." This difference is important because it indicates a discontinuity in the way in which the criterion for conduct disorder is conceptualized between the two versions. As such this discontinuity reveals how possible changes in what constitutes "running away" influences the way in which this scientific disorder is constructed. Ascertaining this discontinuity provides the opportunity to consider an alternative to the notion of the evolving scientific definition.

To emphasize the relevance of scrutinizing the *DSM*, and its notions of the runaway, it is apt to consider the study by Rotheram-Borus et al. (1995). The *DSM-III-R* (APA 1987) played an important role in their study, which focused on mainly Black and Hispanic youths recruited from the Hetrick-Martin Institute in New York City.[15] The measure used to identify conduct problems drew on the *DSM-III-R*, using criteria that included things such as,

> skipped school or work, ran away from home; destroyed property (other than setting fires); teased or fought with younger children; used a weapon in a fight; said things that were not true; stole (with confrontation of the victim . . .); stole (with no confrontation); broke into a house, building, or car; forced someone to have sex with him; were physically cruel to animals; joined with members of a gang to cause trouble; or got in trouble at home. (Rotherm-Borus et al. 1995, 77)

In using this data, this study claimed that, "Whereas most of the problem behaviors occurred at rates similar to heterosexual males, sexual behaviors were not similar" (Rotheram-Borus et al. 1995, 82). Notably, this finding prompts these researchers to speculate about the different "developmental pathways" of male gay and bisexual youths (as compared to male heterosexual youths). Here they state that "many gay youths engage in sexual activity as a means of exploring their sexual orientation, making sexual activity for gay youths normative, as a developmental marker of identity formation" (Rotheram-Borus et al. 1995, 84). Whether such behavior is markedly different from "male heterosexuals" or even is more to do with identity and less to do with pleasure would make for a compelling debate. While acknowledging this debate, I want to emphasize how such notions constitute the psychopathologized queer youth. In this example we can see how the discourse of conduct problems is engaged in the production of the discourse of sexually problematic behavior and nonconforming developmental trajectories.

Notwithstanding the diagnostic emphasis, running away is a debatable issue. Take for example this observation by Savin-Williams, "There is little empirical verification regarding the percentage of runaways who identify themselves as lesbian, gay, or bisexual or the number of lesbian, gay male or bisexual youths who run away from home" (1994, 264). Similarly, there is considerable critique of the ways in which data is collected for studies of GLB youth. This criticism is made by Garafalo, Wolf, Kessel, Palfrey and DuRant, who state,

> Much of what is known concerning the association between gay youth and health risk behaviors is derived from studies using self-select populations such as homeless/runaway youth, youth presenting to sexually transmitted disease clinics, or youth responding to advertisements in gay newspapers or dance clubs. (1998, 896).

●Whilst there is little empirical verification, it is important to note that there are numerous studies that do describe large numbers of runaway gay, lesbian, and bisexual youth.● This is made explicit by Savin-Williams (1994), who cites U.S. figures ranging from 2–3 percent to 6 percent and then argues that these are "probably a gross underestimation because few youths are likely to tell authorities and staff their sexuality" (264). Echoing this view are reports of estimates of GLBT youth on the streets at between "11 percent -35 percent" (Cochran et al. 2002, 773). It is salient to observe in this discussion the incongruence between the diagnostic *emphasis on running away* and the lack of accepted statistical data that can verify it as an issue of substance. Nevertheless, whilst there is limited empirical verification about GLB runaways, this notion of running away forms a key conceptualization in criteria of conduct disorders and in discussions of GLB young people and their supposedly psychopathologized queer behavior disorders.

To borrow from Foucault (1998b), through the analysis of running away psychopathologized queer youth "appears then not as a great continuity underneath an apparent discontinuity, but as a tangle of superimposed discontinuities" (Foucault, 429). This emphasis on the tangle of discontinuities draws attention to the ways in which the notion of the psychopathologized queer youth can emerge as a phantom of continuity. Furthermore, it can be used to raise questions as to why running away is not construed as a positive or helpful behavior (in certain circumstances), but, rather, as necessarily an indicator of psychopathology.

Angle Four: Subjugated Knowledge

Subjugated disqualified knowledges are another angle of scrutiny that can be used to analyze the constitution of psychopathologized queer youth. Foucault (1980) provides a description of subjugated knowledges when he states, "Let us give the term *genealogy* to the union of erudite knowledge and local memories which allows us to establish a historical knowledge of struggles and to make use of this knowledge tactically today" (Foucault 1980a, 83; emphasis in original). This quote indicates the potential value of subjugated knowledges to genealogy, as well as indicating two types of subjugated knowledge, namely "erudite knowledge" and "local memories" or "disqualified knowledge."

The term "subjugated erudite knowledges" refers to those knowledges that have been obscured by dominant knowledge. Foucault terms these "buried knowledges of erudition" (1980, 82), and this sense of being "buried" gives a clue to both their status and their location. These are knowledges that may have competed with dominant knowledges, such as that of the discourses of psychopathologized queer youth. However, these discourses have become buried or concealed by dominant knowledges. One example of these might be the views of those who do not draw on these psychopathologizing discourses. For instance, in a school or education system where notions of conduct disorder are adhered to, alternative teacher perspectives that situate GLB running away as not psychopathological may become subjugated. The presence of such a subjugated erudite knowledge would be important in this case, as it can function as a litmus test for the dominating knowledges. The subjugated erudite knowledge could be used to indicate moments of domination, and thus draw attention to the way in which psychopathological knowledge about GLB youth is produced.

The "disqualified," second type of subjugated knowledges, are knowledges that are bereft of "expertise" and "qualification." These knowledges are "naive knowledges located low down on the hierarchy, beneath the required level of cognition or scientificity . . ." (Foucault 1980, 82). To use these knowledges would require the genealogist to engage in conversations with those that are "low down on the hierarchy." This could mean conducting research with GLB young people who are described by the likes of Fergusson et al. (1999)

as psychopathological. By employing such subjugated disqualified knowledges, genealogy can be thus used to

> entertain the claims to attention of local, discontinuous, disqualified, illegitimate knowledges against the claims of a unitary body of theory which would filter, hierarchise and order them in the name of some true knowledge and some arbitrary idea of what constitutes a science and its objects. (Foucault 1980a, 83)

By engaging in such conversations, the subjugated disqualified knowledges of GLB youth could be drawn on to "entertain claims" against the "unitary body" of knowledge associated with these psychopathologizing discourses. For instance, in contrast to psychopathologized notions of running away, perspectives of young people who are subjugated and disqualified could paint a very different picture of the potential the running away may offer. That is, rather than being depicted by discourses of psychopathologized queer youth as being related to psychopathology, subjugated disqualified knowledges might depict running away as advantageous. It may be depicted as contributing to a young person's survival or the improvement of their life. Through their disqualification, subjugated disqualified knowledges may therefore offer very different perspectives to the dominant psychopathological knowledge—and in so doing present a perspective that can challenge the apparent "unitary" view of psychopathological knowledge.

These two types of subjugated knowledge are therefore valuable tools for critiquing the discourses of psychopathologized queer youth. This point can be interpreted from Foucault's statement that from these two subjugated knowledges it is possible to create "something one might call a genealogy, or rather a multiplicity of genealogical researches, a painstaking rediscovery of struggles together with the rude memory of their conflicts" (1980, 83). Here there is, I argue, great value in the way that this Foucauldian perspective places emphasis on the struggles at play in these instances of domination. It is these very struggles that have the potential to offer different standpoints on the notion of psychopathologized queer youth. The example of accessing the knowledge of GLB young people who have run away is one instance where this would provide an important counterperspective to the dominant psychopathological discourse that would potentially posit them as conduct disordered.

Conclusion

I have argued in this chapter that the emergence of psychopathologized queer youth in the psychopathological literature presents a dangerous turn that concerns itself with those it considers to be sexually and/or gender non-normative. If we accept the perspectives claimed in this literature, then to be a GLB youth necessarily incurs the risk of conduct disorder. I argue the significance in recognizing that this claim of psychopathologized queer youth relies on a post-psychopathological intelligibility of homosexuality. This intelligibility superficially appears not to situate homosexuality as mental illness, but rather situates mental illness as *the risk* wrought by homosexuality. This is, I suggest, a subtle twist, and one that is particularly treacherous in the way in which it cannily interweaves psychopathology with non-normative gender and/or sexual identities. There is therefore the need to be alert to and critical of the practices that draw on this intelligibility to produce discourses of psychopathologized queer youth. As I have discussed, genealogy is one approach that can be employed to catch the intricacies of this discourse. In addition to performing the key task of showing up these discourses, the angles of scrutiny can be drawn on to unsettle the claim that conduct disorder is more prevalent in GLB young people. Similarly, the angles of scrutiny can be used to dispute the assertion that psychopathologized queer youth is the outcome of evolutionary development that favors the heterosexual. Most important, each of these angles of scrutiny can be drawn on to raise awareness of the menace of this dangerous turn and to build an analysis that treats it with scrutiny— and most importantly, much needed suspicion.

Notes

1. Psychiatric and psychological sources are cited throughout this chapter— and in citing these sources I am aware of the risk of appearing to give them some authority. Here it is important to emphasize that this is not my intention. These sources are cited in order to specifically critique the claim that "non-normative" sexual and/or gender identities are linked to psychopathology and, more broadly, to analyze the ways in which notions of youth psychopathology are constructed.

2. Fergusson et al. (1999) specifically refer to "GLB" youth. The identity categories gay, lesbian, or bisexual are often cited in the research literature that concerns itself with this specialist subgroup of youth psychopathology. See for example Lock and Steiner (1999), Fergusson et. al. (1999). I

therefore use the acronym "GLB" throughout this chapter when referring to psychopathological literature that uses this conceptualization. When other identity categories are used the appropriate acronym is included.

3. In *DSM-IV*, conduct disorder is situated under the section "Disorders usually First Diagnosed in Infancy, Childhood and Adolescence." Other mental disorders listed in this section include "Attention-Deficit/ Hyperactivity Disorder (ADHD)," "Attention-Deficit/Hyperactivity Disorder Not Otherwise Specified," "Oppositional Defiant Disorder," and "Disruptive Behavior Disorder Not Otherwise Specified" (APA 1994, 38).

4. In this chapter I concentrate specifically on "behavior disorders." There are likely to be other mental disorders that are also claimed to be linked to GLB youth.

5. The term "queer" is frequently used throughout this chapter as an identity category that indicates a broad range of what could be described as "non-normative" sexual and gender identities.

6. Genealogy has been used in education by several authors, including Laurence and McCallum (1998), and Meadmore and Symes (1996). Interesting queer theoretical use of genealogy includes the recent Ph.D. dissertation by McCully (1998). Foucault's work has been used to examine the construction of mental disorder in several studies, including Robbins' (2000) analysis of Attention Deficit Disorder, Guilfoyle's (2001) examination of the construction of Bulimia and Feder's (1997) analysis of Gender Identity Disorder.

7. For further discussion see Harwood and Rasmussen (2003).

8. The authors explain that this data "was gathered during the course of the Christchurch Health and Development Study, a longitudinal study of a birth cohort of New Zealand–born children who have been studied from birth to age 21 years" (Fergusson et al.1999, 877).

9. Again, these authors refer specifically to "Gay, Lesbian and Bisexual."

10. "Externalizing" problems is frequently used in the psychiatric and psychological literature to refer to behaviors manifested outwardly (as opposed to "internalizing" problems such as "depression").

11. Bailey (1999) goes on to state that "left-handedness" is one of the indicators of developmental aberrance. That left-handedness could be construed to connote aberrance might seem surprising, since it could be presumed that such "wayward" claims have been left to the past of psychiatric science. That Bailey (1999) can include such claims in the article "Homosexuality and Mental Illness" is certainly a salient reminder that such beliefs are not buried in the history of psychopathologizing homosexuality.

12. See also Yarhouse and Throckmorton's (2002) discussion in favor of "reorientation" therapy, which involves attempting to "re-orient" the homosexual to become a heterosexual.

13. The notion of a relation between "internalized homophobia" and psycho-pathology in GLB individuals is often invoked in psychological literature. For example, see Meyer (2003); Lock and Steiner (1999).
14. Each of these refers to an edition of the *Diagnostic and Statistical Manual of Mental Disorders* (APA, 1968, 1980, 1987, 1994).
15. The authors describe this as "a gay-identified community-based agency . . . providing recreational, educational, and social services to gay and lesbian youths" (Rotheram-Borus et al. 1995, 77).

References

Anhalt, Karla, and Tracy Morris, L. 1998. "Developmental and Adjustment Issues of Gay, Lesbian, and Bisexual Adolescents: A Review of the Empirical Literature." *Clinical Child and Family Psychology Review* 1, no. 4: 215–230.

APA. 1968. *Diagnostic and Statistical Manual of Mental Disorders, Second Edition DSM-II.* Washington, D.C.: APA.

———. 1980. *Diagnostic and Statistical Manual of Mental Disorders, Third Edition DSM-III.* Washington, D.C.: APA.

———. 1987. *Diagnostic and Statistical Manual of Mental Disorders, Third Edition, Revised DSM-III-R.* Washington, D.C.: APA.

———. 1994. *Diagnostic and Statistical Manual of Mental Disorders, Fourth Edition, DSM-IV.* Washington, D.C.: APA.

Bailey, Michael, J. 1999. "Homosexuality and Mental Illness." *Archives of General Psychiatry* 56, no. 10: 883–884.

Baumrind, Diana. 1995. "Commentary on Sexual Orientation: Research and Social Policy Implications." *Developmental Psychology* 31, no. 1: 130–136.

Cochran, Bryan N., Angela J. Stewart, Joshua A. Ginzler, and Ana Mari Cauce. 2002. "Challenges Faced by Homeless Sexual Minorities: Comparison of Gay, Lesbian, Bisexual, and Transgender Homeless Adolescents with their Heterosexual Counterparts." *American Journal of Public Health* 92, no. 5: 773–777.

Cochran, Susan, D. 2001. "Emerging Issues in Research on Lesbians and Gay Men's Mental Health: Does Sexual Orientation Really Matter?" *American Psychologist* 56, no. 11: 932–947.

D'Augelli, Anthony R., Neil W. Pilkington, and Scott L. Hershberger, 2002. "Incidence and Mental Health Impact of Sexual Orientation Victimiza-tion of Lesbian, Gay, and Bisexual Youths in High School." *School Psychology Quarterly* 17, no. 2: 148–167.

Dumas, Jean E., Ronald J. Prinz, Emilie Phillips Smith, and James Laughlin. 1999. "The Early Alliance Prevention Trial: An Integrated Set of Inter-ventions to Promote Competence and Reduce Risk for Conduct Disor-der, Substance Abuse, and School Failure." *Clinical Child and Family Psychology Review* 2, no. 1: 37–53.

Elze, Diane. 2002. "Risk Factors for Internalizing and Externalizing Problems Among Gay, Lesbian, and Bisexual Adolescents." *Social Work Research* 26, no. 2: 89–99.

Feder, Ellen K. 1997. "Disciplining the Family: The Case of Gender Identity Disorder." *Philosophical Studies 85*, no. 2–3: 195–211.

Fergusson, David M., L. John Horwood, and Annette L. Beautrais. 1999. "Is Sexual Orientation Related to Mental Health Problems and Suicidality in Young People?" *Archives of General Psychiatry 56*, no. 10: 876–880.

Foucault, Michel. 1972. *The Archaeology of Knowledge*. New York: Pantheon Books.

———. 1977. "Nietzsche, Genealogy, History." Pp. 139–164 in *Language, Counter-Memory, Practice: Selected Essays and Interviews*, ed. Donald. F. Bouchard. Ithaca, N.Y.: Cornell University Press.

———. 1980. "Two Lectures." Pp.78–108 in *Power/Knowledge: Selected Interviews and Other Writings 1972–1977*, ed. Colin Gordon. Sussex: Harvester Press.

———. 1988a. "The Concern for Truth." Pp. 255–267 in *Politics, Philosophy, Culture: Interviews and Other Writings 1977–1984*, ed. Lawrence D. Kritzman. N.Y.: Routledge.

———. 1988b. "Critical Theory/Intellectual History." Pp. 17–46 in *Politics, Philosophy, Culture: Interviews and Other Writings 1977–1984*, ed. Lawrence D. Kritzman. N.Y.: Routledge.

———. 1990a. *The Care of the Self: The History of Sexuality, Volume 3*. London: Penguin.

———. 1990b. *The Use of Pleasure: The History of Sexuality, Volume 2*. N.Y.: Vintage Books.

———. 1991. *Discipline and Punish: The Birth of the Prison*. London: Penguin Books.

Garofalo, Robert, R., Cameron Wolf, Shari Kessel, Judith Palfrey, and Robert H. DuRant. 1998. "The Association Between Health Risk Behavior and Sexual Orientation Among a School-Based Sample of Adolescents." *Pediatrics 101*: 895–902.

Guilfoyle, Michael. 2001. "Problematizing Psychotherapy: The Discursive Production of a Bulimic." *Culture and Psychology 7*, no. 2: 151–179.

Hart, Trevor, A., and Richard G. Heimberg. 2001. "Presenting Problems Among Treatment-Seeking Gay, Lesbian, and Bisexual Youth." *JCLP/In Session: Psychotherapy in Practice 57*, no. 5: 615–627.

Harwood, Valerie. 2003. "Methodological Insurrections, The Strategic Value of Subjugated Disqualified Knowledges for Disrupting Conduct Disorder." *Melbourne Studies in Education 44*, no. 1: 45–61.

Harwood, Valerie, and Mary Louise Rasmussen. 2003. "Applying Foucauldian Angles of Scrutiny to Qualitative Data Analysis." Paper read at American Educational Research Association, Annual Conference, at Chicago.

Hershberger, Scott L., and Anthony D'Augelli, R. 1995. "The Impact of Victimization on the Mental Health and Suicidality of Lesbian, Gay and Bisexual Youths." *Developmental Psychology* 31, no. 1: 65–74.

Hunter, Ian. 1994. *Rethinking the School: Subjectivity, Bureaucracy, Criticism.* NSW, Australia: Allen and Unwin.

Lahey, Benjamin B., and Rolf Loebar. 1997. "Attention-Deficit/Hyperactivity Disorder, Oppositional Defiant Disorder, Conduct Disorder, and Adult Antisocial Behavior: A Life Span Perspective." Pp. 51–59 in *Handbook of Antisocial Behavior*, eds. David M. Stoff, James Breiling, and Jack D. Maser. New York: John Wiley and Sons.

Laurence, Jennifer, and David McCallum. 1998. "The Myth-or-Reality of Attention-Deficit Disorder: A Genealogical Approach." *Discourse: Studies in the Cultural Politics of Education* 19, no. 2: 183–200.

Lock, James, and Hans Steiner. 1999. "Gay, Lesbian, and Bisexual Youth Risks for Emotional, Physical and Social Problems: Results from a Community-Based Survey." *Journal of the American Academy of Child and Adolescent Psychiatry* 38, no. 3: 297–304.

McCallum, David. 1997. "The Uses of History: Mental Health, Criminality and the Human Sciences." Pp. 53–73 in *Foucault, Health and Medicine*, eds. Robin Bunton and Alan Peterson. London: Routledge.

McCully, Susan. 1998. "How Queer: Race, Gender and the Politics of Production in Contemporary Gay, Lesbian and Queer Theatre." Ph.D. dissertation, University of Wisconsin, Madison.

Meadmore, Daphne, and Colin Symes. 1996. "Of Uniform Appearance: A Symbol of School Discipline and Governmentality." *Discourse: Studies in the Cultural Politics of Education* 17, no. 2: 209–225.

Meyer, Ilan, H. 2003. "Prejudice, Social Stress, and Mental Health in Lesbian, Gay, and Bisexual Populations: Conceptual Issues and Research Evidence." *Psychological Bulletin* 129, no. 5: 674–697.

Pincus, Jonathon H. 1999. "Aggression, Criminality and the Human Frontal Lobes." Pp. 547–556 in *The Human Frontal Lobes: Functions and Disorders*, ed. Bruce L. Miller and Jeffrey L. Cummings. New York: The Guilford Press.

Ransom, John S. 1997. *Foucault's Discipline: The Politics of Subjectivity.* Durham, N.C. and London: Duke University Press.

Remafedi, Gary. 1987. "Adolescent Homosexuality: Psychosocial and Medical Implications." *Pediatrics* 79: 331–337.

Rivers, Ian, and Daniel Carragher, J. 2003. "Social-Developmental Factors Affecting Lesbian and Gay Youth: A Review of Cross-National Research Findings." *Children and Society* 17, no. 5: 374–385.

Robbins, Katheryn S. 2000. "The Social Construction of Attention Deficit Disorder: An Ethnography and Archaeology." Ph.D. dissertation, University of Missouri, Columbia.

Rotheram-Borus, Mary Jane, Margaret Rosario, Ronan Van Rossem, Helen Reid, and Roy Gillis. 1995. "Prevalence, Course and Predictors of

Multiple Problem Behaviors Among Gay and Bisexual Male Adolescents." *Developmental Psychology* 31, no. 1: 75–85.

Savin-Williams, Ritch. 1994. "Verbal and Physical Abuse as Stressors in the Lives of Lesbian, Gay Male, and Bisexual Youths: Associations with School Problems, Running Away, Substance Abuse, Prostitution and Suicide." *Journal of Consulting and Clinical Psychology* 62, no. 2: 261–269.

Seidman, Steven. 1993. "Identity and Politics in a 'Postmodern' Gay Culture: Some Historical and Conceptual Notes." Pp. 105–142 in *Fear of a Queer Planet: Queer Politics and Social Theory*, ed. Michael Warner. Minneapolis: University of Minnesota Press.

Shidlo, Ariel. 1994. "Internalized Homophobia: Conceptual and Empirical Issues in Measurement." Pp. 176–205 in *Psychological Perspectives on Lesbian and Gay Issues*, ed. Beverly Green and Gregory M. Herek. Thousand Oaks, Calif.: Sage.

Yarhouse, Mark, and Warren Throckmorton. 2002. "Ethical Issues in Attempts to Ban Reorientation Therapies." *Psychotherapy* 39, no. 1: 66–75.

Chapter Five

Between Sexuality and Narrative
On the Language of Sex Education

Jen Gilbert

Adolescence is one of those mythic figures that the
imaginary, and of course, the theoretical imaginary,
gives us in order to distance us from certain of our
faults—cleavages, denials, or simply desires?—by
reifying them in the form of someone who has not
yet grown up.

—Kristeva 1990, 8

In a reversal of the usual question of what adults can do to cure the problem of adolescence, a recent art exhibit instead asked what the experiences, identities, and representations of youth can teach us about the problem of being human. In reformulating the terms of adult-adolescent engagement, the curator, Francesco Bonami (2003), calls "the adolescent" the "fourth sex." If the female, male, and homosexual are called the first, second, and third sexes respectively, then the adolescent—who, according to Bonami, embodies simultaneously all three positions and none—might be the fourth sex. The adolescent, understood as straddling boundaries, pushing against limits, and living with extremes, unsettles society's belief in maturity, rationality, and order and calls into question the adult's confidence in their own grown-up-ness. Bonami writes: "Adolescence contains the existential anguish of every human being. Only by blocking the memory can man forget the transitory condition of his existence" (12). Sexuality, and especially the sexuality of youth, we might argue, can be too stark and dissembling a reminder of this transition—a feeling of having arrived too late and too early. Sexuality, that intimate gesture of our humanity, is marked by our helplessness. And the adolescent, who is seen as having arrived too early to the complications of intimate relations, has the potential to remind adults that they are too late to repair the vulnerability that now attends the risk of sexuality.

By considering adolescence through the anxieties of adults, anxieties that youth themselves learn to inflame, negotiate, and ignore, this chapter considers how the education of adolescents is affected and organized by the pervasive worries of adults and how the worries of adults harken back to the work of their own adolescence; that is, the work of growing up. To speak of adolescence today is to engage the memories, dreams, disappointments, and worries of adults who have survived their youth, and, owing to this survival, see adolescence as familiar territory. It is notoriously difficult to talk of adolescence as a concept, identity, or experience without getting lost in this crowd. Would it be outrageous then to talk of adolescence as also an adult experience? That is, what of adolescence lives on in the adult?

In this chapter, I explore this conflict down two avenues, both of which stage the meeting of adult and adolescent desires. First, I consider contemporary debates in sex education. If the sexuality of adolescents is troubling and belongs, as Bonami boldly claims, to a different order, then sex education is one arena in which the interests of adults meet and converse with the desires of adolescents. What are the difficulties of imagining an education in sexuality through this constellation of anxiety, forgetting, and desire? Rather than adjudicate the often heated arguments between different proponents of sex education programs, I approach the problem of educating sexuality through questions of language and narrative. One of the most obvious places where the adolescent lives on in the adult is in narratives of growing up. This is both a problem of discourse, asking what grammars, vernaculars, and silences structure and produce theories of "adolescence" and "the adolescent." And, this is a problem of how language does not simply stand outside of sexuality, describing and organizing its effects. According to psychoanalysis, language is also constitutive of sexuality. The capacity for language and the attendant achievement of using narratives to organize the self are a part of what comes to be called sexuality. It is this double sense of language—as discourse and as narrative—that aggravates efforts to talk to youth about sex.

Just Say No

Debates in North America over sex education stage a curious contradiction. While adult experiences of sex are infinitely complicated, filled with emotions such as love, hate, disappointment, anguish and passion, school conversations with adolescents about their sexual lives can be surprisingly sterile. Indeed, despite vigorous debates between advocates of different approaches to sex education, most prominent articulations of sex education for adolescents begin and end with one implicit or explicit sentence: "Just say no." This brief prohibition contains an anxious mixture of fear, judgment, and prohibition that marks the treatment of adolescent sexuality. The anxiety, however, is vague. What should adolescents refuse? How far should the prohibition stretch? The veil of protection that this silence promises to offer adolescents obscures the ambiguity of its reach. Adults worry about saying too much and unwittingly encouraging sexual activity—even through a curriculum of restraint. Cindy Patton (1996) names the problem this way in her discussion of AIDS education:

> Educators had a hard time figuring out how to address young people without igniting sexual desires that, adults believed, might otherwise have lain safely fallow: They did not know if they could extend the mantle of safety that heterosexuality promised without producing a premature sexuality that might so easily go queer. (37)

However, this worry about leading sexuality astray is not outside the adult's dilemma of trying to find a language to narrate the indirection of their own adolescent sexuality. Talk about sexuality is not simply the terrain of sex education; the language of sexuality is intimately connected to narratives of self, friendship, family, and, indeed, learning. Prohibiting or controlling what can or cannot be said about sex also determines what can be said about the self and its desires, dreams, and fantasies. This contradiction is significant and inflects debates around sex education with a tenor of danger: language is conceptualized as an agent of contagion even as it is central both to teaching adolescents and to narrating the complications of selfhood and sexuality.

This inchoate anxiety over how and which language might lead adolescents down the road to saying "no" structures different approaches to sex education in schools. Amid the many and various sex education programs and curricula, increasingly, models of school-based sex education in North America fall into two broad camps[1]: abstinence-only programs and comprehensive programs, which are often, in this political climate, described as abstinence-based programs.[2] First, conservative models of sex education insist that abstinence is the only safe and moral choice for adolescents. This approach is often linked with conservative religious groups and has widespread popularity in the United States owing to, at least, two factors: local control of school boards and the 1996 allotment of federal funds for sex education on the condition that "abstinence from sexual activity outside marriage [is taught] as the expected standard for school-age children" (Lewin 2000). Indeed, research has shown that despite efforts to institute comprehensive sex education programs in U.S. schools in the late 1980s in response to the AIDS pandemic and a growing concern for teenage pregnancy, many school boards have recently abandoned comprehensiveness in favor of abstinence-only.[3]

In abstinence-only programs, language is seen as provocative and infectious. For example, Janice Irvine (2003) observes that in their fight against sex education in schools, the Christian Right equates talking about sex in the classroom with emotional molestation. In this model, talking about sex can exercise a kind of violence on the listener where the student will "catch" the "disease" of sexual desire from an invasive vocabulary. Punitively literal, this equation functions to shut down conversations and, using the rhetoric of protection, expand the silences surrounding sexuality in schools.

Comprehensive programs often respond to this conservatism by insisting that talk about sex is not provocative: it does not put ideas into people's heads, encourage or promote sex or sexual identities, or lead to earlier or more frequent sexual activity. Unlike abstinence-only models of sex education, which see language as contagious, these models of sex education aim to be comprehensive. While conservative educators may withhold information in order to discourage adolescents from experimenting with sex, advocates of comprehensive sex education argue that access to information about sexuality will offer adolescents the tools to just say no, thereby achieving the same result.

There are critiques to be made of both these models that will call attention to the pathologization of sexuality and the refusal to see adolescents as having sexual rights; as having, that is, the right to say yes (c.f., Britzman 1998; Epstein and Johnson 1998; Fine 1992; Patton 1996). However, implicit in both these versions of sex education is a confidence in the capacity of language to name and delimit sexuality. It is a confidence Jeffrey Moran (2000), in his history of sex education in the twentieth century, derides as "instrumentalist." The question that this confidence does not address, and perhaps falls outside of the wish that sexuality could be persuaded into abstention, concerns the ambiguous relationship between language and sexuality. What is the work of talking about sexuality? That is, in what ways does language express and incite sexuality?

This theoretical problematic—central to psychoanalysis—manifests itself in some ordinary ways. For instance, while educators and parents insist on either the harm or harmlessness of sex talk for adolescents— arguing over whether youth need to be protected from sexual silence or sexual speech—we might also recognize the surprise of sexuality in our excited responses to art, poetry, literature, film, or even the more ordinary aspects of language—the tone of someone's voice, the cadence of a foreign language, the spelling of a beautiful word. In these experiences, language can evoke, excite, and agitate—though in somewhat unpredictable ways and places. We may be able to catch something like a sexuality from language, but sexuality does not always answer in the place where it is summoned. We would be hard pressed, for example, to find honest and frank discussions about sexuality in the sex education curriculum.

How might sex education be enlarged to include a theory of sexuality that could notice the pleasures and difficulties of language, of learning to speak one's desire and tolerating the ways desire eludes narrative? An education in sexuality might not only begin with the anxious prohibitions of adults, but with a curiosity about how one loses and finds oneself in language. Following Julia Kristeva into her encounter with Freud, I consider both the inadequacy of language to capture our affective investments in the world and the parallel ways sexuality is experienced as a language, as an attempt at communication and as a container for those aspects of the self that resist comprehension and coherence. How do we use language to discover, obfuscate, and narrate what we want? What languages does sexuality speak? And how do we learn to pose sexuality as a question? These ordinary questions, I suggest, might also become the questions of sex education and the grounds of our conversations with adolescents.

The Language of Sexuality

In stories of sex education, and in the perennial tension "between the need for timeliness and the dangers of suggestiveness" (Moran 2000, 39), the entanglement of sexuality and language confounds any attempt to separate sex education absolutely from pornography, for instance. If, in talking about the risks of death, we might inspire in youth a desire to have sex, we need to consider in more detail the ways language incites and is incited by sexuality. The familiar debates in education over the impact of representation on learning—whether, for instance, cartoon violence causes children to be violent or whether anti-racist representational practices can prevent racism—share a similar logic. And yet, controversies over the stakes of the relationship between experiences and their representations acquire a particular virulence in sex education.

Wendy Steiner (1995) explores the collapse of representation and sex in her study of controversies surrounding art and pornography. She argues that both right-wing critics of "obscene" art and left-wing antipornography activists fail to see how art and representation demand interpretation. She offers the case of Robert Mapplethorpe's photography exhibit as an example. Part of Mapplethorpe's work documents and constructs a gay sadomasochistic aesthetic, incorporating and commenting upon the constructions of masculinity and race. In 1990, his retrospective, "The Perfect Moment," was shut down in Cincinnati, Ohio, and the gallery and its director were charged with pandering obscenity and using minors in nude photos.

During the jury trial, the prosecutor relied, erroneously, on the transparency of meaning in representation. After calling only the police officers who had shut down the gallery as witnesses, the prosecutor held up the photos to the jury of mostly suburban citizens. He then posed the rhetorical question: "You're going to ask, 'Shouldn't we hear something more?' . . . The pictures are the state's case" (32–33). The defense, in turn, brought in an army of experts who all testified to the artistic merit of Mapplethorpe's work and, in the end, the jury was persuaded by "expert" opinion. We might interpret the jury as abdicating to the authority of experts, behaving as many might hope adolescents would in the face of "expert" testimony on the dangers of precocious sexual activity. Steiner, however, offers a more ambivalent formulation:

> artistic meaning, like all meaning, is a matter of interpretation. What the prosecution did not realize is that we react to interpretation; we judge interpretations; there is no such thing as a work [or a word, we might add] that speaks for itself. Obscenity is thus always in the eye of the beholder, and what the beholder sees is subject to influence. (33)

For Steiner, it is the work of interpretation and art's liminal position between reality and fantasy that allows art to provoke thought. She writes: "art is an inherently paradoxical phenomenon whose meaning is always open to varying interpretations . . . those interpretations, though always socially and historically grounded, are also personal, proceeding from a primal yawp of pleasure" (60). Steiner comes close to the psychoanalytic idea that sexuality precedes and makes possible language. According to Freud, we are not able to talk at birth, but we are able to experience pleasure. And because sexuality comes before language, there is, Kristeva (2000) argues, "an inadequacy, an imbalance, between the sexual and the verbal. What the speaking being *says* does not subsume sexuality. Sexuality cannot be spoken or, in any case, it cannot be entirely spoken" (32). This "failure of translation" (37) frustrates our efforts to speak our desire, to find a language that might capture our wants. And yet, to follow Steiner, we might also recognize in this failure and the endless deferment and contingency of meaning the possibility of pleasure.

A similar dynamic is at stake in sex education. In addressing sexuality, sex education eschews the problem of interpretation by relying on the transparency and stability of meaning, what Susan Talburt in chapter one of this volume criticizes as "the fact of sexuality." At the same time, sex education fails to recognize that the work of interpretation, and the surplus of meaning, are intimately tied to experiences of pleasure. The polyvalent nature of sexuality, and the myriad of contradictory meanings that congregate around the word "sex," may be a challenge to the pedagogical wish for transparency, but the play of these meanings in art, or vernaculars, for instance, is part of the pleasure of sexuality.

In one month, the *New York Times* published two different articles on sex education and youth (Lewin 2000; Schemo 2001) that trouble the reliance on the stability and transparency of meaning in sex. The first detailed the results of a survey of 15- to 19-year-old boys showing that the range of sexual practices that boys engage in is shifting to include "noncoital behaviors" like anal and oral sex. Further, researchers speculate that this shift is a response to the increased emphasis on abstinence as "safe sex": "researchers, public health experts and health care workers have found that many young people perceive oral and anal sex as something other [than] sex—and often, even, as abstinence." And because oral and anal sex are not necessarily understood as "sex," many boys believe those activities are risk-free.[4]

During the production of a thesaurus of AIDS-related terms at the AIDS Committee of Toronto, the term "abstinence" was mistakenly placed, for a period, under the rubric of "safer sex." Of course, abstinence is not sex at all, but this error and the reformulation of abstinence in this study both point to the ways AIDS and the increasing focus on abstinence has transformed our sexual landscape. Advocates of abstinence-only programs have long declared that the only safe sex is no sex. There is a peculiar economy of affect at work here. The negation of sexuality (no sex is, of course, not sex) erupts into potential confusion for sex educators as sexuality returns disguised: abstinence is sex that doesn't count as sex.

Three weeks later, the *New York Times* published an article under the headline, "Virginity pledges by teenagers can be highly effective, Federal study finds" (Schemo 2001). In this study, researchers found that if a small group of peers within a school community together pledged to maintain abstinence until marriage, then first experiences with intercourse may be delayed up to 18 months (but not necessarily until marriage). The "virginity pledge" is a movement associated with conservative Christian groups, especially an organization called "True Love Waits." As the article suggests, the efficacy of these pledges is determined by a number of factors:

> [The report] found that virginity pledges did not hold when only one teenager took them, but required the support of like-minded classmates, within limits. Conversely, the pledges' effectiveness began to decline and teenagers stopped delaying sex when the percentage of students signing the virginity pledges increased to more than 30 percent.

Further, when engaging in sexual intercourse after making a pledge, those teenagers are less likely to use contraception than teenagers who never promised to remain virgins. The article concludes with a comment from the coordinator of the "True Love Waits" program: "If you're talking about a person who is not going to keep the pledge anyway, whether or not they would use contraception isn't really something that concerns us. . . . Waiting is what we're striving for here."

Both these articles ask a rather unorthodox question: What is not having sex? If both abstinence-only and comprehensive programs ask youth to not have sex, what are the different ways teenagers are interpreting that demand? The line between "foreplay" and "intercourse" is a perennial dilemma for youth cultures. The first, second, and third base categorization system pre-dates AIDS, but what is new is the reinterpretation of sexual practices through the discourses of abstinence and AIDS education. If parents and educators demand abstinence, youth respond with an inspiring creativity. Youth aren't having unsafe sex because, according to their logic, they are not having sex. And because the focus on abstinence shuts down conversations about different sexual practices, pleasures, orientations, and dangers, youth may not be confronted with information that disrupts their wish that anal sex be neither sex nor risky.

In the studies referred to in these articles parents and educators are seen to rely on the transparency of language both to convince youth to not have sex, and then to convince themselves that the abstinence approach is working. For instance, in the virginity pledge study, researchers only asked youth whether they had sex after making a pledge. They didn't ask about youth's different interpretations of what counts as sex (perhaps out of fear of putting ideas in their heads). The researchers then used their own "passion for ignorance" as evidence of their success (Sweeney 2001). This refusal fails to recognize that sexual practices are interpreted through personal and psychological meanings. In adolescence, having sex—however that is defined—is an overdetermined activity. Here, I use overdetermined in the Freudian sense: the idea of sex is a condensation of various conflicted, contradictory, unconscious, and interrelated meanings. Even though anything can be sexual, certain acts have been burdened with a surplus of meaning. It may be that intercourse means too much. Intercourse, for instance, may mean: pleasure, pain, intimacy, reproduction, love, lust, immaturity, marriage, community, abandon, disappointment, corruption, violation, loss of innocence, ecstasy, hope, betrayal, illness, death, conception, fidelity, etc. . . . Every time a teenager begins to contemplate whether or not they want to be sexually active, they enter into this myriad of meanings and they may get lost in the contradictions. Generally, our response to this confusion is to try and provide youth with the "right" list of meanings: intimacy, marriage, love, responsibility, conception, safety, maturity, etc. . . . This response however, does not make the other meanings go away. To say that sexuality is overdetermined is to say that sexuality is saturated with contradictory and ambivalent meanings.

The adolescents in these studies understand that it is the meanings of sexuality that are the source of pleasure. If we follow Kristeva (2000) and see sexuality as both preceding and inciting language, then we must also see how interpretation itself is a site of pleasure. Sex education programs that take information as the model of learning see interpretation (especially those interpretations that fall outside predictable outcomes) as a failure of learning. The aim is to present clear, concise, and unambiguous information that does not require interpretation. And yet, these studies show how youth are using the language of sex education against itself to create something like a post-AIDS adolescent identity. Between the educational effort to make abstinence "cool" or safer sex ordinary, and the reinterpretation of some kinds of sex as safe enough, adolescents are inventing new forms of intimate relations, new sexual identities, and new kinds of ordinary sex.

The problem for sex education, then, is twofold. First, to talk about adolescent sexuality is to see these new experiences and identities as the grounds for conversation. The language of sex education needs to be large enough to reach out into areas where adults may feel uncomfortable, to follow adolescents into their own sexual cultures and to see those cultures as a source of meaning for adolescents. But, second, and more difficult, no language, no matter how generous or explicit, can secure the meaning of sexuality. The pleasure, as well as the danger, of sexuality is made from the ways sexuality moves through language, refuses to stay in a proper place, and erupts in surprising and unlikely places, experiences, and languages.

In sex education, this imbalance and play between sexuality and narrative means that neither educators nor parents can have the last word on sexuality. Conservatives cannot prohibit sex talk, because any talk can be sexual; but neither can advocates of comprehensive sex education elaborate an accessible language of sex, because sexuality also eludes language and frustrates the desire for comprehension. As Patton notes, this inadequacy has startling effects in sex education: "The language of sex is so imprecise, so polyvalent that it is 'hard' to know when we are talking about sex and when we are talking about business or politics or other weighty matters," such as education, as Britzman adds (cited in Britzman 1998, 63). If education relies on the transparency of language, the translatability of perception into thought, then sexuality, in so far as it comes before and exceeds language, may indeed mark the limit of education.

The Sexuality of Language

But why should sexuality and language be so entangled? What about language evokes and eludes sexuality, and how does sexuality feel like a language? These questions move us away from an instrumentalist understanding of sex education and instead see an education in sexuality as a problem of subjectivity. Culled from her reading of Freud, Julia Kristeva outlines a theory of the subject that is tied to processes of symbolization, of learning to use language to represent psychical experience. According to Kristeva, Freud's work contains three theories of language that each offer both a model of creativity—of how we use language to satisfy our sexual drive—and a theory of failure—of how language fails to be satisfying and feels inadequate. The relation is dynamic and as such is instructive for dilemmas in sex education. If we follow Kristeva, the language of sex education might be enlarged to include considerations of how desire is not only expressed in language, but also how language itself is made meaningful and robust through our attempts to say what we want. That these wants can never be fully articulated and must push against the limits of intelligibility does not mark the failure of language, with the attendant fears of miscommunication and ambiguity. What if, instead, we saw our attempts at finding narratives to name our desires as a kind of learning, as a kind of sex education? Could our theories of language in sex education be transformed by this orientation? Kristeva recognizes the feeling of deadness that comes from transparently equating things with words, and thus, we might read her adventures with Freud as offering up a nascent model of sex education that recognizes the pleasures of miscommunication, dirty jokes, and finding ourselves in unexpected phrases.

In Kristeva's reading, Freud's first theory of language, developed before the *Interpretation of Dreams*, concerns the complex layers of representations that work to create meaning and thus complicate the wish that meaning would stay still and be clear. In particular, Freud distinguished between word-presentations and thing-presentations. A single unit of meaning, Kristeva (2000) writes, "combines a 'closed complex' called *word-presentation* (centered on *sound-image* and including a *reading-image*, a *writing-image*, and a *motor-image*) and an 'open complex' called *object-* or *thing-presentation* (centered on the *visual image* and including *tactile images, acoustic images*, etc.)" (33). Within these two registers of representation, there are many levels of meaning at work. For instance, a word-presentation includes the written word we see, the sound of the word, and the shape of the word being uttered. In this model, representation is layered and the relationship between these different domains of meaning (writing, oral, figural) is conflicted and dynamic. Like the gap that structuralists posit between the signifier and signified, there is, in this model of language, an impasse between thought and perception, what Kristeva calls "failures in translatability" (37).

Consider the example of how the different domains of representation (and representability) are at work in this generic tale of discovering the language of one's desire. A girl was confused by what she wanted and so, she recalls, "During lunch hour at school I'd make my pilgrimage to the Big Dictionary in the school library and look up *intercourse, vagina, penis, homosexual,* hoping a definition might clarify the adult and incomprehensible world" (Lowe 1998, 140). The girl who goes to the dictionary to find the secret of her sexuality negotiates the tension between words and things. The look and sound of the words—penis, vagina, homosexuality—belong to a logic of representation Kristeva calls "heterogenic": not only are the meanings of the terms made in conversation with one another, but within the context of their discovery there is an inaugural confusion between the thing, our perception and memory of the thing, and the word—the symbol that, through thought processes, comes to designate, however inadequately, our experience of the thing.

If Kristeva insists that the relation between word-presentations and thing-presentations is heterogenic, the logic of sex education refuses the creativity of that dynamic and insists upon a linear and transparent relation between the word and the thing. What does it mean, then, that sex education should negotiate this tension between perception and language, where words can become things and things become words? Moran (2000) argues that the history of sex education is a history of response to the ambiguity of language. If information about sexuality can produce sexually responsible adolescents, it was the language of science, apparently neutral and value-free, that would demystify sexuality. Early sex educators believed the silences of Victorianism compelled young people to be curious about each other's bodies. This curiosity could therefore be satisfied and thus eradicated through the presentation of scientific fact: "'scientific' sex education was fundamentally too boring to be suggestive" (49). If adolescents "knew" about sex and were able to discuss sex openly with knowledgeable peers and adults, they would be less inclined to experiment. In most cases, knowledge meant information about the devastating effects of venereal disease, i.e., having the right words to name the wrong actions. Language, as a medium for scientific thought, was meant to instill fear and cure curiosity. Yet, what if Freud was right and the relationship is reversed: language is incited by curiosity?

According to Kristeva, Freud's second theory of language, emerging from his study of dreams, is "optimistic," since language is able to relieve internal pressure and offer us a measure of satisfaction. Through the primary processes of displacement, condensation, and reversal, we are able to bring an otherwise intolerable sexuality into our everyday lives. The capacity for language is a sublimation: a successful substitution for engaging in socially and psychically prohibited activities. In this sense, the capacity to use language is a compensation for the difficult but necessary work of repressing the instincts and entering the social. The effects of this psychical work are what Kristeva simply calls a "story" (38). These stories—dreams, free associations, jokes—are able to bring unconscious contents closer to consciousness and thus offer some relief. This, of course, recalls Patton's observation that it is difficult to know when we are talking about sex since sexuality inspires language, but it might also suggest that there is a less than definite psychical line between having sex and talking about sex. Indeed, we might think of sex as one person having a conversation with another, as actually depending upon one's capacity to use language in the service of desire. In this model, it is possible to understand reading the dictionary as a creative alternative to sexual activity.

Would it be scandalous to suggest that talking about sex, even in scientific terms, even with the rhetoric of prohibition, could engage our sexual desires? In the history of sex education, great efforts have gone into preserving what Moran calls "the chamber of imagery" (40) in adolescents and children. Freud, at his most optimistic, asks us to reconsider the relationship between sexuality and language as being made in unconscious processes and to see language, including the language of sex, as offering the possibility of pleasure. That is, what is it to talk about sexuality (in adolescence, for instance) when language is not neutral but itself sexual and a sublimation of sexuality? This is the question at the heart of Freud's third theory of language.

Rather than thinking of language in purely linguistic terms, Kristeva names Freud's third and more skeptical theory of language, *signifiance*. Language is no longer a privileged route to satisfaction. *Signifiance* is meant to suggest the ways "representation-language-thought" are tied to the death drive. For Freud, the death drive operates in opposition to the life drive, or libido. Whereas the libido is "a binding drive that founds desire, the sexual and love" (47), the death drive unbinds, cuts, and severs. Kristeva suggests two ways to think about the influence of the death drive on language. First, she suggests that in contrast to the optimistic model, in theorizing the death drive, Freud realizes that language is not simply a route for the unconscious to become conscious, but, owing to his work on psychosis, language can also be a place of error. Kristeva writes: "Words not only allow internal things to become conscious but conversely, may also be the source of error and hallucination" (49). Freud saw this dynamic in the traumatic nightmares of shell-shocked soldiers who returned, in their dreams, to the scene of an unrepresentable trauma. In those nightmares and in the delirium of paranoiacs, Freud witnessed a failure at symbolization. If symbolization is the capacity to use language to represent psychical experience and thus tolerate the difference between experiences and their representations, the failure here is to mistake the word, or the symbol, for what it represents. In these cases, language cannot hold the self together, does not feel like compensation for joining the social; instead, the gap between words and things, between experience and representation, becomes a site of psychical disintegration. The error that Kristeva speaks about is a terrible and punishing literalness.

In this shift toward seeing language as a source of suffering, Freud becomes less interested in the structure of language and more concerned with the ways in which the capacity for thought and symbolization emerge in narrative. Narrative, in Kristeva's reading, has the capacity to bind and hold things together and defend against the dissolution that the death drive threatens. If, at the core of subjectivity, there are twin drives for pleasure and destruction, it is only through language, and narrative in particular, that we are able to come close to both surviving and satisfying these urges.

This theory of language offers a radically different understanding of debates over language in sex education. The collapse of the distinction between words and things, experience and representation, suggests the paranoid quality of the debates over sex education. In arguments over what can be talked about in a sex education curriculum, the distance between representation and experience is foreclosed, and suddenly talking about masturbation is tantamount to getting off in public, literally. On December 1, 1994, World AIDS Day, then U.S. Surgeon General Jocelyn Elders was asked, at an AIDS conference, about "the prospects for a 'more explicit discussion and promotion of masturbation' as a means to limit the spread" of HIV (Jehl 1994, 30). Her response, measured and tentative, incited a conservative outcry that resulted in her forced resignation eight days later. "As per your specific question in regard to masturbation. . . . I think that is something that is part of human sexuality and it's a part of something that perhaps should be taught. But we've not even taught our children the very basics" (30).

Elders' tenure as U.S. Surgeon General had been plagued by controversy and opposition. Since her difficult appointment in 1993, she spoke out for the need for comprehensive sex education beginning at an early age; she supported making condoms easily available to youth in high schools; she thought the government should consider legalizing marijuana; and she argued that opponents of her candor on sexual matters exhibit a profound fear of sex (Hilts 1993; Jehl 1994). And yet, despite her outspoken support for these controversial programs, it was the mention of masturbation that led to her termination. Those on the conservative right cried foul, and Bill Clinton, a president later known for his insistence that oral sex was not sex (making him an unwitting accomplice in the redefinition of abstinence as sex that doesn't count as sex), decided that masturbation crossed some imaginary line. One thing at stake in these controversies is a refusal to distinguish between talk of masturbation and actual masturbation. This punishing literalness is an example of what Hanna Segal (1991) calls a "symbolic equation" (35) and demonstrates how symbolization can fail to ward off the anxiety associated with the death drive and sexuality.[5]

Kristeva (2000) describes narratives as "stories full of gaps, silences, awkwardness—in a way, novels deprived of an audience" (65). This conception of narrative suggests the ways our worries, hopes, fears, anxieties, fantasies, and desires are contained in language and organized in stories. The narrative gives form to affect, contains the unruliness and destructiveness of our fantasies, and yet, remains awkward and somewhat inarticulate. Our narratives of adolescence, then, contain our anxieties about sexuality, struggle with and against desires that cannot be named, and protect the fragility of our grown-up-ness.

Is it any surprise that Kristeva would elsewhere name the adolescent as the privileged narrator? Kristeva (1990), borrowing from Helene Deutsch, calls this frontier creature "the eternal adolescent." Rather than see this adolescent as corresponding to youth that we might meet in the context of sex education, perhaps "the eternal adolescent" is an aspect of adolescence that Kristeva would like to salvage for adults:

> This may sound odd, because we know that the eternal adolescent is immature and capriciously fragile, moving from depression to hysteria, from amorous infatuation to disappointment. But eternal adolescence also indicates a certain suppleness of agencies, an adaptability, a capacity to modify oneself according to the environment and the other, as well as against them. It is this aspect that it is important to cultivate, not only when one listens to patients but also when one reads literary texts. (51)

Kristeva accords the eternal adolescent a privileged relation to narrative. The eternal adolescent maintains "a certain openness in one's psychical apparatus" (51) and is therefore able to experience the range of affects that erupt into texts and narrative. If adults can sometimes seem to have more in common with the shell-shocked soldiers or paranoiacs who are caught in a recurring nightmare—just say no, just say no—perhaps this conception of the adolescent is more willing to risk the devastation of losing: losing love, losing language, losing oneself.

One of the most difficult questions we can ask of ourselves when we work to conceptualize a conversation with youth that acknowledges and respects the difficulties and pleasures of sexuality is a question posed mainly to ourselves: What is the difference between adolescents and adults? The question is routinely approached from the vantage of the adult who wishes to understand the development of adolescents so that they may effectively intervene into youth "problems." Incisive critiques of this vantage work to unhinge "adolescence" from a long list of damaging stereotypes: "storm and stress," "raging hormones," apathetic, discontent, narcissistic, and a long list of the usual suspects. Kristeva, however, allows us to notice how these narratives of experience emerge from adults' forgetful remembering of their own adolescence and how youth, in turn, encounter and engage these narratives in their efforts to imagine their place in the world.

The barriers to having honest conversations with adolescents do not, therefore, simply belong to the structural obstacles of addressing sexuality in schools. It is not enough to elaborate and expand discourses of sexuality in schools. While traditionally sex education has been concerned with pregnancy, reproduction, safety, and the beginnings of life, to move beyond the opposition between silence and speech, the curriculum of sex education must also address love, friendship, disease, and fears of mortality (Britzman 1998). These large existential questions are posed in relation to sexuality, and herein lies the difficulty of sex education: it is through the obscure experience of sexuality that we encounter the most urgent questions of life. Learning from and about sexuality asks us to confront our vulnerabilities and to imagine how this thing we call the self is made from the fragility of our relations with others and the world. If we must create institutional and curricular spaces to discuss issues of sexuality, love, and loss, we must also recognize the difficulty and pleasures of narrating these experiences in schools and during adolescence, both those lived and remembered.

Notes

1. For a discussion of the history of these programs, see Moran (2000), Irvine (2003), and Levine (2002). It is important to note that the hegemony of these programs is most prevalent in school-based curricula. Outside the schools, in community health centers, AIDS organizations, and youth serving agencies, sex education takes on many guises, many of which are not oriented toward abstention and take seriously youth's right to enjoy their bodies. The good news for youth is that school-based sex education may be the least relevant and least persuasive education they receive. That said, the purpose of my discussion here is limited to probing the ways the complicated relationship between language and sexuality is recognized and defended against in school-based sex education programs.

2. Weis and Carbondale-Medina (2000), in a study of an abstinence-based program, suggest some of the ways girls can find room for curiosity about their bodies and sexualities in a program that gives them permission to not

have sex. Their study suggests that the quality of a sex education program is affected by the spirit of openness and inquiry, not simply whether a sex education program stresses abstinence or comprehensiveness.

3. At the recent meeting of the UN Children's Conference, delegates attempted to compose an international agreement to improve the living conditions of children. The drafting of this agreement broke down over heated discussions of children's and youth's access to sexual and reproductive health services and education. As Saunders (2002) reports, "The United States, the Vatican and fundamentalist Islamic nations had refused to sign the agreement unless it stated that abstinence was the only acceptable approach to AIDS and sex education in UN-supported aid programs." In this strange alliance, the United States' position was opposed by Roman Catholic countries in Latin America, Poland, members of the EU, and Canada. An agreement was reached only after reference to the capital punishment of children was deleted (some states in the United States allow for the execution of youth under 18) and only a vague mention of reproductive health issues was included. This controversy suggests the extent to which United States domestic policy influences foreign affairs. Because the United States contributes the largest amount of foreign aid to developing nations, other members of the UN could not afford to draft the agreement without the participation of the United States or chastise the United States for its puritanical and mean-spirited position.

4. See also Remez 2000.

5. Hanna Segal (1991) offers a related clinical vignette: She was working with a psychotic patient in a hospital who had, since his illness, given up playing the violin. When she inquired why he had abandoned playing the violin, "[he] answered with violence, 'Do you expect me to masturbate in public?'" (35). In this example of concrete thinking, "the symbol is so equated with the object symbolized that the two are felt to be identical. A violin *is* a penis; playing the violin *is* masturbating and therefore not to be done in public" (35).

References

Bonami, Franscesco, ed. 2003. *The Fourth Sex: Adolescent Extremes.* Milan: Charta.

Britzman, Deborah. 1998. *Lost Subjects, Lost Objects: Toward a Psychoanalytic Inquiry of Learning.* New York: State University of New York Press.

Epstein, Debbie and Richard Johnson. 1998. *Schooling Sexualities.* London: Open University Press.

Fine, Michelle. 1992. "Sexuality, Schooling and Adolescent Females: The Missing Discourse of Desire." Pp. 31–60 in *Disruptive Voices: The*

Possibilities of Feminist Research. Ann Arbor: University of Michigan Press.

Hilts, Philip. 1993. "Blunt Style on Teen Sex and Health: The New Surgeon General Meets Controversy Head On." *New York Times*, 1.

Irvine, Janice. 2003. *Talk About Sex: The Battles over Sex Education in the United States*. Berkeley: University of California Press.

Jehl, Douglas. 1994. "Surgeon General Forced to Resign by White House." *New York Times*, December 10, 1, 30.

Kristeva, Julia. 1990. "The Adolescent Novel." Pp. 8–23 in *Abjection, Melancholia, and Love: The Work of Julia Kristeva*. Ed. John Fletcher and Andrew Benjamin. New York: Routledge.

———. 2000. *The Sense and Non-sense of Revolt*. New York: Columbia University Press.

Levine, Judith. 2002. *Harmful to Minors: The Perils of Protecting Children from Sex*. New York: Thunder's Mouth Press.

Lewin, Tamar. 2000. "Survey Shows Sex Practices of Boys." *New York Times*, December 19.

Lowe, Bia. 1998. "Waiting for Blastoff." Pp. 135–142 in *Queer Thirteen: Lesbian and Gay Writers Recall the Seventh Grade*. Ed. Clifford Chase. New York: Rob Weisbach.

Moran, Jeffrey. 2000. *Teaching Sex: The Shaping of Adolescence in the 20th Century*. Cambridge, Mass.: Harvard University Press.

Patton, Cindy. 1996. *Fatal Advice: How Safe-Sex Education Went Wrong*. Durham, NC: Duke University Press.

Remez, Lisa. 2000. "Oral Sex Among Adolescents: Is it Sex or is it Abstinence?" *Family Planning Perspectives* 32, no. 6: 298–304.

Sauders, Doug. 2002. "International Compromise Rescues Accord." *Globe and Mail*, May 11.

Schemo, Diana Jean. 2001. "Virginity Pledges by Teenagers Can Be Highly Effective, Federal Study Finds." *New York Times*, January 4.

Segal, Hanna. 1991. *Dream, Phantasy and Art*. New York: Routledge.

Steiner, Wendy. 1995. *The Scandal of Pleasure: Art in an Age of Fundamentalism*. Chicago: University of Chicago Press.

Sweeney, Jennifer Foote. 2001. "The Virginity Hoax." Salon.com, January 12.

Weis, Lois, and Doris Carbonnel-Medina. 2000. "Learning to Speak Out in an Abstinence-Based Sex Education Group: Gender and Race Work in an Urban Magnet School." Pp. 26–49 in *Construction Sites: Excavating Race, Class, and Gender among Urban Youth*, ed. Lois Weis and Michelle Fine. New York: Teachers College Press.

Part II

Rethinking Youth Practices

Chapter Six

Safety and Subversion

The Production of Sexualities and Genders in School Spaces

Mary Louise Rasmussen

Identity is constructed in the temporal and linguistic mobilisation of space, as we move through space we imprint utopian and dystopian moments upon urban life. Our bodies are vital signs of this temporality and intersubjective location. In an instant, a freeze-frame, a lesbian is occupying a space as it occupies her.

—Munt 1995, 125

The Foucauldian notion of dividing practices is the focal point of this chapter. I will consider how spatial dividing practices are produced through an analysis of the regulation of sexualities in school spaces. More specifically, I turn my attention to the production of dividing practices that produce "safe spaces," "queer spaces," and that enable the production of subversive spatial acts that "imprint utopian and dystopian moments" (Munt 1995, 125) within and around high school settings in the United States. My aim is to interrogate some of the implications that ensue from these various attempts to produce spaces that construct and are constructed by the politics of identity. I will commence my analysis by elaborating upon my conception of Foucault's notions of dividing practices and heterotopias.

Dividing Practices

Dividing practices are one of three modes of objectification of subjects identified by Foucault in his essay *The Subject and Power* (1982), the others being scientific classification and processes of subjectivization. Foucault writes that these dividing practices might cause the subject to be divided inside himself or divided from others. "This process objectivizes him" (Foucault 1982, 208). For the purposes of this chapter I will analyze both of these aspects of dividing practices, focusing on the ways in which they are interiorized and on the ways that individuals are divided from others.

In the introduction to *The Foucault Reader* (1984), Paul Rabinow argues that Foucault conceives of dividing practices as operating to produce social and personal identities through spatial and discursive manipulation (Rabinow 1984, 8). Given this conception of dividing practices, the lesbian, gay, bisexual, transgender, and intersex (LGBTI) identified teachers and students, who form the central focus of this chapter, may be understood as a group "given an identity through dividing practices" and who thus become the object of "diverse applications" of power and knowledge. Following this conception of the productive role of dividing practices, it is possible to interrogate how this group forms relations within and around this mode of objectification, and, how these dividing practices are utilized in the name of reform, salvation, and domination.

Sexuality and Spatial Dividing Practices

any sexual identity can assume space and space can assume any sexual identity . . . space is produced, and it has both material and symbolic components.

—Bell and Valentine 1995, 18; emphasis in original

I think it is somewhat arbitrary to try to
dissociate the effective practice of freedom by
people, the practice of social relations, and the
spatial distributions in which they find themselves.
If they are separated they become impossible to
understand. Each can only be understood through
the other.

—Foucault 1984, 247

The epigraphs above both emphasize the relational temperament of space and how this intersects with people's ability to construct identifications. The following discussion of spatial dividing practices is underpinned by this notion of space as a relational production, shifting according to the places, times, and bodies with which it interacts. In a brief essay entitled *Of Other Spaces*, Foucault elaborates on this notion of space as relational. He writes:

> The space in which we live, which draws us out of ourselves, in which the erosion of our lives, our time, our history occurs, the space that claws and gnaws at us, is also, in itself, a heterogeneous space. In other words, we do not live in a kind of void, inside of which we could place individuals and things. We do not live inside a void that could be coloured with diverse shades of light, we live inside a set of relations that delineates sites which are irreducible to one another and absolutely not superimposable on one another. (Foucault 1986, 23)

If space is considered as relational, then it is inevitable that schools and the communities that inhabit and interact with them will be the site of complex tensions, tensions that are irreducible to other spaces. In *Of Other Spaces* Foucault also discusses the notion of heterotopia to consider spaces "that have the curious property of being in relation with all the other sites, but in such a way as to suspect, neutralize, or invert the set of relations that they happen to designate, mirror, or reflect" (Foucault 1986, 24). He argues that these heterotopic spaces "obviously take quite varied forms, and perhaps no one absolutely universal form of heterotopia would be found" (24), and he goes on to elaborate six principles that may be used to provide a "systematic description" (24) of this notion of heterotopia. I use this Foucauldian notion of heterotopia to consider how certain spaces related to sexualities and secondary schooling may distort, neutralize, or invert their "designated" functions. One such space is the school prom; I consider how a space ostensibly designed as the preserve of heterosexuality may simultaneously be the space of sexual subversion.

But first I will briefly introduce three of the principles of heterotopia. In the first principle Foucault puts forward the notion of heterotopias of deviation, "those in which individuals whose behavior is deviant in relation to the required mean or norm are placed. Cases of this are rest homes and psychiatric hospitals, and of course prisons" (25). In his third principle Foucault contends "the heterotopia is capable of juxtaposing in a single real place several spaces that are in themselves incompatible" (Foucault 1986). In describing his fifth principle of heterotopia, Foucault writes that:

> Heterotopias always presuppose a system of opening and closing that both isolates them and makes them penetrable. In general the heterotopic space is not freely accessible like a public space. Either the entry is compulsory . . . or else the individual has to submit to rites and purifications. . . . There are others, on the contrary, that seem to be pure and simple openings, but that generally hide curious exclusions. Everyone can enter into these heterotopic sites, but in fact this is only an illusion: we think we enter where we are, by the very fact that we enter, excluded. (Foucault 1986, 26)

In the "safe spaces" and "queer spaces" analyzed below, various strategies are deployed, ostensibly to offer protections to LGBTI-identified secondary students. I consider the protections these spaces purport to provide, and pose the question of whether these spaces may be conceived as heterotopic, merely creating the illusion of protection and inclusion.

This discussion of sexuality and heterotopic space in schools also reflects a trend within queer theory toward a focus on sexual spaces that are not "easily produced as transgressive . . . creating a forum in which those spaces not commonly considered 'sexual' might be discussed as productive of queer selves . . . working from the premise that all spaces have queers in them, and all actions are performed by queers" (Hemmings and Grace 1999, 391). Members of school communities possess a variety of sexual and gender identifications. They are compelled to rub up against one another within and around school settings, thus they are all complicit in the production of all manner of sexed and gendered selves.

Safe Space?

I think schools have a long way to go still and that they are not the safe environments that they need to be. And I think it's really sad because I think one of the major ways that homophobia still has a huge impact, and transphobia especially has a huge impact on people's lives, is that youth who are GLB or have non-traditional gender identities or whatever, they basically are denied access to an education because they are not safe in schools, and they don't feel welcome in schools.

—Jaron Kanegson[1]

The above characterization of schools as unsafe places for students and teachers due to the homophobia and transphobia that occurs within their surrounds was a sentiment echoed by all the participants in my research. This sentiment is also echoed in educational research that has characterized schools as unsafe places for LGBTI-identified students and teachers (Bloom 1999; De Crescenzo 1994; Griffin 1994; LeCompte 2000). In response to the notion that schools may be unsafe, there has been a trend toward the development of discourse that promotes "safe spaces" within and outside schools for LGBTI-identified teachers and students. Given this trend I use the notion of heterotopic spaces to consider the absences, inversions, and counteractions that might be associated with the "curious property" of the "safe space."

Robert Boostrom, in his analysis of the usefulness of "safe space" in educational discourses, argues that the trope of "safe spaces" might be seen as "a response to the menace of an alienating world" (Boostrom 1998, 404). However, Boostrom is critical of "safe space" tropes in educational discourse because he argues these tropes may work as a tool censoring critical thinking and create a place in which teachers rule out conflict (407). Following on from Boostrom, it is possible to consider more closely questions such as: What does a safe school look like? How might a school be made safe? Who is a school being made safe for? Or, alternatively, from whom does the school need to be protected? Is there such a thing as a "safe space"? And, finally, who gets to decide what's safe and what's not?

While an exploration of all these questions is beyond the scope of this chapter, I will consider some of them in the context of a brief analysis of the Safe Schools Coalition of Washington (SSCW) and of comments made by a participant in my research regarding the use of "safety transfers" in New York City (NYC) public schools. The safety transfer allows public school students to move to another school as a priority on the grounds that their safety is compromised at their existing school. SSCW describes its mission as "to help make Washington State schools safe places where every family can belong, where every educator can teach, and where every child can learn, regardless of gender identity or sexual orientation."[2] The first recommendation of the Safe Schools Resource Guide revolves around the provision of "explicitly protective/inclusive policies" for people who belong to a minority group based on their sexual or gender identity (Reis 1997, 1). The first foundation of these protections, supposedly integral to the development of "safe spaces" in schools, endeavors to address "the misunderstanding that one's sexual orientation is a behavior" (1). Yet, by tying the construction of "safe spaces" to essentializing tropes of identity, the SSCW produces its own spatial exclusions.

People allowed into the "safe spaces" supposedly provided by the safe schools framework are those who conceive of their gender or sexual identification as somehow fundamental. As such, these "safe spaces" might be described as heterotopic, insofar as they "presuppose a system of opening and closing that both isolates them and makes them penetrable" (Foucault 1986, 26). When students adopt LGBTI-identifications, these may be considered a rite of entry into the "safe space" that SSCW endeavors to produce. On the other hand, students who defy sexual and gender norms may not be deemed worthy of the protections offered by "safe space" if they refuse to stand under the umbrella of LGBTI identifications.

In her discussion of "safe-sex" education, Cindy Patton demonstrates the problems inherent in creating such spaces that reinforce the heterosexual/homosexual binary:

> Heterosexism demands that we name partners and limit sexuality to a narrow range of cross-gender behaviors. To demand a narrow gay identity—even implicitly . . . runs the risk of duplicating this form of oppression. To refuse to claim that everyone any of us has ever had sex with is thereby "gay" is not to degay our community: rather, it is to complicate and confound heterosexuality, to create more space for sexual alliances, not less. (Patton 1996, 154)

Patton's analysis of "safe sex" education offers a valuable intervention into the "safe space" discourse. Ultimately the *safety* of spaces within and around schools may be diminished rather than enhanced by rhetoric that delimits the creation of "safe spaces" through the use of essentializing tropes of identity. Furthermore, the refusal to claim "that everyone any of us has ever had sex with is thereby 'gay'" as indicated by Patton above, allows for a more complex envisioning of the notion of "safe space" in school settings, encompassing a broader range of people, and potentially creating school spaces that are more inclusive of a wider range of behaviors and identifications.

While the trope of "safe space" is ostensibly designed for the protection of the rights of the individual, it has also been deployed as a means to remove troublesome students. Below, one of the U.S. participants[3] I interviewed in my research project describes the way schools used the notion of safety to remove a transitioning transgender student from the school space:

> there was an enormous amount of pressure put on the student, an MTF [Male to Female], to not cross dress, and transition publicly at school . . . even though the student was not a problem like to the school environment so much. What they did was safety transfer the student. . . . Instead of dealing with the issue, bringing in people to do education or trying to change the environment they just safety transfer the student out.
>
> The guidance counselor that the student had was like telling the student that you need to go to Hetrick-Martin and not be here. . . . [T]he student did not want to leave the school and had no plans to leave that school. . . . It's really not what the Hetrick-Martin Institute or Harvey Milk High School [HMHS] has done. . . . It's what the Board of Education or certain schools perceive it [HMHS] as. That is, anytime they have a lesbian, gay or transgender student . . . they cannot deal with that student, and [they] stick them in an all gay school.

Foucault contends that "[s]pace is fundamental in any form of communal life; space is fundamental in any exercise of power" (Foucault 1984, 252). This is exemplified above where the safety transfer reflects an "exercise of power" to preserve the public space of the school within the confines of a heteronormalizing framework. Thus, tropes of "safe space" can be used as a mechanism to remove students that trouble the heterosexual/homosexual binary under the guise of providing for their safety. In this instance, as in the case of the safe schools program, there is a sense that everyone can enter into a "safe space," but these heterotopic spaces only offer the illusion of inclusivity. In practice, it appears acts of entry into these "safe spaces" are predicated on a process of exclusion from the hetero norm.

As Beverley Skeggs notes in her study of visibility and sexuality in leisure spaces, "[t]he production of 'safe gay spaces' is an impossibility . . . [and represents a failure] to challenge the legitimacy of those who create the desire for safety in the first place" (Skeggs 1999, 228). Following Skeggs, I contend the safety transfer described above is indicative of a failure to interrogate heteronormalizing behaviors within the school. The transfer also reflects discomfort caused by the occupation of school space by transitioning students and signifies how "safe space" discourses may be co-opted by the desire to preserve high schools as heteronormalizing spaces.

On the surface, tropes of "safe space," like notions of inclusion, are difficult to critique. However, on closer scrutiny it is apparent this trope operates as a dividing practice producing material and symbolic exclusions of particular individuals from the imaginary realm of "safe space." As the above examples indicate, it is also necessary to take into account the power relations that underlie the invocation of "safe space" in educational contexts and to determine whose interests are served by the construction of such spaces.

Queering Safe Space

Another form of "safe space" that manifests in the United States comes in the form of high schools specifically catering to the needs of LGBTI-identified young people. In the subsequent analysis I am not focused on determining whether these schools provide a positive educational experience for the students who attend; rather, I am interested in interrogating the rhetoric that supports and opposes the construction of high schools that spatially divide young people based on their sexual and gender identifications.

These schools that cater to students who adopt LGBTI identifications are often deeply invested in tropes of "safe space" and tropes of LGBTI young people as "at-risk." One such school, the Harvey Milk[4] High School (HMHS) located in New York City, is one of numerous services provided by the Hetrick-Martin Institute (HMI).[5] The origins of the Institute, as indicated by the reference to protection in its former name, lay in the construction of "a safe and supportive environment [for] . . . lesbian, gay, bisexual, transgender and questioning youth between the ages of 12 and 21 and their families."[6]

There is some ambivalence within HMI about the existence of schools like the HMHS.[7] Christopher Rodriguez,[8] a participant who works at HMI, argues that such schools exist because of failures in the school system, situations in which students are:

> not getting the resources and support they need in their communities or their community schools. . . . Ideally, one of the things we are going to do is transform the public schools of NYC, but that is a long time in coming. So until those schools are transformed and able to support all of the young people there in all of the ways they need to be supported, we are going to continue to support alternative programming like this that is going to meet specific needs.

In the above quote there is a sense that HMHS, by its very existence, is indicative of the failure to accommodate all students within the mainstream space of the NYC Board of Education. Such spaces are thus ongoing testaments to the spatial exclusions produced by homophobia and transphobia in educational settings.

Programs such as HMHS have received criticism from within and outside LGBTI communities. One of the biggest ongoing criticisms of HMHS, according to Joyce Hunter, one of the schools' founders, is:

> this whole issue of isolating the kids. In fact people said we were ghettoizing them . . . they said why would you isolate this group of kids . . . why are you not going for integration. . . . People have to understand that these young people have isolated and ghettoized themselves to the streets . . . there are a group of kids who have been so traumatized by the school system that they are just not going to go back. And so this school provided a place for them to get a safe education.

HMHS has also been criticized by people who have religious objections to the spatial division of students based on their sexual and gender identifications. The Walt Whitman Community School (WWCS) in Dallas is another school catering primarily to young people who identify as LGBTI.[9] WWCS has been critiqued for its "promotion of the gay agenda" by "segregating a minority population under a 'paradigm of exclusion fuelled by the morally-suspect agendas of militant special-interest groups'" (Martin 2001). Steve Baldwin, a former California State Assemblyman, in a report on "the gay agenda in our public schools"[10] contends that students attending programs such as HMHS and WWCS "are subjected to unrelenting homosexual propaganda with no information allowed about programs that have successfully counseled homosexuals to return to the heterosexual lifestyle."[11] Clearly, the educational spaces created by the construction of these schools are the subject of much emotive debate, for and against their existence.

Partially in response to critiques akin to those above, these schools have developed discourses that seek to produce the educational spaces they create as necessary havens in an alienating world. An example of the production of such a discourse appears in the following extract. A teacher at WWCS in Dallas, Wally Linebarger, in the course of an interview with Tim Martin, notes:

> Few people criticize hospitals, for example, for segregating the sick in order to best treat them. Similarly, some students who are living in gay or lesbian environments and struggling with their sexual identity need special attention in order to best function in the larger, mainstream society. We're kind of like an educational hospice along the way to college and life. (Martin 2001)

The series of medical metaphors, alluded to by Linebarger above, construct sexual identity as akin to a sickness in need of treatment prior to the restoration of students to mainstream society. The association Linebarger draws between LGBTI-identified students and their need for "special attention" (Martin 2001) is also evident in the following excerpt from a promotional brochure produced by the EAGLES Center[12] in Los Angeles:

> Some people say the EAGLES Center is a gay ghetto. We say that our students were already segregated at their previous schools by their peers, teachers, administrators, and, sometimes, themselves. They now need a safe haven in which to recuperate from physical and psychological abuse.

Returning once again to Foucault's notion of heterotopia, I argue that these havens and hospices may be conceived as "heterotopias of deviation" (Foucault 1986, 25). These spaces effectively work to reinscribe categories of deviant and normal students because they are produced in order to cater to students who are classified as deviant, by virtue of their sexual and gender identifications. The production of such spaces also reinforces Angus Gordon's suggestion that adults who identify as LGBTI have a tendency "to reduce adolescence to a stable site of either shame or abjection in gay and lesbian narrative" (Gordon 1999, 20). This narrative perpetuates a belief in the need and desire to produce "heterotopias of deviation" (Foucault 1986, 25) for the protection of abject young people who identify as LGBTI.

While I argue that the spaces produced above are not unproblematic, there is also no doubt that many of the young people who attend HMHS, EAGLES, and WWCS are thankful to receive support services that go beyond those provided in mainstream high school settings. However, it is also important to consider some of the implications that ensue from the construction of these programs as "safe spaces" that "save [LGBTI-identified young people] from. . . . possible death, because we are able to offer them so many opportunities that they probably wouldn't otherwise have" (Christopher Rodriguez).

In fact HMI's relationship with students is much broader than the provision of educational services. Rodriguez notes that HMI also offers students access to "counseling services, and socialization activities, and training opportunities, and case management." According to Rodriguez these services are fundamental in enabling the young people attending HMHS to complete their studies and graduate from the program. Such a model of comprehensive support services has clear associations with the case management of other groups of people depicted as abject by the broader society.

I recognize that these discourses of protection are, in part, strategically motivated. Portraying these young people as vulnerable reinforces these school's requests for continued financial support. This strategy is apparent in the following comments made by Verna Eggleston, HMI's executive director, in the *HMI Reporter*:

> It bears repeating that these and other initiatives can only be realized with donor support. Homophobia, unfortunately, is not going away. Young people are coming out at earlier ages than ever before, and many continue to face ostracism in their schools and in their homes. Places like HMI are still necessary in the year 2001 and, as far as we can tell, will continue to be necessary in the years to come. . . . We here at HMI remain committed to this vulnerable population. . . . (Eggleston 2001)

While Eggleston and her peers emphasize the problems caused by homophobia in mainstream educational spaces, it is apparent that the factors that drive students into requiring the services provided by these "safe spaces" go beyond discrimination based on sexual and gender identifications. The young people who use these services, at least in Los Angeles and New York, are, as Rodriguez states, mostly:

> from working poor backgrounds. It is . . . roughly 80–85 percent,[13] a population of young people of color. The largest numbers of which are Latino and African American. We have almost equal numbers of young men and women in the program now, who are coming... from families in crisis, or communities in crisis.

Considering that the young people who use these services are racially/ethnically and economically marginalized, it appears that their sexual and gender identifications are but one factor contributing to their marginalization.

In her analysis of the ways in which "safe sex" education works to construct young people of color as "already lost," Cindy Patton argues that, unlike their white counterparts, young people of color are often considered to be:

> Geographically situated "where the trouble is," the risk faced by youth of color becomes a public, collective phenomenon, rather than a private, individual one. [These young people are] Viewed as hard-to-reach, potentially already lost. . . . (Patton 1996, 61)

Patton's analysis has resonances in the rhetoric produced in relation to schools such as HMHS and the EAGLES Center. Yet within the public rhetoric produced by these schools, rather than being characterized as "already lost," the young people of color are rarely mentioned. Homophobia and the oppression of young people are two elements that can be woven into a narrative that will appeal to a broad range of donors within and outside LGBTI-identified communities. Vikki Bell, drawing on the work of Judith Butler, argues that "one site of the construction of difference can act as the 'unmarked background' for another" (Bell 1999, 5). The exclusion from the public rhetoric of these programs of the economic and racial dividing practices imbricated in young people's need for their services elides the complexities that sustain young people's ongoing need for the services they provide. Thus race and class may, in certain instances, become the unmarked background in discussions of sexuality and schooling.

This analysis of some of the spatial dividing practices that operate within these programs is not intended as an argument in favor of their dissolution. It is a call to reexamine the factors that contribute to the spatial division of economically disadvantaged, young people of color in educational programs cast solely under the rubric of providing services to LGBTI-identified young people. It is also hoped this analysis will prompt further consideration of the role these programs must inevitably play in reinscribing these young people's status as "potentially already lost" (Patton 1996, 61), while simultaneously struggling to provide these same young people with essential services and educational opportunities.

The spatial dividing practices that reinforce the marginal position of programs such as these, and the young people that utilize them, are not only to be found in the rhetoric they produce or the physical relocation of students. The EAGLES Center in Los Angeles is spatially and symbolically isolated from the Los Angeles Unified School District (LAUSD). Of the two campuses of the Center that I visited, one was located in the basement of a high-rise building in Hollywood that had been abandoned by all other tenants, and the other was located in the rooms of a small shop front. According to a promotional brochure produced by EAGLES, the LAUSD only provides teaching salaries and a few basic items. The Center must find funds for "technology, books, educational materials, supplies, field trips, social services. . . . Even our housing has to be at no cost to the district. Our students need stability; they need a permanent site for the program (from 1992 through August 1997 we have moved 13 times!)."[14] These campuses of the EAGLES Center, charged with the mission of catering to LGBTI-identified young people who are "at-risk," appear to be at risk themselves, by virtue of their marginal spatial and economic status.

In contrast to the EAGLES Center, the HMHS occupies a more well-resourced premises, including traditional school spaces such as classrooms and a cafeteria. The physical layout of HMHS reflects Rodriguez's statements below about what the young people want from the school:

> They want a high school with teachers that they can develop relationships with, they want a school bell, they want a lunch period, they want books, folders and homework to take home and bring back everyday. What they really seek is to have an experience like every young person has during the high school years.

Rodriguez's description of students' expectations of HMHS speaks to their desire for a normalizing school experience. On some levels it appears that temporal dividing practices employed at HMHS, such as school timetables and bells, are symbolic of a desire among students and staff to compensate for the students' spatial division from the mainstream school system.

All of the schools described above strive to provide "safe spaces" to young people who, for a variety of reasons, have rejected and/or been rejected by mainstream high schools. They deploy and produce a range of spatial dividing practices in an effort to provide students with another route to educational qualifications that may enable them to move out of these liminal spaces and into mainstream high schools, colleges, or jobs. There is an awareness among those involved in these schools that their "physical, social and curricular space is reproductive of social relationships and values in society but there is also a sense that the transmission of these relationships is susceptible to mediation and contest" (Armstrong 1999, 83). By virtue of their existence, these schools create spaces that illuminate the exclusions produced by wider social and educational relations of power. These relations of power continue to be simultaneously contested and reinscribed by the people involved in the heterotopic spaces outlined above.

The Invention of Sexualities and Genders in School Space

Because space is relational, it has the capacity to produce certain "practices of freedom" (Foucault 1996) and certain exclusions. In the following section I consider some of the intersections between spatial dividing practices and the heteronormalization of school communities. Following Felicity Armstrong's analysis of the *Struggle for Space in School,* I argue that these spatial dividing practices often reproduce "values and meanings which . . . sustain differences and exclusions. These values and meanings are seen as natural because of the familiarity of the practices and discourses which surround them" (Armstrong 1999, 76). And because these "values and meaning are seen as natural," they too become a "familiar and poorly known horizon" (Foucault 1997, 144). While heteronormalization is familiar in school spaces, sometimes school spaces are the scene of subversive spatial acts. One such act, Krystal Bennett's crowning as a prom king, momentarily disrupted processes of heteronormalization. Ironically, this act, which was performed last year at Ferndale High School in Washington state, was only made possible by the dividing practices that produce discrete sexual and gender identificatory categories in Australia and the United States.

My decision to focus on this particular act is informed, in part, by Susan Talburt's analysis of the directions of ethnographic inquiry relating to people who are LGBTI-identified. Talburt argues "ethnographic inquiry into gay and lesbian subjects has been limited by its disciplinary and sociocultural locations and must move beyond the production of realist representations that voice and make visible identity and experience . . . "(Talburt 1999, 529). The ensuing analysis comprises an attempt to move beyond the desire to merely make LGBTI-identified people visible in research, by focusing on the enactment of an unconventional educational act and the ways it intersects with power relations in schools. In this analysis I am mindful of the intersections of space, bodies, and texts and their relations to the "making of the material spaces we inhabit" (Threadgold 2000).

In this analysis of Krystal Bennett's reign as prom king, I am also informed by Foucault's contention that:

> . . . despite all the techniques for appropriating space, despite the whole network of knowledge that enables us to delimit or to formalize it, contemporary space is perhaps still not entirely desanctified. . . . To be sure a certain theoretical desanctification of space . . . has occurred, but we may still have not reached the point of a practical desanctification of space. And perhaps our life is still governed by a certain number of oppositions that remain inviolable, that our institutions and practices have not yet dared break down. These are oppositions that we regard as simple givens. . . . All these are still nurtured by the hidden presence of the sacred. (Foucault 1986, 23)

The proliferation of discourses that emerged around Bennett's election as prom king may be read as a vindication of Foucault's contention regarding "the hidden presence of the sacred" (23) in the production of space. It is possible that Bennett's election provoked so much debate because it disturbed one of the most sacred spaces of U.S. secondary school cultures, the school prom: the space where heteronormalizing discourses that permeate school cultures are ritually reproduced and exemplified by the selection of a prom king and queen.

Krystal Bennett—Prom King

This year, in Ferndale, Washington, students elected a woman prom king. And not just any woman, but a big, butch, out dyke who brought her girlfriend to the prom. The openly gay senior, Krystal Bennett, saw it as a great political statement. Parents got on the phone and complained, and now the principal says there will be clearer guidelines about who can and cannot be nominated; I am sure it will be based on gender (like only boys can be

kings—well, tell that to Murray Hill).[15] *This system*
will work for a while to squash the gay kids from
reigning as queens, and the butch dykes from
flagrantly waving their scepters; however, the
administrative bigots will get tripped up again when
the first openly transgendered student wants to be
nominated. It'll happen, and I can't wait to
chaperone that prom.

—Taormino 2001

In the spring of 2001, as reported above, Krystal Bennett[16] was nominated as prom king by her senior class at Ferndale High School in Washington state. Bennett's reign as king provides an opportunity to trace discourses that emerge when a ritual designed to reinforce heteronormalizing discourses within the school space is subverted.

I now turn to an analysis of media coverage of the Ferndale prom, the reaction of Ferndale High School's principal, and I consider some of Bennett's own comments on her reign as king. Michelle Esteban, a local television news reporter, produced a story about the Ferndale prom. She reports: "There was nothing unusual about the voting process, but who [the students] picked for their prom king was very unusual. Ferndale's prom king is Krystal Bennett, an openly gay senior" (Esteban 2001). In a taped interview with Esteban that takes place on the grounds of Ferndale High, Bennett states, "I really wanted to win and was excited about it . . . but because it didn't seem realistic, I didn't take it as seriously as I felt about it" (Esteban 2001). Bennett is aware that a woman being crowned king will have wide ramifications and notes that this event is "one the entire school is going to hear about, one everybody is going to have to address, one that's really going to directly affect the administration and the staff" (Esteban 2001). This interview on the Komo4 News supports Bennett's claim that this subversive spatial act did have ramifications beyond the school space. The principal reports receiving various types of feedback from community members about Bennett's reign as king. Esteban goes on to note, "The school says it got about 10 calls from the community, a few complaining, but most callers were just curious" (Esteban 2001).

There is no sense in Esteban's report of a community decrying the immorality of Bennett's reign. However, the student body president at Ferndale is reported in the Associated Press as saying, "I guarantee the vast majority of our school thinks there is something a little bit

disgusting or very wrong about homosexuality. . . . [But] if you think
it's wrong, try to change them in a loving fashion."[17] When Esteban
asked the principal of Ferndale High School, David Hutchinson, about
Bennett's nomination, he says, "It was okay. They're [the students]
telling Krystal that we support you" (Esteban 2001). Somewhat contra-
dictorily, Esteban reports, "Krystal thinks most of the students voted
for her as a joke, but she says she is going to get the last laugh" (Esteban
2001). Bennett has been harassed by classmates since the vote and is
reported to be considering leaving Ferndale because she says, "I'm not
sure if I want to surround myself with negativity."[18] Students' reaction
to Bennett's election is by no means uniform; other students are
reported as saying the vote to elect Bennett was sincere and that, "When
they announced who the king was, there was a distinct group of people
cheering. . . . I'm glad she came out and that she was accepted like that
in our school."[19]

There is no consensus at the school about why Bennett was elected
king, or about how students responded to her election. However, the
discursive explosion surrounding Bennett's election is indicative of the
provocative nature of this event, taking place in this space, at this
particular moment in the United States. Bennett's reign as king also
garnered national media interest (it was featured in *USA Today*,[20] on
the Fox News Channel,[21] and in LGBTI community newspapers and
websites). Gay and lesbian proms may still attract some local media
coverage, but they no longer warrant the degree of national attention
that Bennett's election provoked. (In fact, lesbian and gay proms are
now so frequent in some parts of the United States they are almost in
danger of becoming passé.) So why should the election of a woman as
prom king be so newsworthy? Is it possible that Bennett's story has such
currency because it not only challenges discursive dividing practices
relating to sexual identifications, but also because it challenges divisions relating to gender identifications? Effectively, Bennett's election
momentarily reconfigures the sacred space of the prom and exposes its
contingent foundations.

While it appears that everybody at the school knew about Bennett's
performance, it was not one that school authorities were eager to have
repeated. David Hutchinson, the principal, appears in the final section
of the News4 report, headed "Unlikely It'll Ever Happen Again."
Hutchinson states that Bennett's reign as king "is one way to deal with
homosexuality, but it may not be the best way . . . in this venue it wasn't
as appropriate" (Esteban 2001). The *Seattle Times* reports that in
response to Bennett's election, the "high school is crafting a policy to
ensure that at future proms, the king will be male, the queen female."

There is no discussion in the interview of why Hutchinson believes Bennett's election was inappropriate "in this venue." Maybe the reporter perceived that Hutchinson's objections would be so obvious that such a question did not even bear asking. It appears *natural* that the heteronormalizing prerogative traditionally attached to the venue of the prom requires protection from future disruptions akin to that produced by Bennett. Paradoxically, the need to establish guidelines determining who is fit to be king and queen bears testimony to the vulnerability of the supposedly "natural" relations produced within the space of the school prom.

Once again, many questions relating to sexual and gender identifications are absent from educational discourses, even when they pertain to the election of lesbian prom kings. By associating Bennett's reign with a strategy for dealing with homosexuality, Hutchinson also assumes that lesbians are the only women who desire the king's crown. Presumably a woman could desire to be king without desiring other women, just as a man who is straight-identified might fancy himself a prom queen.

Bennett's election, and the discourses it produced, operates to disrupt the heteronormalizing production of social and personal identifications relating to sexuality and gender in educational contexts. In the epigraph to this section, Tristan Taormino also suggests another reason why Bennett's election may provoke debate. Bennett's election points the way to other disruptions of school space, such as "when the first openly transgendered students wants to be nominated" king or queen (Taormino 2001). However, the schools' response to Bennett's election, and the lack of reported opposition to this strategy of prohibiting women from being elected kings and men queens is a salient reminder of the persistent reinscription of spatial dividing practices that reinforce heteronormalizing processes in educational contexts.

Conclusion

Heterotopia, sexuality, and schooling are juxtaposed and interweaved throughout this chapter in order to study the subversion of heteronormalizing spaces as well as the potential problematics of "safe spaces" and "queer spaces." This study of heterotopia and spatial dividing practices disrupts narratives of oppression that are too often associated with LGBTI-identified young people. While these narratives of risk may serve some strategic purposes, they may also serve to reinforce the heterosexual/homosexual binary, and thereby to limit people's agency in the production of sexual and gender identifications.

The study is also informed by Friedrich Nietzsche's assertion of the "importance of 'little deviant acts' in a life where accumulated tensions are always becoming naturalized and moralized" (Connolly 1998):

> For nothing *matters more* than that an already mighty, anciently established and irrationally recognized custom should be once more confirmed by a person recognized as rational. . . . All respect to your opinions! But *little deviant acts are worth more.* (Nietzsche in Connolly 1998, 114, 115)

Dennis Sumara and Brent Davis ponder "how curriculum might begin to insert itself into the tangled web of ignorance that currently exists in and around discourses about sexuality" (Sumara and Davis 1999, 200). The actions of people like Bennett challenge the heteronormative underpinnings of existing discourses produced in relation to the spaces and places of sexualities, genders, and schooling. And because these actions challenge normative conventions of sexuality and gender, they also act as a conduit for conversation that might momentarily be inserted into school curricula, destabilizing the "tangled web of ignorance that currently exists." But the actions described above are fleeting, and, as Hutchinson's remarks indicate, they may be closed down as quickly as they are opened. But, as Nietzsche suggests in his reference to "little deviant acts," the fleeting nature of such actions does not diminish their ability to underscore the contingent foundations of identifications and the potential of subversion to trouble the production of heteronormativity, even in some of schooling's most sacred spaces.

Notes

1. Jaron Kanegson was one of the participants in my research relating to the production of discourses related to sexualities and schooling in high school settings in Australia and the United States. As part of this research I interviewed people in both countries who work in programs designed to support LGBTI-identified teachers and students. At the time of the interview, Kanegson worked at the Lavender Youth Recreation and Information Center (LYRIC) in San Francisco. Part of Kanegson's role at LYRIC involved the provision of support services to students within and outside San Francisco schools.
2. See inside front cover of Reis (1997).
3. Not all of the participants in my research agreed to be identified, which is why some are named in this chapter and some remain anonymous.
4. The name Harvey Milk honors the city supervisor of San Francisco. Milk was elected in 1977 and was assassinated a year later by a conservative

political opponent. "Founded in 1984, the Harvey Milk School is the . . . result of HMI's collaboration with the New York City Board of Education. The Harvey Milk High School is the first and largest accredited public school in the world devoted to the educational needs of lesbian, gay, bisexual, transgender, and questioning youth"; see http://www.hmi.org/main.html, accessed June 4, 2001.

5. The HMI was founded in 1979 in response to an incident in a NYC group home. A 15-year-old boy was beaten and sexually assaulted by other residents. Group home staff addressed the incident by discharging the young man, explaining to him that the attack would not have happened if he were not gay. When Emery S. Hetrick and A. Damien Martin learned of the case, they marshaled the support of concerned adults and founded the Institute for the Protection of Lesbian and Gay Youth (IPLGY). The Institute was renamed in their honor after their deaths. This information is drawn verbatim from the Institute website; see http://www.hmi.org/main.html, accessed June 4, 2001.

6. See http://www.hmi.org/main.html, accessed June 4, 2001.

7. In June 2002 the Harvey Milk High School received a $3.2 million grant from The Board of Education in New York to expand the school, increase the number of student places, and become a full academic institution with the power to grant diplomas.

8. At the time of the interview Rodriguez was associate executive director of Policy and Public Information at HMI.

9. The WWCS opened its doors in 1997. Unlike HMHS and the EAGLES Center, students attending WWCS are required to pay tuition, as it is a private school and therefore receives no support from the local school district. In the 2003–2004 school year WWCS suspended operation, as it was unable to obtain accreditation from the Southern Association of Colleges and Schools; it hopes to reopen in 2004–2005.

10. See Baldwin, http://www.libertocracy.com/Transfer/Articles/Education/queer/GayAgenda.htm, accessed July 5, 2001.

11. See Baldwin, http://www.libertocracy.com/Transfer/Articles/Education/queer/GayAgenda.htm, accessed July 5, 2001.

12. The Los Angeles Unified School District (LAUSD) supports three centers, known collectively as the EAGLES (Emphasizing Adolescent Gay Lesbian Education Services) Center. It is officially recognized as a branch of the LAUSD Central High School. Since the time of interview the EAGLES Center has been renamed the OASIS. Founded in 1992, the EAGLES Center brochure states that it "primarily targets at-risk gay, lesbian, bisexual and transgender youth between the ages of 14 and 21."

13. Students at the EAGLES Center are also predominantly young people of color, see http://search.lausd.k12.ca.us/cgi-bin/fccgi.exe?w3exec=school.profile.content and which=8581, accessed July 5, 2001.

14. This text is drawn from a promotional brochure produced by the EAGLES Center.

15. Murray Hill is a drag king based in NYC. In 1997 he ran for mayor as a write-in candidate; see http://eastvillage.about.com/library/weekly/aa112797a.htm, accessed July 11, 2001.
16. To see an interview with Bennett about her reign as King, go to http://www.komotv.com/news/story_m.asp?ID=10882, accessed December 19, 2001.
17. See http://www.foxnews.com/story/0,2933,25235,00.html, accessed November 21, 2001.
18. See http://www.foxnews.com/story/0,2933,25235,00.html, accessed November 21, 2001.
19. According to a news report in the *Bellingham Herald* by Jim Donaldson and Kari Thorene Shaw. An excerpt of the report was posted on the GLSEN website, see http://www.glsen.org/templates/news/record.html?section+12 and record+737, accessed November 21, 2001.
20. May 20, 2001.
21. May 21, 2001.

References

Armstrong, Felicity. 1999. "Inclusion, Curriculum and the Struggle for Space in School." *International Journal of Inclusive Education* 3, no. 1: 75–87.

Baldwin, Steve. 1999. "Report on AB 101 and the Gay Agenda in our Public Schools." See http://www.libertocracy.com/Transfer/Articles/Education/queer/GayAgenda.htm accessed 05/07/01.

Bell, David, and Gill Valentine, 1995. "Introduction." Pp. 1–27 in *Mapping Desire: Geographies of Sexualities*, ed. David Bell and Gill Valentine. London: Routledge.

Bell, Vikki. 1999. "Perfomativity and Belonging: An Introduction." *Theory, Culture and Society* 16, no. 2: 1–10.

Bloom, Leslie Rebecca. 1999. "Interpreting Interpretation: Gender, Sexuality and the Practice of not Reading Straight." *International Journal of Qualitative Studies in Education* 12, no. 5: 331–345.

Boostrom, Robert. 1998. "'Safe Spaces': Reflections on an Educational Metaphor." *Journal of Curriculum Studies* 30, no. 4: 397–408.

Connolly, William. 1998. "Beyond Good and Evil: The Ethical Sensibility of Michel Foucault." Pp. 108–128 in *The Later Foucault: Politics and Philosophy*, ed. Jeremy Moss. London: Sage.

De Crescenzo, Teresa, ed. 1994. *Helping Gay and Lesbian Youth*. New York: The Harrington Park Press.

Eggleston, Verna. 2001. "Executive Director's Comments." *HMI Reporter*, spring.

Esteban, Michelle. 2001. "Ferndale High School Elects Female Prom King." *Komo4 News*, http://www.komotv.com/news/story_m.asp?ID=10882, accessed 20/06/01.

Foucault, Michel. 1982. "The Subject and Power." Pp. 208–226 in *Michel Foucault: Beyond Structuralism and Hermeneutics*, ed. Hubert. L. Dreyfus and Paul Rabinow. New York: Harvester Wheatsheaf.

———. 1984. "Space, Knowledge, and Power." Pp. 239–256 in *The Foucault Reader*, ed. Paul Rabinow. London: Penguin.

———. 1986. "Of Other Spaces." *Diacritics*. Spring: 22–27.

———. 1996. "Ethics of Concern for the Self as a Practice of Freedom." Pp. 432–449 in *Foucault Live (Interviews, 1961–1984)*, ed. Sylvere Lotringer. New York: Semiotext(e).

———. 1997. "For an Ethics of Discomfort." In *The Politics of Truth: Michel Foucault*, ed. Sylvere Lotringer and Lysa Hochroth. New York: Semiotext(e).

Gordon, Angus. 1999. "Turning Back: Adolescence, Narrative, and Queer Theory." *GLQ: A Journal of Lesbian and Gay Studies* 5, no. 1: 1–24.

Griffin, Jacqui. 1994. *SchoolWatch Report: A Study into Anti-Lesbian and Anti-Gay Violence in Australian Schools*. Sydney: Author.

Hemmings, Clare, and Felicity Grace, 1999. "Stretching Queer Boundaries: An Introduction." *Sexualities* 2, no. 4: 387–396.

LeCompte, Margaret D. 2000. "Standing for Just and Right Decisions." *Education and Urban Society* 32, no. 3: 413–429.

Martin, Tim. 2001. "To be Gay, and Happy, at School." Student.Com, http://www.student.com/article/gayschool/2001 accessed 22/02/01.

Munt, Sally. 1995. "The Lesbian *Flaneur*." Pp. 114–125 in *Mapping Desire: Geographies of Sexualities*, ed. David Bell and Gill Valentine. London: Routledge.

Patton, Cindy. 1996. *Fatal Advice: How Safe-Sex Education Went Wrong*. Durham, NC.: Duke University Press.

Rabinow, Paul. ed. 1984. *The Foucault Reader*. London: Penguin.

Reis, Beth. 1997. *Safe Schools Resource Guide*. Seattle: Safe Schools Coalition of Washington.

Skeggs, Beverley. 1999. "Matter out of Place: Visibility and Sexualities in Leisure Spaces." *Leisure Studies* 18: 213–232.

Sumara, David and Brent Davis, 1999. "Interrupting Heteronormativity: Toward a Queer Curriculum Theory." *Curriculum Inquiry* 29, no. 2: 191–208.

Talburt, Susan. 1999. "Open Secrets and Problems of Queer Ethnography: Readings from a Religious Studies Classroom." *International Journal of Qualitative Studies in Education* 12, no. 5: 525–539.

Taormino, Tristan. 2001. "Porn Queens and Prom Kings." *Village Voice*, New York, http://www.villagevoice.com/issues/0121/taormino.shtml, accessed 18/05/01.

Threadgold, Terry. 2000. "Poststructuralism and Discourse Analysis." Pp. 40–58 in *Culture and Text: Discourse and Methodology in Social Research and Cultural Studies*, ed. Alison Lee and Cate Poynton. St. Leonards, NSW: Allen and Unwin.

Chapter Seven

Scout's Honor

Duty, Citizenship, and the Homoerotic in the Boy Scouts of America

Andrea Coleman, Mary Ehrenworth, and
Nancy Lesko[1]

Scouting is an institution akin to the flag and the constitution as a commonplace representation and evocation of "America." The statistic that 20 percent of all American boys[2] are scouts may underplay its considerable cultural weight as a shaper of citizens and the nation. The intimate relations of "America" and the Boy Scouts (BSA) were aggressively promoted by Theodore Roosevelt and youth policymakers in the early 1900s as an antidote to urban devirilization of young men (Macleod 1983). The first *Boy Scouts of America Handbook* promoted the organization as necessary to "combat the system that has turned such a large proportion of our robust, manly, self-reliant boyhood into a lot of flat-chested cigarette smokers, with shaky nerves and doubtful vitality" (quoted in Shapiro 1997, 22). Outdoor life was prescribed to strengthen individuals' physical and moral health and to rescue the nation. The current Scout Oath maintains this emphasis on love of country in its opening lines: "On my honor, I will do my best to do my duty to God and my country and to obey the Scout Law" (www.scouting.org). While woodsy images and "morally straight" narratives of scouts may appear anachronistic, scouting still evokes strong emotional responses and involvements, in part because of the vast army of public schools, churches, and other civic organizations such as the United Way who actively provide support.[3] The long and intimate relations of

"America" with the Boy Scouts made it a national story when the BSA met queer scout activists at the Supreme Court.

In June 2000, the United States Supreme Court issued a 5–4 decision in *The Boy Scouts of America v Dale* supporting the right of the BSA to exclude homosexual scouts. This right was based on the BSA's status as a private organization. James Dale had been an assistant scoutmaster in New Jersey and a member of the BSA for twelve years. In college Dale came out and held the office of president of the campus lesbian and gay alliance. The publication of that information led to his expulsion from the BSA. His case followed another gay scout's 1986 case in which the BSA exclusionary policy was also upheld.

Although the Supreme Court dubbed the BSA a private organization (despite the fact that the President of the United States is the Honorary President of the BSA), the Dale decision led to a sustained firestorm of publicity and public policy revisions. Many school districts and churches declared that they would no longer support the BSA by providing space for meetings free of charge. For example, in Philadelphia the two sides are still struggling to align a city policy that prohibits discrimination on the basis of sexual preference with the Boy Scout's ban of openly gay leaders. The Philadelphia Scouts have lost a half million dollars in funding from the United Way and the Pew Charitable Trusts because of their discriminatory policy, and the area's 48,000 scouts will have to vacate their city-owned building. Local communities across the United States were split by the longstanding belief in and material support for local troops and the equally avid belief in and support for nondiscriminatory policies. Debates across the country were heated and sustained. Individual troops that took a stand against the BSA policy lost their troop charters, such as the mountaineering troop in Sebastopol, California (www.scoutingforall/articles/2003082601.shtml, retrieved January 8, 2004). In a replay of U.S. "Don't Ask, Don't Tell" military policy, BSA troops can only include gay members if the members and the troops don't let anyone know about it.

The Dale decision also led to the founding of a protest movement, Scouting for All, which has collected 90,000 signatures on its petition to the BSA to change its homophobic policy. In this chapter we utilize the award-winning documentary film *Scout's Honor* (2001), about Scouting for All's founder, Steve Cozza, to critically examine the narratives, images, feelings, and desires that circulate across queer scouts, youth activism, the BSA, and "America." In so doing, we are working in the messy and crowded spaces of stories of democracy, feelings and desires for the nation and for young men and women, and fantasies of what it means to live and participate as a citizen in the United States today. We consider how something we want to call "democratic" survives among youth active around sexual identity issues. Our focus is primarily on how the film narrates the construction of the political subject, that is, the ways "we" understand queer youth activists' relationship to the political world and to themselves. In other words, we are concerned with the film as *civic education*, and ask: How does the film narrate Steve Cozza's political activism against the homophobic policy of the Boy Scouts of America? How does the film help construct the realm of the political? What effects does the portrait of Steve as a young, "natural" superhero have for queer activism? What alternative stories, images, desires, or memories are available to queer this narrative of natural youth activists?

Sexuality and Nationality

In our recognition of the complexity of political struggles by marginalized groups, we locate our analysis in the scholarly body of work known as radical democratic citizenship studies (Rasmussen and Brown 2002), and here we briefly outline some of our specific theoretical positions. One starting point is our recognition of the significance of nationalism in shaping identity (in and out of the BSA) and in providing legitimacy and language for activism around the rights of sexual minorities (Parker, Russo, Sommer, and Yeager 1992; Shapiro 1997). The Scouting for All movement legitimates its agenda in part by appealing to the un-American nature of discrimination and the right to organized protest guaranteed in the Bill of Rights. But the individuals who hold and claim this nationality and these rights are often stereotypical liberal heroes, who are "born" as fully formed subjects in isolation. The quintessential American liberal hero who acts for justice is "not contingent, struggled for, or made in material conditions" (Vaughan 1997, 82). These naturalized heroes, our activists, are the main characters in a metastory of "U.S. history as a 'march of liberty' with the Constitution providing a legal framework in which the orderly expansion of liberty could take place" (Swidorski 1997, 29). The march of liberty story omits political and economic struggles among contesting groups or classes, and enshrines the Constitution and the Supreme Court as the foundation of our democratic society, with particular importance given to the First Amendment freedoms, the linchpins of "our" democracy (Swidorski 1997, 30).

Sexuality has no historically demarcated place within this progressive march of liberty anchored in the constitution story. "Sexual citizenship" is a term little explored in citizenship studies (Lister 2002), although George Mosse's (1985,1996) work directly links a particular form of heteronormativity with the 1930s nationalism of Germany and France. "The male body," claims Mosse, "was thought to symbolize society's need for order and progress, as well as the middle-class virtues such as self-control and moderation" (1996, 9). The body was overtly linked with nationalist sentiment in the period before and during World War Two in ways that have been subsumed since then. Nevertheless, the erotic quality of civic relations is implicit in much current work on nation and citizenship. As Parker et al. (1992) point out, nationalism is regularly couched as "a *love of country*: an eroticized nationalism" (1). The terms of this love relation always involve a "deep horizontal comradeship," a "fraternity," as nationalism favors a distinctly homosocial form of male bonding (5). The BSA is also characterized by such relations.

Heteronormative public policies and the dematerialized assumptions of the march of liberty metastory continue to make queer legal activism a significant national narrative. Ironically, political activity and current definitions of nation, sovereignty, and citizenship, as they are taken up in public policy debates over civil rights, adoption, and marriage, are increasingly located on the terrain of sexuality (Goldberg-Hiller 1997, 101). While the public sphere may have been shrunk into the private by neoliberal policies and policymakers (Duggan 2002), the "march of liberty" also has to contest with more rainbow flags. And this current moment is the context for this analysis: when the public attention to virulent homophobic policies, referenda, and neoliberal gay intellectuals (Duggan 2002; Goldberg-Hiller 1997) coexists with the use of law and civil rights legacies to support gay political subjectivity and, specifically, youth activism. In what follows we examine some of the storylines of citizenship, subjectivity, and nation when the march of liberty and the BSA encounter Steve Cozza and Scouting for All.

Scout's Honor: The Film

Scout's Honor begins with a collage of documentary and propaganda clips portraying scouts since the founding of the BSA, in heady visions of boys and men in the woods, in tents, and on parade, in various stages of undress, costume, and regalia. The archival footage depicts presidents from Teddy Roosevelt to JFK to Bill Clinton meeting with representatives of the BSA. "Scouting is the largest youth movement in the country. One out of every five American boys is a Scout," is emblazoned on the screen as an introduction to this story. Through footage of former presidents, the film nostalgically weaves scouting into the fabric of "natural" American boyhood. The film then moves from interviews with and media footage of Tim Curran, the first scout to be publicly expulsed from the organization for being homosexual, and James Dale, to interviews with Steve Cozza, his troop leader, his family, and his friends. Film clips of Cozza publicly campaigning for Scouting for All are interspersed with more intimate conversations with Steve, his family, and his friends. The film closes with Cozza receiving his badge for Eagle Scout and his avowal, even as he assumes his award, to continue to battle the BSA over their exclusion of gays "because the Boy Scouts are wrong."

   Scout's Honor is a complex text in that it is simultaneously documentary and pedagogy. Analyzing this text requires a method that takes into account the inconsistent, contradictory, and tenuous hegemony of dominant discourses. We begin, therefore, with the film studies concept of modes of address, looking at how Elizabeth Ellsworth (1997) borrows the concept in order to explore the incoherent, unknowable spaces of pedagogy, and how she summarizes its meaning with the question: "Who does this film think you are?" (22). Ellsworth explains that all films have desired audiences, and whether that audience is the broadest possible mass or a tiny niche, filmmakers "make many conscious and unconscious assumptions and wishes about the who that their film is addressed to and the social positions and identities that their audience is occupying" (24). Therefore, the film creates an assumed subject position that situates the viewer within various power relations and identity constructions. Filmmakers play on recognized tropes, operate within specific genres, and offer up certain character types that are designed to correspond to the knowledge of a particular audience. Ellsworth offers the example of films like *Jurassic Park*, intended for twelve-year old, suburban white boys, which are "pitched to the positions that such boys are assumed to occupy" (24). In order for the audience to "get it," to recognize the narrative genre and tropes with the least effort and confusion, to enjoy the film in the way it was intended to be enjoyed, they must take up the desired, twelve-year old, suburban white boy position. Ellsworth shows how films work to achieve the audience they desire, pushing their viewers to certain positions, reinscribing those positions, and making the positions seem more real in the world.

   One problem with this desired subject position is that "the viewer is *never* only or fully who the film thinks s/he is" (26). Ellsworth's point is that a film's mode of address and an individual's response will never wholly correspond, regardless of the degree to which a person may look like the intended viewer. Therefore, one way to analyze the representations of queer youth offered in *Scout's Honor* is to ask, "Who does *Scout's Honor* think the viewer is?"

The Implied Viewer

The title of the film takes up the phrase "scout's honor," a colloquial assurance of truthfulness based on the premise of Boy Scout integrity. Implicit in the title is the assumption that the viewer shares universal notions of honor, of scouting, and of their synonymous relationship. The film calls on this assumption and reiterates it by addressing us in particular ways: as participants in commonsense democracy; as neoliberals; and through homonormativity.

Is There a Scout in All of Us? A Commonsense Address

Castronova and Nelson (2002) note that "commonsense democracy depends on antidemocratic moves that encourage our participation in a romantic ideal of civil life while discouraging our participation in gritty dialogues about the political (pre)conditions for community" (3). Cozza's activism and its enactment as pedagogy exemplify the notion of a romantic civic ideal in the way that Cozza is able to protest while remaining a Boy Scout and eventually becoming an Eagle Scout. His is a peril-less situation, a romantic vision of activism on *behalf of others*.

Unlike James Dale and Tim Curran, both of whom were ousted from the Scouts as adults for their public performance as gay males, as a straight, adolescent activist, Cozza is in no danger of expulsion. Others around him fall, including his father, who is expelled, and his scoutmaster, Tim Rice, who is also expulsed for supporting Steve's cause. But Cozza himself cannot be touched, in real and metaphoric ways. Steve's heterosexuality serves as a form of armor in this battle, one that he calls on reluctantly but consistently to ensure his safety, and imply ours. This armor is reinforced by Cozza's youth, which serves as another shield, particularly as Steve seems peculiarly desexed in the film. Nor do any gay adolescents or adolescents who are sexually active at all appear in the film to interrupt the notion that boyhood is a period of innocence. In this way the film colludes with Cozza's careful delineation of himself as pure boy.

Cozza's boyish purity is a scoutish purity, as originally described by G. Stanley Hall, the child psychiatrist whose definitions of adolescence particularly influenced the founding of the BSA as a means of gathering boys at the age of twelve in order to protect them from the onset of puberty and its manifest dangers (Macleod 1983). Macleod notes that "Hall made it clear that teenage sexuality was unavoidable, but his romanticism suggested a program of sublimation through religious idealism and enthusiastic activity: the adolescent would be a young Galahad" (109). It is as such a Galahad that Cozza appears in the film, constructed publicly by adults as a "good kid" who represents the intersection of safe discourses: outspoken youngster fighting for what he thinks is right, and youth as embodiment of family values, tolerance, and justice. He has other layers to his armor (churchgoer, white suburbanite, center of nuclear family and circle of friends). And in a paradox that emerges in the tacit struggle for discursive definition, one of Steve's most potent defenses is his identity as a Boy Scout. Metaphoric understandings of the Boy Scouts as good American boys lend Steve near invincibility, at least while he may still safely be constructed as a boy and participant-activist.

Steve's is a secure position from which he may indeed disrupt the Boy Scouts' vision of themselves as noble and cause them considerable unrest. The way the film situates Cozza suggests the possibility that activist roles may be endured publicly because they are framed within liberal discourses of tolerance that intersect with unspoken assumptions of adolescents as nonthreatening. In the way that Cozza hesitates and then calls on his heterosexuality, it also suggests ways for adolescents to manipulate storylines, taking up the ones publicly that give them power in contested situations, although that power may be fleeting, limited, and vulnerable.

The narrative trajectory of progress in Scout's Honor runs alongside a narrative of natural citizenship and participatory democracy. According to Curran, "the American people are evolving on questions of gay rights." He points out that the BSA is the sole remaining nonreligious youth organization in the United States that discriminates against gays. Curran focuses on the discriminatory nature of a single Scout policy, rather than heteronormative Scout culture, and recalls the historical role of the courts in eventually rectifying legal errors in accordance with the Constitution. However, projects that link legal parity to material equity elide the system's common failure to enforce the rights recognized by the Court. Further, a rights doctrine relies on the notion that the world is divided into a public sphere, which enforces the law, and a private sphere in which people are free to pursue their individual interests—a proposition that ignores not only the interdependence, even collapse, of public and private spheres, but also the history of unequal access produced through such a social pattern (Kennedy, 1998). Curran reinforces this public/private distinction by insisting that the BSA include gays because it does not matter that they are gay—a self-annihilating paradox.

Shrinking the Arena of Discontent: A Neoliberal Address

In the way that it contains gayness as nonthreatening and implicitly accepts the notion that morally straight is a position to which all decent men aspire, *Scout's Honor* tranquilizes fears of the unknown terrain of queer moralities. Like Sullivan's appeals for gay access to marriage and the military, the documentary seeks that we "embrace politics if only ultimately to be free of it" (189). In this embrace, as Duggan (2002) notes, there is the loss of any "vision of a collective, democratic public culture or of an ongoing engagement with contentious, cantankerous queer politics. Instead we have been administered a kind of political sedative" (189). We see the effect of this sedative in the proposition that morally straight is universally defensible.

In the public arena, both supporters and detractors of gays' inclusion in the BSA utilize the traditions of the Boy Scouts as well as particular passages from the BSA oath, especially its central pledge to remain morally upright. The BSA leadership asserts that being a homosexual is incompatible with moral uprightness; moral uprightness necessarily rests on the rock of heterosexuality. James Dale explains what he thinks scouting means: "I think what the scouting program teaches is self-reliance and leadership. Giving your best to society. Leaving things better than you found them. Standing up for what's right. . . . This policy [exclusion of gays] really goes against everything this program taught me" (Lewis-Denizet 1998, 2). Dale's is a sentimental version of the scouting storyline. He tells it as an American story of family values and young leadership. It is a heroic, mythic coming-of-age story, desexualized, with the *Dale* decision as the unpredicted tragic ending, a kind of narratological shipwreck (Currie 1998) where the narrative of the past (young American boys, true and strong, becoming men without sexuality) collides with the present (men with men in spaces other than the BSA), making certain identities (such as men with men in public spaces and the BSA) impossible. Dale's need to be a gay scout is more than simply a political agenda. It is a claim that he exists at all. James Dale's interview in *The Advocate* closes with his description of Steve Cozza's plan to generate a million signatures to overturn the BSA decision. "This boy is my hero."

At the nexus of this narratological shipwreck is Steve Cozza, author, character, narrator, who tells the story of the BSA, his story, and the story of the gay man whom he loves, as stories of friendship, mentorship, and endurance. Steve Cozza defines his family friend, Robert Espindola, a gay man, as teaching him family values and moral uprightness—to live according to principles of justice and fairness. When Steve's dad first told him about the BSA's policy against gays, Steve immediately thought of Robert.

> The Boy Scouts told me it was immoral and wrong to be gay. I thought, Wait a minute, Robert is not wrong. That doesn't make sense. I definitely put his face to it right away. . . . [Robert] had been teaching me family values and about God and moral issues ever since I was 7. And here the Boy Scouts were talking about he's immoral. It turned me off. (Gallagher 2001, 2)

Steve reported that his decision to take a stand against the Boy Scouts resulted from his putting Robert Espindola's face to the Scout's policy. He added that he had to take a stand against the Scouts because accepting the policy would have amounted to "turning my back on my friends" (May 22, 2001, *Advocate*, 2). Steve tells his story thus, as a natural story of a young friend loyal to his mentor. He calls on the homosocial traits that the BSA endorses, weaving them closely within a context dear to conservatives of any faction, of church, family, and community.

The Emergence of the Lie: A Homonormative Address

The conservative moralism that emerges as the film progresses is reminiscent of what Duggan calls a "new strain of gay moralism" that followed radical AIDS activism, a moralism that advocated for monogamous gay marriages, a moralism that was antidemocratic, antiegalitarian, and assimilationist in the extreme (2002, 182). The film constructs Cozza as a straight, white, normal male, his family as hypernormal, and his gay role model as a morally straight, white, male church-camp counselor. The film implies that we should be like Steve, not like those for whom he advocates, or rather, that they too are like him (Curran, Dale, other gay Eagle Scouts, Espindola) and we can be like them if we are like them in the ways they are like Cozza, in the ways they are morally straight. Mosse (1996) reminds us that "it is the normative—that which is considered normal—which motivates most people and determines their perceptions of society" (12). And so it is homonormative notions that drive Cozza's activism and audience participation in it, and that circumscribe queer existences in a move that refuses to recognize queer or its seductiveness.

In this way, the space created by Cozza's willingness to include gays in the Scouts reflects a buried master narrative that Sedgwick names in other circumstances as "the overarching lie," namely, that even those who want to help gays predicate their work on anything but the desire for a gay outcome for kids (1993, 76). And it feels in *Scout's Honor* that Cozza's choice of narrative shifts in consciousness. Cozza seems to name his heterosexuality as a means of making clear that he (representing straight youth) remains "safe" despite his closeness to what he names as his "role model," Robert Espindola (representing gay men, also here named as infected with HIV). Thus, Cozza constructs his identity as straight as a means to demonstrate how safe it is to be around gays. But this construction of heterosexuality reenacts a master narrative of homophobia by shaping the dream of queer as an ugly dream.

Steve's activism has roots in family values, in his many years of friendship with Robert Espindola, and by a love of scouting, especially the camping trips and ways that the Scouts inspired boys to work for others. In *The Advocate* interviews with Steve and James, each is portrayed as somewhat of a natural activist. In 1986, Tim Curran was kicked out of the Eagle Scouts when they discovered that he was a member of a gay youth group. Seventeen years later, in *Scout's Honor*, Curran explains that "joining the Boy Scouts when [he] was fourteen was a natural step." Sexuality and Scout identity are innate qualities that are normalized through biological inevitability. Further, activism is simultaneously dematerialized and materialized. In *Scout's Honor*, we see Steve at home with his family in Petaluma, California, shooting hoops, skateboarding; the film works hard to portray him as a regular guy, although his mother dubs him fearless. He jokes, argues a bit with his dad, needs to be encouraged to do his homework and speaks eloquently about the ups and downs of his national campaign. This regular-ness sits side-by-side with an extraordinary activism on behalf of gays, although the very notion of "gay" has a "regular" quality to it, a way of containing what might be construed or constructed as queer identities within safe, conservative, homonormative boundaries of citizenship.

Steve Cozza, gay advocate, and the gay cast of characters, including Dale, Curran, and Espindola, are normalized, positive representations. Luhmann (1998) points out two assumptions that ground calls for positive imagery. First, visibility politics advocating lesbian and gay inclusion targets a straight audience and "sees homophobia as a problem of ignorance, of not knowing any lesbian and gay folks" (143). Accordingly, normalized images of lesbians and gays allow straight people to understand that "they" are just like "us" and leads to the end of discrimination. For example, Espindola is "like" Steve in his values if not in his sexual practices. Second, Luhman explains that a politics of inclusion also assumes that a young, queer audience will benefit from exposure to positive lesbian and gay role models. Like Luhman, Talburt (2000) underscores the limitations of positive representation and argues, "projects that teach tolerance (to straights) and offer role models (to queers) create necessarily distorted knowledges through partial, normalized images and depend on intact identities that can be rationally seen and received" (8).

The process of determining positive imagery has everything to do with the "who" that creates the image—her location within relations of gender, race, class, ability, religion, age, sexuality, geography—as well as her assumptions regarding the viewer or participant. There is no path to objective imagery, and representations necessarily fulfill some expectations while neglecting others. For this reason, Luhmann (1998) identifies a crucial failing of identity politics as the desire "to expand the definition of *normal* to include lesbians and gays rather than attacking and undermining the very processes by which (some) subjects become normalized and others marginalized" (144). A more productive question may be, How do these representations work in the film?

Scout's Honor depends on an essentialist understanding of sexuality as a universal and apparently biological human trait. Like other media projects around queer youth activism, some of the heroes of *Scout's Honor* are gay folks who publicly define themselves in opposition to a heterosexual majority. Similarly, in the summer of 2002, *The Advocate* published an issue dedicated to exploring the lives of gay and lesbian youth. On a predominantly red, white, and blue cover, the headline "Young and Gay in the USA" is printed over the photo of 21-year-old Mark Beierschmitt, a Pennsylvania native whose story is featured in the MTV documentary *True Life: I'm Coming Out*. Beierschmitt, white, handsome, muscular, and clad in a red sleeveless t-shirt and blue jeans, resembles a contemporary Captain America who substituted a rainbow-studded belt buckle for the more ambiguous blue jumpsuit. In the issue's feature article, author Erik Meers (2002) quotes from interviews with eight queer-identified young people and notes that Beierschmitt's coming-out narrative is an archetypal tale for today's gay youth. According to Meers, the story "illustrates an important reality: Although this generation has unprecedented support services and a legion of out role models, young gays' basic struggle to come to terms with their sexual identity remains deeply personal and incredibly difficult" (58).

According to Meers, "no one knows the difference between private acceptance of one's sexuality and public coming-out better than Joel Relampagos" (62), who came out on MTV's *True Life*. Although Meers points out that Relampagos' decision to come out to his parents on national television was a source of extreme anxiety, by overcoming his fear Relampagos "was able to make his personal turning point into a highly visible resource for other youth" (62). In Meers' narrative, gay identity is forged through the act of coming out, when youth are transformed from confused adolescents to confident young people, and are subsequently equipped to lead the less fortunate out of the closet and into the "new-found freedom" of fixed sexual identity (62).

The modes of address of both *Young and Gay* and *Scout's Honor* depend on the reader or viewer to recognize one's sexuality as essential and fixed. Taken for granted is that young, gay heroes (Beierschmitt, Cozza) either are or they aren't gay. Counter to essentialist understandings of sexuality, constructivist notions emphasize the elasticity of human sexuality and focus on the way sexuality is molded by or a product of social beliefs and values; "embodied in cultural myths, social relations, or language, sexuality is foremost a mental concept, not a biological phenomenon" (Sears 1998, 83). A constructivist critique of *Young and Gay* and *Scout's Honor* would question the ways that sexuality is constructed as both self-evident and natural. Essentialist/ constructivist debates have a long history in the academy across multiple disciplines and crystallize around questions of origin, positing a natural or cultural basis for sexuality. Recently, however, many critics have found that the debate has grown unproductive. Hence, many theorists have begun searching for alternative methods for thinking about sexuality.

Comfort and Terror

An analysis of queer youth activism has important implications for research that seeks to address issues of sexual and gender difference in the classroom. Specifically, underlying our investigation is an uneasiness with activist discourses that construct gay identities as fixed categories to be liberated, celebrated, or conflated with notions of "normal" American boyhood. However, we are mindful also of identity politics as a key means by which activists work to make society— particularly schools—safer for youth who are queer-identified or - perceived. Researchers such as Susan Talburt (2000) acknowledge limitations of identity categories but also emphasize ways that group identity "can be understood as creating new spaces for intervention" (62). Although we recognize the import of expanding understandings of identity politics, we are drawn to pedagogical spaces that are opened through the contradictions, absences, and ruptures in coherent lesbian and gay identity categories.

In order for *Scout's Honor* to succeed, the audience must take up the position offered by the program's address. Like Cozza, the audience must be courageous, compassionate, and derive a clear understanding of sexual difference: a Scout either is or is not gay. Further, the audience should be willing to participate in this understanding because the process also reaffirms their own subjectivity—their normalness. But what happens when the viewer is not the person the film wants them to be? What if the person tuning in to the show is a lesbian-identified woman who sometimes sleeps with men? What if the viewer is a straight-identified, middle-aged man who had sex with men on numerous occasions during his youth? Or a gay-identified male who only came out in middle age? How do these viewers respond to Cozza's certainty that he's not gay?

Ellsworth contends that ways in which a film is off target in its production of audience identities are not cause for alarm. On the contrary, she claims that the power of the text is produced through this misalignment. "The difference between who an address thinks its audience is and the who that the audience members enact through their responses, is a resource available for both filmmakers and audiences as they engage in meaning-making, cultural production, and the invention of new social identities" (37). As an analytic method, modes of address disrupt claims that the media is an omnipotent cultural purveyor that shapes an acquiescent population. Instead, the effects of media projects must be understood as mediated, partial, not fully controllable. Further, a project's modes of address are never unified and are subject to disruption. For example, *Scout's Honor* inscribes the notion of "gay" and "gay Scout" as something safe, contained, disciplined, something not disruptive, something pseudo-conservative, something closer to straight than to queer. Thus "gay" acts as a disciplinary term within and through the film. It denies, makes invisible, and negates other notions of sexual identities, notions such as "queer."

Cozza's armor of heterosexuality complicates the film's address by further exposing the homosexual to vulnerabilities. It is a melancholic performance, in the way that Butler names the melancholia that marks the destruction of the homosexual (1990, p. 81). It is a melancholia that arises from the sense of something being destroyed all over again, a sense that latent, deep-rooted, near invisible homophobia saturates the language, and possibly the hearts of even those who stand in opposition to discrimination against "gays." (In *Scout's Honor* "gay" is constructed as some kind of unified identity untroubled by continuums of bisexuality, trangenderedness, or other possibilities.) The argument framed in *Scout's Honor* is that children aren't in danger of becoming gay by having mentors who are gay. "My dad went to Catholic school and he was taught by nuns, but he didn't become a nun," jokes Cozza to great acclaim in his public-speaking tours. Audience members find this comparison overtly reassuring in *Scout's Honor*. It is an argument that clearly works in making a Scouts that includes gays continue to appear a safe space. But it is an argument that, while overtly reassuring to heterosexual identity, terrorizes the homosexual all over again. Implicit in this argument lies the deep-rooted idea that there is, indeed, something terribly wrong with homosexuality, something from which we need to protect children.

Apple describes Gramsci's notion of hegemony as something that is truly total, that is lived at depth, that saturates the consciousness and constitutes the limits of commonsense (1990, 5). It is that kind of hegemonic homophobia that is at work in Cozza's appeal that including gay Scouts as leaders won't affect the children in gay men's care. It is a silent and pervasive understanding that we would never take up the storyline of the homosexual by choice, because it is an ugly one. Jameson asserts that such "buried-master narratives" act as a central way of understanding the world and creating meaning. He posits "not the disappearance of the great master-narratives, but their passage underground as it were, their continuing but now *unconscious* effectivity as a way of 'thinking about' and acting in our current situation" (1979/1984, xii).

But if we look not only at the narrative but at the spaces created by that narrative, we see that the vision of "gay" remains a vision of outsider, of alienation, of death. It would be impossible, now, for instance, for Cozza himself to come out in the space he has constructed for the homosexual or for the heterosexual because he has inscribed these as possibly conjoined but inherently separate spaces. Such an act would destabilize the comfortable spaces he has defined through his construction as straight boy. Articulating ideals of tolerance, which he performs as the inclusion of the "other" from the safe side of the binary, Cozza makes impossible the idea of a continuum between homosocial and homosexual. And it is *as* this implicit continuum that the Boy Scouts have the potential to be read as a space both public and private, in which the homoerotic cannot be effaced without eradicating the homosocial binds that constitute the Boy Scouts.

Mythic Achievements of Manhood: The Homosocial/Homoerotic

The notion of a safe, "morally straight" gay scout is interrupted throughout the film in several key ways, so that the film potentially acts as a pivot-point between boundaries in places where it is unsuccessful in controlling what Duggan calls "cantankerous queer politics." *Scout's Honor* demonstrates some possibilities for disruption when we resist the position that seems to be asked of the viewer, when we refuse to ignore the bodies that are so highly visible and erased in the film, when we read the film as the collision of public myths with private bodies. It is a text in which the narrative trajectory suggests ideas of progress in public notions of the homosexual at the same time that the text reaches backward to mythic images of American boyhood that suppress the homoerotic. At the nexus of notions of youth, of activism, of American manhood, and of homosexuality, *Scout's Honor* performs metaphorically as an unstable ideological space in which possibility is simultaneously inscribed and constrained.

Despite their overt homophobia, the Boy Scouts perform metaphorically as a space in which males choose to be with other males exclusively in settings that are public and settings that are private, in which they learn what it is to be men, in which they come of age in ways that are informed by the mythic. Sedgwick speaks of the way that "because 'homosexuality' and 'homophobia' are, in any of their avatars, historical constructions, because they are likely to concern themselves intensely with each other and to assume interlocking or mirroring shapes . . . it is not always easy (sometimes impossible) to distinguish them from each other" (1985, 20). Sedgwick thus warns us to look for how notions of homosexuality may mask or serve as vehicles for homophobic constructions. But it is possible to use this ideological construction to demonstrate the long-term, continual, consistent presence of the homoerotic also. In this way, when we look at the Boy Scouts as an American myth, as the space in which boys become men in the presence of other males, it feels as if homophobic denial is produced primarily as a means of masking the embeddedness of the homoerotic in this mythic story. It is because the homoerotic is such a persistent strand in this narrative that the homophobic has to be constantly reiterated.

Taking oaths of fraternal brotherhood, dedicating themselves to serve others, apprenticing themselves to greater mentors, demonstrating their achievements in public and private trials of endurance, the Boy Scouts inhabit the mythic storyline of American superheroes. We see in the Boy Scouts the embodiment of national homosocial desires for a male world. They are becoming Batman, Superman, Captain America. Like these comic-book superheroes, they wear their uniforms only for public display, but they bear themselves both publicly and privately as upholders of democracy and manhood. And like these superheroes, it is the way they perform masculinity that marks their membership. For the form of masculinity they enact and reiterate is what Connell names "hegemonic masculinity," marked by the subservience or invisibility of women and the public performance of feats of macho force (1996, 209).

It is an entirely male world, one that is informed by mythic notions of manhood in which males test each other, mold each other, and strive to achieve control of themselves and also of their world. In their carrying of flags, wearing of costume and insignia, striving to perform notions of American manhood, the Boy Scouts in *Scout's Honor* carry on the tradition of the comic-book superheroes they emulate. "Democracy needs mythmakers," writes Urbinati (2000, 41), and the Boy Scouts represent myth woven into their very fabric, including the closely woven myths that this is a male world, and that this male world exists as an asexual one. In this way the male Boy Scout as a body remains ephemeral, an impossibility. Butler speaks of the "matrix of intelligibility" through which certain kinds of identities, which she names as those in which gender does not follow from sex and desire does not follow from sex or gender, cannot exist (1990, 24). But it is also impossible for identities to exist in the absence of desire. We know this in the way we inhabit bodies ourselves, in the sense we have of desire informing our ways of experiencing the world. To be in the world without desire is to inhabit a world without purpose or joy or presence. And so the Boy Scout, devoid of desire, is only partly a male, or he is only partly in this world, which means that we read his identity as impossible, as camouflaged, or as mythic.

It is only as mythic beings that the Boy Scouts may perform masculinity as asexual entities. This myth collides, however, with the physical entity of private bodies, those bodies who don and strip their Boy Scout uniforms, who give pleasure and pain to themselves and to others, in the daily transactions of boys and boys and men. In the novel *The Amazing*

Adventures of Kavalier and Clay, Michael Chabon describes the mythic endeavors of Sammy, his comic-book illustrator, as informed by "a longing—common enough among the inventors of superheroes—to be someone else; to be more than the result of two hundred regimens and scenarios and self-improvement campaigns that always ran afoul of his perennial inability to locate an actual self to be improved" (2000, 113). It is only superheroes who achieve masculinity without locating the self, which is why ultimately theirs remains a mythic form of masculinity.

The narrative of the Boy Scouts as boys becoming men fragments at this fundamental disconnect between masculinity as a performance and the rejection of the body. Derrick shows us how sometimes when we see a narrative break down like this, what we are seeing is the conflict between internal narrative trajectory and the force of outside oppressive discourses (1997). In this way, for instance, the force of the homoerotic acts as a disruptive force in the Boy Scouts' way of authoring themselves. The intelligibility of the narrative of masculine self-construction disintegrates because the homoerotic is in collision with homophobic discourse. Looking at narrative disruption in certain novels, Derrick posits that "the homophobia of the text works to suppress or repress something *it itself is producing*" (1997, 47). We can read *Scout's Honor* this same way, as a fantastical space in which queer desires are produced and sublimated in the processes of achieving acceptable manhood.

It makes sense then that we see in *Scout's Honor* ways that the Boy Scouts act as a space in which men not only learn to be male in accord but also in opposition to each other. Something has to happen with suppressed desire in this utterly male domain. As long as narratives of desire remain incoherent, the emergence of the homoerotic and the possibility of a continuum between the homosocial and the homosexual are suppressed. But it is a precarious incoherency, always threatened by its own production in this world where males choose to only be with other males, where male bodies exist in close proximity to each other, where the desire to be like other males is consistent with the desire to be with other males but where ways to love other males remain ambiguous. "For a man to be a man's man is separated only by an invisible, carefully blurred, always-already-crossed line from being 'interested in men'" notes Sedgwick (1985, 89). And so we see men at war with each other in *Scout's Honor* as the Boy Scouts go to war with Dale and Curran, because their very coherency as gay Boy Scouts threatens the (heterosexist) authorial intent of the Boy Scouts to remain incoherent.

Making the Private Public:
The Boy Scouts as a Homoerotic Space

With black and white clips of Boy Scouts carrying flags in municipal parades, meeting in public schools, and standing behind the president in the Oval Office, *Scout's Honor* constructs the Boy Scouts as a public space, one in which notions of American manhood and of citizenship are conflated. At public ceremonies spanning the last hundred years, Boy Scouts speak their Oath: "On my honor, I will do my best to do my duty to God and my country and to obey the Scout Law." The language of this oath inscribes the concept that these duties are unitary, that personal honor, duty to God, duty to country, and allegiance to the Scouts act as cohesive forces. Yet, as Caldeira notes in *The Making and Unmaking of Democratic Spaces*, "to look for spatial practices and forms of citizenship in the making . . . is to encounter contradictory tendencies" (2000, 225). So too, the film makes contradictory modes of address, as Steven Cozza demonstrates a site of conflict in the tension between personal honor and allegiance to the Scouts.

Thus we see Steve Cozza articulate his understanding of the Oath as one that makes allegiance to Scout policy impossible, because he reads their policy of discrimination as innately dishonorable. Cozza threatens the stability of the public space created by the Boy Scouts in a unique way, because he is a radical antidisciplinary force acting from within. He is unwilling to quit the Scouts and the Scouts are unable to expel him, and Steve speaks as an insider, calling on the very language structures that shape the Scouts to destabilize their public honor. He is insider in other ways, too; he is an insider to the dreams of boyhood and manhood that shape the public dream that is the BSA.

In describing the spaces of democracy delineated by dimensions of action, decision, and time, Urbinati holds forth that the work to be done in delineating liberatory democratic spaces is "that of creating dreams and vision, of challenging one narrative with another" (2000, 41). And so we have to pay attention to what these dreams are that we create from the residue of the ones that we challenge. We see Cozza doing that work, challenging the narratives of gay as predator, gay as contagious, gay as immoral, and gay as outsider, with storylines of gay as mentor, gay as moral, gay as intimate; or we can compress these narratives into gay as churchgoer/community-member/friend-mentor/sick-but-can-still-be-hugged. This is a dream empty of desire. But it is not the only way to dream of scouts.

We could dream of the Scouts as a homoerotic space. Telling the story this way, as a story of love between men, also has the potential to reconceptualize the Boy Scouts as a place where danger is truly dared, as the BSA sing in their anthem. Reconceptualizing the Boy Scouts as a homoerotic public space means infusing the language used to describe it with desire. It means seeing "paranoid homophobic responses" to the BSA as sites of potential disruption, as markers of the homoerotic surfacing in societal consciousness. In 1954, for instance, Wertham published *Seduction of the Innocent,* in which he attacked comic-book narratives such as *Batman and Robin* for a raging homoerotic subtext. Wertham's text acted as a stage for what in current queer discourse we might term paranoid homophobia. But of course, Wertham was right, the homoerotic is firmly embedded in comic-book superhero narratives. Robin does live alone with Batman in his cave. They do learn to care for the world by caring for each other. So it may be a homophobic tendency to excavate this homoeroticism in order to suppress it, but it is not a paranoid one; indeed, in some ways, it is a marker of the latent potency of the homoerotic—a sign that it is achieving coherency.

This struggle over narrative control, as it were, occurs in theaters that are intra-institutional as well as intertextual and in ways that are metaphysical and metaphorical. The Boy Scouts are intimately conjoined with their gay Eagles whom they so violently expulsed, indeed, it is through the violence of their rejection that we may read the fear of unacknowledged conjointness. "Violence sublimates same-sex desire and reinforces paranoid distances between men," writes Derrick (1997, 81). The intensity of this paranoid homophobia mirrors both the depth to which the homoerotic remains unspeakable and the potency of it as a presence. Neither Dale or Curran are able, in *Scout's Honor,* to name one of the pleasures of the Boy Scouts as the way it is a homosocial/homoerotic space. They call instead on mythic structures of American manhood—it is a space where morality is constructed in interaction with God and Country, where goodness reigns; but never, ever, is it possible in *Scout's Honor* to name the Boy Scouts as a space where men *like* to be with other men, where desires that are overwhelmed or interrupted in other more *heterosexual* arenas may be fulfilled. And yet that is the space, nevertheless, and perhaps in spite of itself, that the film avows. It is thus that we see the persistence, the enduring life of the homoerotic.

Although Curran, Dale, and Cozza have failed to change either the BSA or the legal status of gay Scouts, this film moves its viewers to pride and optimism. How can failure and exclusion be read optimistically? Lauren Berlant (2002) understands the "formalist pedagogy of liberal democracy" as training citizens to "read the details of national/democratic failure as evidence of successes said to be imminent in its political form" (145). The constitutional march-of-progress story and the idealistic young Galahad images and words of Steve Cozza stir pride and optimism. Queer politics and institutional violence against gays are ultimately quieted by the "normative affect of liberal optimism" (145). *Scout's Honor* incites us to consent to liberal-hegemonic optimism about "America" and suggests *eventual* queer participation in the march of progress, while carefully instructing viewers in how to misread the facts and effects of past queer activism. Berlant's analysis suggests that this documentary offers a queer politics shipwreck that marks the realization that this way of telling the past makes impossible certain futures. Citing this shipwreck as the wreck of narratives that were never real anyway because they were narratives in which queer desires remained invisible opens up dilemmas and possibilities for viewers and queer citizens.

If we acknowledge queer desires as submerged forces, we could retell this story as a public story of private love between men, which is a story more destabilizing and more sustaining. Read this way, *Scout's Honor* suggests that it would be productive to introduce new scripts into this conversation, including one of: I'm gay, that's one reason I love the Boy Scouts. This is also a more plausible storyline. To maintain belief in scouting as simultaneously a masculine coming-of-age story and a story defused of desire calls on hallucinatory gestures that are simply impossible for this audience to maintain, even in the face of texts such as *Scout's Honor* that work hard to fix adolescence as immune to desire. There is no immunity, though, for desire, as we know in our own hearts and our own bodies, in the way we refuse this story and yearn for others.

Notes

1. All three authors contributed equally to this chapter.
2. This statistic opens the film, *Scout's Honor*, which focuses on the Boy Scouts. The respective Scouting websites provided these membership figures: 2.8 million girls in GSA and 3.3 million boys in BSA.
3. The support of the Mormon Church for the BSA is especially interesting. In an article about Brigham Young University's (run by the Mormons) new major in Scouting, *Newsweek* provided this view of the Church of Jesus Christ of Latter-Day Saint's (LDS) close relationship with Scouting: "The Boy Scouts are the official boys' youth group of the LDS, and more than one in nine Scouts are Mormons. Critics say the church exerts

disproportionate influence through membership on the national advisory council and vigorous fund-raising" (www.scoutingforall.org/aaic/2003112801/shtml, retrieved January 8, 2004).

References

Apple, Michael W. 1990. *Ideology and Curriculum*. New York: Routledge.
Berlant, Lauren. 2002. "Uncle Sam Needs a Wife: Citizenship and Denegation." Pp. 144–174 in *Materializing Democracy: Towards a Revitalized Cultural Politics*, ed. Russ Castronovo and Dana D. Nelson. Durham, N.C. and London: Duke University Press.
Butler, Judith. 1990/1999. *Gender Trouble*. New York: Routledge.
Caldeira, Teresa. 2000. "The Making and Unmaking of Democratic Spaces." Pp. 224–233 in *The Pragmatist Imagination*, ed. Joan Ockman. New York: Princeton Architectural Press.
Castronovo, Russ and Dana D. Nelson. 2002. "Introduction: Materializing Democracy and Other Political Fantasies." Pp. 1–21 in *Materializing Democracy: Towards a Revitalized Cultural Politics*, ed. Russ Castronovo and Dana D. Nelson. Durham, N.C. and London: Duke University Press.
Chabon, Michael. 2000. *The Adventures of Kavalier and Clay*. New York: Picador.
Connell, R. W. 1995. *Masculinities*. Berkeley: University of California Press.
Currie, Mark. 1998. *Postmodern Narrative Theory*. London: Palgrave.
Derrick, Scott. 1997. *Monumental Anxieties: Homoerotic Desire and Feminine Influence in 19th Century U.S. Literature*. New Brunswick, N.J.: Rutgers University Press.
Duggan, Lisa. 2002. "The New Homonormativity: The Sexual Politics of Neoliberalism." Pp. 175–194 in *Materializing Democracy: Towards a Revitalized Cultural Politics*, ed. Russ Castronovo and Dana D. Nelson. Durham, N.C. and London: Duke University Press.
Ellsworth, Elizabeth. 1997. *Teaching Positions: Difference, Pedagogy, and the Power of Address*. New York: Teachers College Press.
Fine, Michelle. 1992. "'The Public' in Public Schools: The Social Construction/Constriction of Moral Communities." Pp. 101–113 in *Disruptive Voices: The Possibilities of Feminist Research*, ed. Michelle Fine. Ann Arbor: The University of Michigan Press.
Fine, Michelle, and Lois Weiss. 2000. "Construction Sites: An Introduction." Pp. xi-xiv in *Construction Sites: Excavating Race, Class, and Gender Among Urban Youth*, ed. Michelle Fine and Lois Weiss. New York: Teachers College Press.
Frug, Gerald. 2000. "Public Space / Private Space." Pp. 82–89 in *The Pragmatist Imagination*, ed. Joan Ockman. New York: Princeton Architectural Press.

Gallagher, John. 2001. "Making a Difference." *The Advocate*, May 22, 1–7 (retrieved December 6, 2002 from www.findarticles.com).

Goldberg-Hiller, Jonathan. 1997. "Talking Straight: Narrating the Political Economy of Gay Rights." Pp. 89–101 in *Tales of the State: Narrative in Contemporary U.S. Politics and Public Policy*, ed. Sanford F. Schram and Philip T. Neisser. Lanham, M.D.: Rowman and Littlefield.

Jameson, Frederic. 1979/1984. "Foreword." Pp. vii-xxi in *The Postmodern Condition: A Report on Knowledge*, ed. Jean Francois Lyotard. Minneapolis: University of Minnesota Press.

Kennedy, Duncan. 1990. "Legal Education as Training in Hierarchy." Pp. 38–58 in *The Politics of Law: A Progressive Critique*, ed. David Kairys. New York: Pantheon Books.

Lewis-Denizet, Benoit. 1998. "The Model Boy Scout." *The Advocate*, April 14, 1–4. (retrieved December 6, 2002 from www.findarticles.com).

Lister, Ruth. 2002. "Sexual Citizenship." Pp. 191–208 in *Handbook of Citizenship Studies*, ed. Engin F. Isin and Bryan S. Turner. London: Sage.

Luhmann, Susanne. 1998. "Queering/Querying Pedagogy? Or, Pedagogy is a Pretty Queer Thing." Pp. 141–155 in *Queer Theory in Eductation*, ed. William F. Pinar. Mahwah, NJ: Lawrence Erlbaum.

Macleod, David. 1983. *Building Character in the American Boy: The Boy Scouts, YMCA, and Their Forerunners, 1870–1920*. Madison: University of Wisconsin Press.

Meers, Erik. "The Young and the Restless." *The Advocate*, June 25, 2002, 57–67.

Moritz, Meg. 2001. *Scout's Honor*, ed. Tom Shepard: New Day Films.

Mosse, George L. 1985. *Nationalism and Sexuality: Middle-Class Morality and Sexual Norms in Modern Europe*. Madison: University of Wisconsin Press.

———. 1996. *The Image of Man: The Creation of Modern Masculinity*. New York: Oxford University Press.

Parker, Andrew, Mary Russo, Doris Sommer, and Patricia Yaeger. 1992. "Introduction." Pp. 1–18 in *Nationalisms and Sexualities*, ed. Andrew Parker, Mary Russo, Doris Sommer, and Patricia Yaeger. New York and London: Routledge.

Rasmussen, Claire and Michael Brown. 2002. "Radical Democratic Citizenship: Amidst Political Theory and Geography." Pp. 175–188 in *Handbook of Citizenship Studies*, ed. Engin F. Isin and Bryan S. Turner. London: Sage.

Schram, Sanford F. and Philip T. Neisser, ed. 1997. *Tales of the State: Narrative in Contemporary U.S. Politics and Public Policy*. Lanham, M.D.: Rowman and Littlefield.

Sears, James T. 1998. "A Generational and Theoretical Analysis of Culture and Male (Homo)Sexuality." Pp. 73–105 in *Queer Theory and Education*, ed. William F. Pinar. Mahwah, NJ: Lawrence Erlbaum.

Sedgwick, Eve Kosofsky. 1985. *Between Men: English Literature and Male Homosocial Desire*. New York: Columbia University Press.

———. 1990. *Epistemology of the Closet*. Berkeley: University of California Press.

———. 1993. "How to Bring Your Kids Up Gay." Pp. 69–81 in *Fear of a Queer Planet: Queer Politics and Social Theory*, ed. Michael Warner. Minneapolis: University of Minnesota.

Shapiro, Michael J. 1997. "Winning the West, Unwelcoming the Immigrant: Alternative Stories of 'America.'" Pp. 17–26 in *Tales of the State: Narrative in Contemporary U.S. Politics and Public Policy*, ed. Sanford F. Schram and Philip T. Neisser. Lanham, M.D.: Rowman and Littlefield.

Shukla, Sandhya. 2000. "Dialectics of Place and Citizenship." Pp. 248–253 in *The Pragmatist Imagination*, ed. Joan Ockman. New York: Princeton Architectural Press.

Swidorski, Carl. 1997. "Constitutional Tales: Capitalist Origin Stories and U.S. Democracy." Pp. 27–38 in *Tales of the State: Narrative in Contemporary U.S. Politics and Public Policy*, ed. Sanford F. Schram and Philip T. Neisser. Lanham, M.D.: Rowman and Littlefield.

Talburt, Susan. 2000. *Subject to Identity: Knowledge, Sexuality, and Academic Practices in Higher Education*. Albany: State University of New York Press.

Urbinati, Nadia. 2000. "Democracy's Mythmakers." Pp. 34–41 in *The Pragmatist Imagination*, ed. Joan Ockman. New York: Princeton Architectural Press.

Vaughan, Leslie J. 1997. "Native Son: Stories of Self-Creation in the Judicial Politics of Clarence Thomas." Pp. 76–88 in *Tales of the State: Narrative in Contemporary U.S. Politics and Public Policy*, ed. Sanford F. Schram and Philip T. Neisser. Lanham, M.D.: Rowman and Littlefield.

Wertham, Frank. 1954. *Seduction of the Innocent*. New York: Rinehart.

Chapter Eight

Agency in Borderland Discourses

Engaging in Gaybonics for Pleasure, Subversion, and Retaliation

Mollie V. Blackburn

It was not unusual for me, a white woman in my thirties, to walk up to the red brick row home in the middle of a block on a two-lane, one-way street in Center City, Philadelphia and see a group of young people hanging out on the four cement steps with wrought-iron railings on both sides and, while walking up the steps, hear one of them say to another, "'Sup cunt?" Typically, although not always, it was a Black young man performing femininity (Butler 1989) or a male-to-female transgendered person offering such a greeting. The first few times I heard this I probably did not understand what was being said, but once I understood, I bristled at the use of the word "cunt." Immediately I wanted to tell youth not to use that word because it insulted women. Over time, through many conversations with the youth, I came to understand the complicated ways in which these youth used this and many other words—words and ways of using them that together we came to call "Gaybonics."

In this paper, I look at the ways these youth make use of Gaybonics for pleasure and subversion in a queer youth center that I'll call the Loft, in the larger surrounding queer community, on a public bus, and in a public school. By looking beyond the homophobia that queer youth experience in their lives and looking instead at the ways these youth subvert these experiences into experiences of pleasure, I complicate the vulnerable positionality of these youth as victims with their powerful positionality as agents. This is not to say that they are either victims or agents; rather, they are both simultaneously. Because there is significant literature that reveals the former positionality (Britzman 1997; Eaton 1993; Gray 1999; Murray 1998; Owens 1998; Rofes 1995; Savin-Williams 1994; Unks 1995; Youth Voices 1996), I focus on the latter. In particular, I explore the ways in which youth use a Borderland Discourse to elicit pleasure and to subvert oppression, and, when their borders are violated, they shift from this Discourse in order to retaliate against hatred, thus positioning themselves as agents.

Borderland Discourses

Queer youth often experience heterosexism and homophobia in the forms of neglect, isolation, and abuse (Owens 1998; Rofes 1995), which complicate the identity work of lesbian, gay, bisexual, transgender, and questioning (LGBTQ) youth. According to Deborah Britzman (1997), "While gay and lesbian youth are busily constructing their sexual identities, they always encounter contradictory and hostile representation of their identity work" (194). These contradictions and this hostility require that "gay and lesbian youth must rearticulate received representations of heterosexuality with their own meanings while imaginatively constructing gay and lesbian aesthetics and style" (Britzman 1997, 195). Queer youth both elicit pleasure *from* and subvert homophobia *with* language in this imaginative identity work.

According to sociolinguist James Gee, language "encapsulate[s], carr[ies] through time and space, meaning, meanings shared by and lived out in a variety of ways by the social group" (116). However, as Gee (1996) notes, "Language is but a 'piece of the action,'" a piece that has "value and meaning only in and through the Discourse of which it is a part" (149). A Discourse, Gee asserts, is a way of being in the world, a "sort of identity kit which comes complete with the appropriate costume and instructions on how to act, talk, and often write, so as to take on a particular social role that others will recognize" (127). The youth who I represent here use Gaybonics to recognize and be recognized by those within their predominantly Black, queer youth community, but the flip side of this is that they also use it to avoid being understood by those outside of the community.

The use of a Discourse to exclude those outside of a particular community resonates with the ways in which bell hooks (1994) writes about the use of vernacular by those who have inequitable access to traditional notions of power. She asserts that "marginalized and oppressed people attempt to recover [them]selves and [their] experiences in language. [They] seek to make a place for intimacy. Unable to find such a place in standard English, [they] create the ruptured, broken, unruly speech of the vernacular" (175). She goes on to say that vernacular works to "more than simply mirror or address the dominant reality" (175), instead the vernacular subverts that reality. For example, she writes about marginalized and oppressed people making "English do what [they] want it to do" by "tak[ing] the oppressor's language and turning it against itself" and by "mak[ing] [their] words a counter-hegemonic speech, liberating [them]selves in language" (175). Although hooks refers specifically to what she calls Black vernacular, a parallel can be drawn to Gaybonics used by queer adolescents. Raymond, in her discussion of queer adolescent identities, asserts that the "mores, languages, codes, and signifiers," or Discourse, of a queer adolescent subculture "reflects a kind of knowledge that may be inaccessible to others" (116). I show that queer Black youth with whom I worked liberated themselves in language, as hooks says, by making their language inaccessible to their oppressors, as Raymond says, thus eliciting pleasure among themselves and subverting homophobia and other forms of oppression, particularly ageism and racism.

Gee uses the term "Borderland Discourses" to describe "community-based Discourses" that allow interactions "outside the confines of public-sphere and middle-class," and in this case I would add homophobic, ageist, and racist "elite Discourses" (162). Gee's notion of Borderland Discourses can be informed by Gloria Anzaldúa's (1987) description of borderlands as "vague and undetermined place[s] created by the emotional residue of an unnatural boundary" (3). Borders are unnatural boundaries, she claims, that are "set up to define the places that are safe and unsafe, to distinguish *us* from *them*" (3). Gaybonics works to create such a border—one that distinguishes safe from unsafe and us from them so that communication among some is facilitated while that among others, particularly potential oppressors, is hindered.

I explored with youth their understandings of Gaybonics in a youth-run LGBTQ center in Philadelphia. This exploration was a piece of a larger one of literacy performances in the center. The youth at the center are almost entirely from urban communities, and although they are diverse in terms of race, class, and gender, among other aspects of their identities, the population is predominantly Black male. I focus on Story Time, a literacy-based group that I initiated with my partner and facilitated for over three years. I particularly focus on a youth-initiated project within Story Time in which youth in the group created a dictionary of the gay vocabulary. The data encompasses field notes and audiotapes of the group meetings and documents shared and produced in the context of these meetings. The project took place over five months, during which the project was proposed and conceptualized; the dictionary was drafted, edited, and revised; and reflections were made about the significance of such a vocabulary. All of the youth represented by the data in this paper self-identify as something other than straight, and all but two of them self-identify as Black. The data were not only analyzed by me, but also by the youth. Drawing from these data and analyses, I illustrate and examine the ways in which these youth used Gaybonics to elicit pleasure and subvert anticipated oppression in order to position themselves as agents in a world that often works against them.

The project was first proposed when I wondered aloud how youth learned to communicate with one another in the center; I asked how they learned to "read" one another (in the Freirian [1991] sense of reading the world, as opposed to the way these youth used it, which I later came to understand as a way of insulting someone). Their responses suggested that indeed, this was something that needed to be learned. Take, for example, an interaction I shared with Trey and Shane,[1] two young Black gay men, in Story Time:

Trey: Y'all should have a class on that.

Shane: You should have a group on reading [queer youth in this community], Trey.

Trey: Yeees.

Mollie: Tell me what you would do, tell me how you would . . .

Group: [laughter]

Shane: Chiiiile.

Group: [laughter]. . .

Mollie: Hold it, wait, tell me how you would teach a class on reading.

Trey: Chile I'd put down different vocabularies first.

Quentin, another young Black gay man who was a part of this discussion, suggested that people should have opportunities to "just throw [their own interpretations] in" to the vocabulary list, conveying his belief that the language was alive, varying from one perspective to another and changing over time, a belief that was confirmed as we edited and revised the dictionary.

Although the discussions were focused on the words they used, the youth recognized that communicating with one another was about more than this. For example, in this same meeting, the youth discussed the meaning of the word *fierce*:

Trey: If I said your hair looked fierce . . . that'd be a bad thing.

Group: [laughter]

Quentin: But but your hair could be fierce and it could be a good thing too, like, *chile your hair is fierce*, like.

Trey: I use fierce as a bad way.

Shane: That's how I use it.

Trey: I use fierce as a bad way.

Group: [unintelligible]

Shane: But they will know by your facial expressions.

Trey: They be like you be like, *oh chile your hair is fierce.*

Group: [laughter]

Shane: They will know by your facial expressions, that you know like, one track is hanging right here, you know.

Group: [laughter].

So, even though these youth said they would start teaching people how to communicate with one another by focusing on vocabulary, they acknowledged that communication also includes body language, for example. As we continued to explore Gaybonics together, it became evident to me that we were not just talking about particular words. Rather, we were talking about a particular "Discourse" or way of "being in the world" (127), to use Gee's (1996) language. I use Trey's term, "the gay vocabulary," in reference to the words and Shane's term, "Gaybonics," in reference to the larger Discourse that includes this vocabulary but is much more than that.

It also became clear to me through this exploration that we were not just talking about one Discourse in isolation from others. Not only were we talking about a Discourse associated with the queer youth community, we were also talking about this Discourse in relationship to a Discourse associated with the Black Community; that is, Ebonics. I use the term "Ebonics" even though I recognize the risk of this word being misinterpreted as it was following the Oakland resolution of 1996. By

"Ebonics" I do not mean "'broken' English, . . . 'sloppy' speech, . . . 'slang,' . . . [or] some bizarre lingo spoken only by baggy-pants-wearing Black kids," (Smitherman 1998, 30). Instead, Ebonics refers to "'Linguistic and paralinguistic features which on a concentric continuum represent the communicative competence of the West African, Caribbean, and United States slave descendants of African origin'" (Williams quoted by Perry and Delpit 1998, 209). Theresa Perry (1998) describes the "power, beauty, [and] complexities" (12) of Ebonics and points to literacy acts associated with it that "function for freedom, for racial uplift, leadership, citizenship" (14).

In referring to this Discourse, I have elected to use "Ebonics" rather than "African American Vernacular English" or "AAVE" for several reasons. Perry (1998) argues that vernacular is only one variety of what she calls "Black Language/Ebonics" (4). Therefore to use AAVE is to exclude multiple varieties of Black Language/Ebonics, which include "oral and written, formal and informal, vernacular and literary" (Perry 1998, 10). While Perry describes the vernacular as just one variety of Black Language/Ebonics, Ernie Smith (1998) argues that Ebonics is not a vernacular dialect of English at all (57). He illustrates that Ebonics is, instead, "an African grammar with English words" (55). In 1973, a caucus of Black scholars committed to defining "'black language from a black perspective'" (Williams quoted by Smitherman 1998, 29) coined the word "Ebonics," which literally means black sounds (Smith 1998, 54). With this commitment and intention in mind, I use the word "Ebonics."

Similarly, I use the word "Gaybonics" because it was coined and used to name language of queer Black youth from a queer Black youth perspective. Although these youth did not elaborate on this particular word choice, and I did not push them to do so, I imagine that both the word "Gaybonics" and that which it represents are intricately intertwined with "Ebonics." Certainly the word, being directly derived from "Ebonics," suggests this relationship. Also, the youth who engage in Gaybonics are typically, although not always, Black. Further, like Ebonics, Gaybonics is a linguistic choice that is deeply embedded in feelings and situations of oppression. It has power that is significantly distinct from standard English, or what some consider to be the "discourse of power" (Fordham 1999), raising the question of whether there can be one discourse of power and suggesting that different discourses have different power in different contexts. In fact, Fordham (1999) asserts that Ebonics is a weapon in what she describes as guerilla warfare against racism and for the "liberation of a people and reinforce[ment of] their Black identity" (288). I agree with her claim and further assert that Gaybonics is also a weapon against hegemonic oppression, including homophobia as well as racism and ageism. In these ways, the intricate relationship between Gaybonics and Ebonics and between sexual and racial identities is significant, as this chapter illustrates.

The youth used both Gaybonics and Ebonics in much the same way that Anzaldúa uses multiple Discourses in *Borderlands* (1987). That is, these Discourses exist "at the junctures of cultures," cross-pollinating and creating what Anzaldúa calls "the language of the Borderlands" (preface). This is evident in the former example, in the use of the word "fierce." I have since learned that, in some communities, Black women more typically use the word "fierce." In this data, Black gay men, perhaps performing femininity, used and defined the word. While it is a word that can be associated with Ebonics, its use here—by men instead of women—associates it with Gaybonics. Thus, the word as it is used here is located in both Discourses simultaneously. As we worked on the dictionary together, we ran into this overlap repeatedly. Initially we tried to distinguish one Discourse from another but eventually agreed that the overlap exists and that to distinguish them was an artificial task. In fact, it seems to me that Gaybonics is a subDiscourse of Ebonics because while it is not used by all those who use Ebonics, it is not typically used by those who do not use Ebonics at all. While it is not my purpose to neatly locate Gaybonics relative to Ebonics, I pay some attention to times in which youth make stylistic shifts in language in order to achieve particular functions, or what Blom and Gumperz (1972) call metaphorical code switching.

In particular I consider the relationship between the use of these Borderland Discourses and the identities of the youth who engage in them. Sociolinguist Nikolas Coupland (2001) asserts that linguistic style "operates primarily in the expression of identity and relational goals" (190). Similarly, A. C. Liang concludes that the "process of negotiation between individuals, intentions, and social and cultural forces illustrates the intimate connection between language and identity" (307). While Liang's work is helpful because it focuses on sexual identities, particularly lesbian and gay identities, it fails to consider racial identities. However, Rusty Barrett (1999) studies the speech of African American drag queens. He suggests that race and sexuality cannot be explored in isolation from each other when he states that the "complete set of linguistic styles together index a multilayered identity that is sometimes strongly political with regard to issues of racism and homophobia" (313). He concludes that the "polyphony of stylistic voices and the identities they index serve to convey multiple meanings that may vary across contexts and speakers" (327). Building on this work, I analyze different stylistic voices, or what I'm calling Borderland Discourses, to reveal and make sense of the multiple meanings being conveyed and what difference these meanings make in the lives of those engaging in the Discourses.

Pleasure and Subversion in a Queer Youth Center

As young people engaged in Borderland Discourses in this queer youth center, they elicited pleasure through humor and intimacy. Black folklorist J. Mason Brewer (1978) asserts that humor elicits a "feeling of power in the midst of misery," is intended to amuse, and makes people feel better about themselves (x). It is this understanding of humor with which I am working here. That the youth engaged in Borderland Discourses to humor one another was evident throughout the three years that I spent at the center.

When we worked on the dictionary together in Story Time, the group not only identified and defined words that they considered to be a part of the gay vocabulary, they also performed the words in use. Inevitably the group laughed together as they performed. As in the interaction between Trey and Shane when they explained what "fierce" meant, Trey performed the word when he said, "Oh chile your hair is fierce," and Shane complemented the performance with an image of one track of hair hanging in the wrong place. They played off of each other and humored the group, as evidenced by the group's laughter. Through these performances, youth illustrated ways in which language can be used to exert power over others, particularly those who are the objects of the criticism, to make themselves feel better, and most outstandingly to amuse one another.

Examining the gay vocabulary also served to create a sense of intimacy among those who engaged in the Discourse. But to engage in the Discourse, they had to learn it. When I asked youth how they learned Gaybonics, I was told:

Quentin: You pick it up.

Trey: I picked it up when I started coming here when I was like seventeen, I started listening to the vocabulary, and stuff like that . . .

Trey: [Quentin] didn't even think he was going to get the uh vocabulary.

Quentin: No, he had to teach me, I had to keep asking, What does that mean? How do you use that?

Here, Trey said that he learned Gaybonics through observation, and Quentin said that he learned it from more overt teaching. This teaching and learning played a significant role in developing intimacy among youth in the center. Janice, a young Black bisexual woman who came to Story Time, talked about the importance of such opportunities to teach and learn the Discourse of any given community when she said, "I think here, I didn't understand most of the slang, but like people taught me, it wasn't like, like in high school, people weren't like *well you're not a part of us or whatever,* looking at me like I'm crazy." Here, Janice implied that being taught Gaybonics at the center made her feel more a part of the community.

However, just as engaging in a particular Discourse makes some people feel more included, it makes others feel excluded. According to Quentin, "there is definitely a culture at the Loft or a culture among young gay people, if you can't understand [Gaybonics], then you can't really fit in." During this same discussion, Karen, a young Black lesbian who came to Story Time, said that, "if the in-crowd doesn't deem you worthy to fit in, then they're not going to take you under their wing and educate you on the lingo." In this conversation, Quentin and Karen conveyed that the relationship between knowing Gaybonics and being a part of their predominantly Black, queer youth community are integrally intertwined and those who do not know the Discourse are excluded from the community. Therefore one could not assume that, just because a young person came to the Loft, he or she was a part of the community there.

Just a few weeks after this Story Time conversation, a group of youth played a game called "When the Wind Blows." While observing the game, the use of Gaybonics to exclude became particularly apparent to me. To play the game, there is one fewer chair than there are players. The one standing player says, "The wind blows for anyone who," and completes the sentence with a phrase that reveals something true for him- or herself and ideally for other players as well. Everyone for whom that statement is true stands up and finds another chair. The person without a chair then makes a statement that is true about him- or herself, and thus the game continues. During this particular game, I noticed that some players were using the gay vocabulary, which hindered those who did not understand the words. I mentioned this at the following meeting of Story Time. I said:

Mollie: When we were playing that When the Wind Blows game, when people were using private words I tried to say "say what you mean," or "define it," because I think that can feel really isolating or outcasting, you know, feel like you're on the outside of that community as opposed to the inside . . .

Theo: What do you mean by private words?

Dara: Yeah, I was going to ask that.

Mollie: Uh, wor, ok, like if I asked the que, if we're playing When the Wind Blows, you know the game, right?

Dara: Uh huh.

Mollie: And I say, um, "the wind blows for anybody wearing a gilda," and nobody knows [that gilda means wig].

Group: [laughter]

Thunder: [Is] that what she said? I said that.

Mollie: Did you say that?

Thunder: I feel so bad.

Mollie: No, no, no don't. I'm telling you why, but if five people don't know what it is . . .

Quentin: Yeah.

Mollie: It kind of makes you feel stupid. . . .

Shane: Out of those five people, like three of them got wigs on.

Mollie: Right.

Group: [laughter]. . .

During the game, Thunder, a young Black gay man, exerted power over the people who didn't know the gay vocabulary by using words some people did not know, effectively preventing those people from playing at least one round of the game. While some people could not play the game, he could. Thus, using the gay vocabulary here made Thunder feel better about himself. The group's laughter suggested amusement, not only in the incident but also in the telling of the incident. Thus, this incident, as well as the telling of it, served to humor many of the youth involved.

Still, there was at least one person in the group who did not seem to be amused. This was Steve, who seemed to identify with those who did not understand the Discourse. Steve is a young Asian American gay man who came to the center sporadically and never particularly connected with the youth who came more regularly. He said:

> people feel that uncomfortable because they don't relate to the same things because they're not from here, they're from outside, and there are like things about, I don't really, I find it more interesting the people who don't come here, they come here once and they leave, I generally become friends with them, I relate to them a lot more than the people who are already here. I don't know why that is.

Admittedly, I, as well as others in the group, assumed a defensive stance in response to his comment. I suggested that he think more about why he did not relate to people at the center, suggesting that he assume responsibility for this disconnect, and one of the youth verbally agreed with me. Another youth asked how his comment connected with the conversation we were having about language, suggesting that his comment was off-topic. Although Steve did not respond to my comment or the youth's question, Quentin and Shane made an effort at locating his comment in our conversation about language. They said:

> Quentin: I think that language does [have to do with feeling like an outsider in the center] because there are people here, and I think it happens to a lot of people when they come, um, if they integrate themselves, you'll feel like you're speaking two different languages but over the time, you'll either incorporate it or keep your own but understand what the people are saying.
>
> Shane: I do, I personally do think that the language has something to do with [feeling like an outsider in the center].

Then Shane went on to give an example of the ways in which not knowing Gaybonics could hinder a youth's effort to develop intimacy with those in the center. Even though the group would not assume responsibility for someone's positionality as an outsider, they acknowledged that one's faculty with Gaybonics had something to do with whether one felt a part of the community.

What was not articulated but I believe was embedded in this conversation was the racialized nature of the Discourse. Trey, a Black gay man who uses Ebonics, said he just picked up on Gaybonics. Quentin, a Black gay man who does not typically use Ebonics, said he had to be taught Gaybonics. The Black women in the group, both of whom use Ebonics, still described the need to teach Gaybonics. However, Steve, who is gay but is not Black, who does not use Ebonics, neither picked up on nor was taught Gaybonics. In other words, it seems that Gaybonics is not a Discourse for all queer youth at the Loft; rather, it is specifically a Discourse for Black queer youth.

Several weeks before this conversation, I suggested that the youth used Gaybonics to position some people as insiders and others as outsiders within their predominantly Black, queer youth community. I was told that they did not do it *on* purpose, but that doing it did serve *a* purpose. Quentin told me that the exclusion was not necessarily intentional, but instead it was a "part of the culture." Further, Thunder asserted that youth engaged in Gaybonics in ways that constructed borders within their community in order to practice for other communities where they needed to construct such borders to protect themselves from the homophobia that they experienced. He said:

> Thunder: I feel like the vocabulary, the gay vocabulary is like our way of defense in the straight community.
>
> Quentin: True.
>
> Thunder: When you're out there
>
> Mollie: Say more about that. What do you mean that it's your defense?
>
> Thunder: Ok, all right, by you playing around with your friends and you saying stuff *oh chile, you tired* [ugly], *you like a rock* [extremely ugly, like a rock]. Y'all kiki [joke] and laugh but it's like practice, it's like, you are, how should I say, training yourself for the salt that's to come when you get out there in the real world because, here in the Loft, we're here, we're comfortable, we can kiki and laugh.
>
> Mollie: So you're developing defense mechanisms?
>
> Thunder: We're developing defense, and you know, it quickens your reflexes to come back up with something more witty and more like *uh, gag-nation,* you know what I'm saying?
>
> Mollie: So it's a way of dealing with abuse?
>
> Thunder: Right.

Here, Thunder referred both to language more typically associated with Ebonics, such as "tired," as well as that associated with Gaybonics, such as "kiki." He suggested that this language is not only about the pleasure that comes from humor and intimacy within his predominantly Black queer youth community, but it is also about constructing borders within this community as practice for subverting homophobia, or "the salt that's to come," outside of this community. However, in addition to being practice for a world that is often heterosexist and homophobic, I imagine that this use of Discourse was also a reflection of what these youth practice regularly in their world that is also often racist. In other words, perhaps their use of Gaybonics not only serves to create borders between themselves and heterosexists and homophobes but also between themselves and racists. This use of a Borderland Discourse to evade oppression is reminiscent of Holt's finding that Black people in the United States "learned that masking linguistic meaning was (and still is) a central weapon" (as cited by Fordham 1999, 279). The youth at The Loft revealed that the work of engaging in a Borderland Discourse to include some and exclude others served as one way of subverting anticipated cruelty both inside and outside of the center.

   This way of practicing with language for protection reminds me of Audre Lorde's (1984) discussion of The Dozens, which she describes as "A Black game of supposedly friendly rivalry and name-calling; in reality, a crucial exercise in learning how to absorb verbal abuse without faltering" (171). These exercises, which among these youth are not only a Black game but also a queer game, serve to entertain but also to subvert and retaliate against hatred, as I illustrate and explore next.

Pleasure, Subversion, and Retaliation beyond the Center

That the youth use Borderland Discourses to subvert oppression out-side of their queer, youth, and predominantly Black community became evident when I received a note from a young Jewish gay man who used to come to the center quite often, but, while I was there, had only visited during his breaks from college. He had come to a meeting of Story Time during which we worked on the dictionary, so he knew about the work we had done. His note said that one of his coworkers at a local queer bookstore ran a "new LGBTQ etc. magazine," and that he was "really interested in publishing a piece dealing w/that dictionary (excerpts maybe?)." I read the note aloud at the next meeting of Story Time and asked them how they wanted me to respond to the note. I was surprised when the youth rejected the invitation to publish excerpts from the dictionary. I had imagined that the opportunity to publish their work would be somehow validating, but Karen said, "I don't think the dictionary should be in the magazine because then everybody would know the T [truth], if you're talking about somebody, and then they've read the magazine, then they're going to know you're talking about them." Thunder and Shane agreed and said:

> Thunder: You tell him no, it's just not a good idea.
>
> Shane: Tell him thanks but no thanks.

Their response to the note communicated to me how literally Gaybonics offered them spaces in which to communicate outside of their predominantly Black, queer youth community.[2] I understand their rejection of this offer to publish the dictionary to be less about keeping the gay vocabulary from homophobes, who would most likely not read the publication, but to be more about keeping the language from the older, predominantly white, queer community. In fact, by using the word "T" to mean truth, a word used in some Black communities, Karen implied that the "everybody" to whom she was referring was not-Black, rather than not-queer. By using a Discourse unfamiliar to those outside of their queer, young, and predominantly Black community, they "ma[d]e a place for intimacy," (175) to use hooks' (1994) words.

Not only did the use of Gaybonics as a Borderland Discourse serve to create intimacy, as hooks says, and mutual recognition, as Gee says, it also served to position the users of this Discourse as agents who subverted ageism and racism by creating a border that hinders those outside of that border from understanding what those inside of the border are saying, a strategy they practiced within their community. If the dictionary were published, then the border between us and them, between safe and unsafe, as Anzaldúa says, would be threatened. Those outside of their community would then have information that would facilitate their understanding of conversations occurring inside of their community. Thus, youth would lose some of the privacy that Borderland Discourses offered. By rejecting the offer to publish the dictionary, these youth positioned Gaybonics as protection against those outside of the Discourse.

While the previous example suggests that these youth used Gaybonics to subvert those within the local queer community but outside of their Black queer youth community, the following example illustrates the ways one of these youth, Thunder, used Gaybonics in an effort to subvert homophobia in the larger community, what he calls "the real world." He said:

> Thunder: So when you get out in the real world you on this, let's say you on the judy-ass 23 [a disliked bus route], and you know . . .

Karen: Oh! The longest ride ever.

Thunder: The longest ride ever.

Group: Where does the 23 go?

Karen: It goes all, it's the longest ride in Philadelphia.

Thunder: And, and it's like, I'm going to give an example. Now, . . . So I'm with my best friend and we're sitting there we're kikiing and cackling [laughing] in the back of the bus talking about stuff, gossip. And trade [masculine men] very graciously get up on the bus at what? Broad and Erie.

Karen: Yes honey.

Trey: That's ghetto.

Thunder: And they come all the way to the back of the bus. They're talking. They stop and listen to our conversation, and we talking talking.

Up to this point, Thunder and his friend used Gaybonics as a way of subverting the homophobia they expected to encounter on a public bus, particularly a bus on this specific route. Although Thunder did not explicitly state that the two were using Gaybonics, he implied this by telling the story in the context of a discussion about the Discourse and by using the gay vocabulary as he described the encounter. For example, he set the scene by saying that he and his friend were "kikiing and cackling," instead of using standard synonyms, like joking and laughing. In Gee's (1996) words, Thunder and his friend used a Borderland Discourse to communicate "outside of the confines of public sphere . . . Discourses," (162) even in a public sphere. Thus, they worked to subvert homophobia.

However, the limits of subversion through Gaybonics were made evident as Thunder continued telling about the encounter. He said:

Thunder: They stop and listen to our conversation, and we talking talking, and we didn't realize that they're cackling! And you know we're talking and then [they] was like, "You noticing something?" [I] Said, "Yeah. Why are you all up in my business?"

Group: [laughter]

Karen: You said that?

Group: [laughter]

Trey: Did she [he] ever.

Thunder: And they [said], "You faggot ass." [And I said,] "Is that all you can say, you cunt? Look at your Timberlands, they are leaning like the Eiffel Tower" . . .

Group: [laughter, clapping]

Thunder: . . . we're talking about the 23.

Mollie: But you are also talking about people hurting people, not about boots at all.

Thunder: Well, we were talking about, but he tried it [my patience], and as soon as he said *faggot*, the defense went schzing!

Trey: Yes.

Thunder: "Look at your cornrows. They need to be rebraided. They look like they are hanging by what? A string."

Group: [laughter]

Thunder: And that was it.

Here, Thunder continued to use Gaybonics, both in Story Time—to humor the group—and on the bus—to create intimacy with his friend and to subvert anticipated homophobia.

However, it became apparent that Thunder and his friend would no longer be able to subvert the trade men's homophobia with Gaybonics when the men intruded upon their conversation, not only by listening to but also interrupting it. This intrusion suggested that the trade men were making *some* sense of the conversation, although *what* sense they made is unknown. Thunder's use of the word "trade" to describe the men suggests that they *could* have been a part of the local queer community and therefore could have had access to the Discourse of Gaybonics. The word "trade," according to the gay vocabulary, suggests that although the men appeared masculine and could be perceived as straight, they were, from Thunder's perception, gay men who did not want to be recognized as such. Whether they were straight or gay was irrelevant; what mattered was that at least in this context they were homophobic. They could have been straight homophobes, or, as Thunder suspected, gay men struggling with internalized homophobia. Either way, their homophobia—not their sexuality—was a threat to Thunder and his friend, who were, at least in this instance, out gay men.

This is not to say that only the trade men were threatening to the out gay men. I imagine that the threat was mutual and that it began before the verbal interaction. Perhaps the trade men were threatened by the mere presence of out gay men because they feared that suspicions might be raised about the sexuality of all of the men in the back of the bus, including them. Perhaps the out gay men were threatened by the overt masculinity of the trade men, and the trade men felt implicated in something the out gay men said. Perhaps that's when they called Thunder and his friend "faggot-ass," disrupting the intimacy between Thunder and his friend, proving subversion of hatred through language inadequate, and thus making Thunder and his friend more vulnerable.

Thunder responded to this slur with a metaphorical code switch (Blom and Gumperz 1972). That is, Thunder responded not by engaging in Gaybonics, but rather, by engaging in a Discourse that, at least in this particular interaction, was more dominant. The shift from Gaybonics is particularly evident by his use of the word "cunt." He did not use it as it is defined in the dictionary of the gay vocabulary, where it is described as an adjective meaning "cute, happy" or "feminine" and as a noun meaning "a friend." Rather, he used it more like it is used in the mainstream, to the extent it is used in the mainstream, as a derogatory word for female genitalia or women more generally. One thing that Thunder knew about these men is that they were masculine, and he suspected that their masculinity was important to them. From his perspective, he could make them vulnerable by calling their masculinity into question by not only referring to them as women but by doing so in a derogatory manner. By using "cunt" in this threatening way, Thunder shifted *from* using Gaybonics into the larger Discourse of Ebonics. In particular, Thunder used short quick metaphorical jabs or "snaps"; in other words, he began "playing the dozens" (Percelay, Ivey, and Dweck 1994). Percelay, Ivey, and Dweck assert that "[t]he dozens illustrates the force of the spoken word, and is the ultimate expression of fighting with your wits, not your fists" (23). In this fashion, Thunder went on to ridicule the homophobes' shoes and hairstyles, thus retaliating against them.

While the incident on the bus was a somewhat threatening one, it was also a humorous one. In fact, The Dozens is recognized as a "comedic art form . . . [b]orn out of a shared experience of pain and prejudice" (Percelay, Ivey, and Dweck 1994, 21). Certainly humor was the tone of the telling in Story Time. Thunder's peers supported him with encouraging phrases, laughter, and applause. In fact, I am the only one who made a critical remark, which I did when I told him that he was perpetuating a cycle of people hurting people when he criticized the homophobe on the bus. What I did not understand when I made that comment was that while he may have been perpetuating a cycle of people hurting people, he was ending a cycle in which the homophobe is the oppressor and the out gay man is the victim. Lorde (1984) asserts that "it is not difference which immobilizes us, but silence" (44). By retaliating against the homophobes, by refusing to remain silent, Thunder asserted his agency. Although he was still victimized by the men, his positionality was complicated and improved by his agency. In Lorde's (1984) language he was "not only a casualty," but "also a warrior" (41).

Thus, on the bus, Thunder used Gaybonics to amuse his friend, engage in an intimate conversation with him, and subvert homophobia; but when the limits of this Discourse in this context became apparent, Thunder shifted to Ebonics in order to retaliate against the homophobia of the trade men and humor his friend. Further, in Story Time, he humored the group with his retelling of the incident in hybrid Borderland Discourses that represented both his sexual and racial identities. In this way, Thunder used Borderland Discourses to position himself as an agent in the homophobic context of a public bus in an urban area of Philadelphia that is populated largely by people of color as well as within this queer youth center.

Agency or Activism?

These youth used Gaybonics, as well as Ebonics, to elicit pleasure through humor and intimacy among those inside of their queer, youth, predominantly Black community. Just as this use of such Discourses in the center created intimacy, or a sense of insiderness for some, it, simultaneously, created a sense of outsiderness or exclusion for others. Thus the youth practiced at creating borders that distinguished us from them, to use Anzaldúa's words, positioning them to subvert the oppression that they experienced outside of their community—whether that oppression took the shape of homophobia, as with the trade men on the bus; ageism and racism, as with the older white queer community; or otherwise. While these youth used Gaybonics to effectively subvert some anticipated cruelty, there were times when subversion proved inadequate. At these times, the Discourse-defined borders were violated. As a result, these youth shifted from the use of Gaybonics into another, more dominant Discourse in order to retaliate against these oppressors. Thus, they positioned themselves as agents.

This study shows that young people will use language to position themselves as agents. I am reminded of Fordham's (1999) study that revealed Black high school students choosing to use Ebonics and resisting the use of the standard dialect, finding the former more affirming and liberating. She depicts one English teacher in particular who insisted that her students use standard dialect in classroom conversations. However, students refused, even though they exhibited their knowledge of the dialect on exams. Fordham describes this teacher as being "in constant emotional struggle" over this dilemma (274). In this study, students positioned themselves as agents by carefully engaging in Discourses in order to accomplish their own goals, rather than the goals of the teacher. The youth in Fordham's study, as well as the study represented here, support Michel Foucault's (1990) claim that "we must not imagine a world of discourse divided between accepted discourse and excluded discourse, or between the dominant discourse and the dominated one; but as a multiplicity of discursive elements that can come into play in various strategies" (100).

If we as educators and educational researchers know that students will use language to position themselves as agents, then we need to work with that information. We need to dispel the myth that there is one discourse of power. We need to understand what different Discourses do for different students. We need to recognize and value the power of different Discourses. For example, the youth represented in this chapter engaged in Gaybonics in order to protect themselves from homophobes, as well as ageists and racists. Thus, the Discourse did important work for these youth, and to insist that these youth not use this Discourse did and does not make sense. If, however, we feel like the Discourse is in some way harmful, as I did in the game of "When the Wind Blows" and as I now understand it to be for youth like Steve, it does not make sense to allow the use of the Discourse to go uninterrogated. However, this does not mean squelching the Discourse. Instead it means talking about what work the Discourse does for some youth and against other youth; it means knowing that there are some things we do not know and may never know; and it means facilitating discussions with youth about ways of accomplishing the goals of all youth involved. Conversations about the power and problems of Gaybonics could have helped youth in this study make more conscious and informed decisions about ways of using language to assume agency. Similarly, conversations about the power and problems of any Discourse, including but not limited to the standard dialect, can help students to make better decisions about their own language use and agency.

While agency is imperative, it is also inadequate. For example, in this paper, while youth asserted their agency by using Borderland Discourses, thus constructing or reifying borders that protected them, they also hindered communication across differences. In other words, while they positioned themselves as agents, they did not position themselves as activists. I suggest that teachers and educational researchers need to help our youth become not only agents but also activists. Chela Sandoval (2000), in her book *Methodology of the Oppressed*, elaborates on the relationship between "activism and the agent" (235). She writes about agency as a "mechanism for survival" and activism as a generation and performance of a "higher moral and political mode of oppositional and coalitional social movement" (157). I have illustrated the ways in which agency can be asserted through Discourses to please, humor, create intimacy, subvert, and retaliate against; but agency can also be asserted to accomplish the work of social and political change. This is the work of an activist. Sandoval asserts that agency and activism, in conjunction, intensify each other. She describes a "*new* morality of form that intervenes in social reality through deploying an action that re-creates the agent even as the agent is creating the action— in an ongoing, chiasmic loop of transformation" (157). So, according to Sandoval, the work of social change strengthens the one engaging in the work and vice versa.

Lorde (1984) talks about action as a conversion of anger into the "service of our vision and our future is a liberating and strengthening act of clarification" (127). Drawing from her, I am reminded of the times in which I squelched anger, such as when Steve spoke about how the center was an unwelcoming place for him. I placed blame on him for feeling disconnected, rather than hearing his anger, validating his feelings, and facilitating a discussion surrounding what he had said. What would it have been like if I had fostered dialogue in which we explored anger and conflict? What could we have learned about one another and our worlds? What if in Story Time, when invited to publish the dictionary, we, as a group, instead offered another text as an alternative, perhaps an editorial in which youth explained the ways in which they experienced the queer community in Philadelphia, as Black youth?

There are times, however, in which an activist stance does not make sense. Lorde (1984) asserts that while anger can be converted into activism, hatred cannot. She claims that anger occurs among peers who share goals of change, but that "hatred is the fury of those who do not share our goals, and its object is death and destruction" (129). While the men in the back of the bus did not work to destroy one another literally, they did work to do so metaphorically. Thus, this context was not one for activism.

But what about school? Is school such a context? In the same meeting of Story Time that Thunder told the group about the incident on the bus, he also told about an incident in his urban public high school, where he was out as a gay man. He described an interaction between himself and a classmate who he knew to have had same-sex encounters but who was not out as gay. This particular interaction began with the classmate making homophobic comments around Thunder. Here, Thunder described his response to the classmate's homophobia:

> Thunder: Now I took that [gay] vocabulary to school one day. That was in high school. Someone just irked my patience and I had some T [truth or gossip], I had some major T on him. So I just kind of just spilled it out.
>
> Karen: You blew it up, you blew it up.
>
> Thunder: And he [gagging sound]. And I spilled some more, and he gagged some more. I spilled some more.
>
> Group: [laughter]

The vocabulary to which Thunder referred was the gay vocabulary; however, again, by using the word "T" for truth or gossip, he suggested that his use of Gaybonics and Ebonics was intertwined. In this interaction in school, much like on the bus, Thunder was threatened by another man's homophobia, perhaps internalized homophobia, and he used Borderland Discourses to protect himself and retaliate against the oppressor, thus asserting his agency. So, here, school was not a context for activism. But could it have been? What if his purpose had been to confront and change the classmate's homophobia rather than retaliate against it? Or, what would it have been like if Thunder's classmate had felt safe enough to solicit advice from Thunder as an out gay young man in their urban public high school? What if he had tried to communicate across differences rather than reify and intensify those distances? What if he were using language to engage rather than to subvert or retaliate against?

Further, what would it be like to create school as a context where conflict was understood as a catalyst for learning? What would it be like to create school as a context for hearing and knowing differences? Where people may come as victims and casualties, agents and warriors, but also to become activists for social change? Can school be such a context? I believe it can be, and that, as educators, I believe this is our work.

Notes

1. All names of people in this chapter are pseudonyms.

2. I received permission from the youth represented in this paper to use and define the vocabulary included for academic purposes.

References

Anzaldúa, Gloria. 1987. *Borderlands/La Fronteras: The New Mestiza.* San Francisco: Spinsters/Aunt Lute.

Barrett, Rusty. 1999. "Indexing Polyphonous Identity in the Speech of African American Drag Queens." Pp. 313–331 in *Reinventing Identities: The Gendered Self in Discourse,* ed. Mary Bucholtz, A. C. Liang, and Laurel A. Sutton. New York: Oxford University Press.

Blom, Jan-Petter, and John J. Gumperz. 1972. "Social Meaning in Linguistic Structure: Code-Switching in Norway." Pp. 407–434 in *Directions in Sociolinguistics,* ed. John J. Gumperz and Dell Hymes. New York: Holt, Reinhart and Winston.

Brewer, John M. 1978. "Introduction." Pp. ix–x in *Encyclopedia of Black Folklore and Humor,* ed. Henry D. Spalding. Middle Village, N.Y.: Jonathan David Publishers.

Britzman, Deborah P. 1997. "What is This Thing Called Love?: New Discourses for Understanding Gay and Lesbian Youth." Pp. 183–207 in *Radical Interventions: Identity, Politics, and Difference/s on Educational Praxis,* ed. Suzanne de Castell and Mary Bryson. Albany: State University of New York Press.

Butler, Judith. 1989. *Gender Trouble: Feminism and the Subversion of Identity.* New York: Routledge.

Coupland, Nikolas. 2001. "Language, Situation, and the Relational Self: Theorizing Dialect-Style in Sociolinguistics." Pp. 185–210 in *Style and Sociolinguistic Variation,* ed. Penelope Eckert and John R. Rickford. New York: Cambridge University Press.

Eaton, Susan. 1993. "Gay Students Find Little Support in Most Schools." *The Harvard Educational Letter* 9, no. 4: 6–8.

Fordham, Signthia. 1999. "'Dissin' 'the Standard': Ebonics as Guerilla Warfare at Capital High." *Anthropology and Education Quarterly* 30, no. 3: 272–293.

Foucault, Michel. 1990. *The History of Sexuality: An Introduction, Volume 1.* New York: Vintage.

Freire, Paulo. 1991. "The Importance of the Act of Reading." Pp. 21–26 in *Literacy in Process,* ed. Brenda M. Power and Ruth S. Hubbard. Portsmouth, N.H.: Heinemann.

Gee, James P. 1996. *Social Linguistics and Literacies: Ideology in Discourses.* 2nd ed. London: Taylor and Francis Ltd.

Gray, Mary. L. 1999. *In Your Face: Stories From the Lives of Queer Youth.* New York: Harrington Park Press.

hooks, bell. 1994. *Teaching to Transgress: Education as the Practice of Freedom*. New York: Routledge.

Liang, A. C. 1999. "Conversationally Implicating Lesbian and Gay Identity." Pp. 293–310 in *Reinventing Identities: The Gendered Self in Discourse*, ed. Mary Bucholtz, A. C. Liang, and Laurel A. Sutton. New York: Oxford University Press.

Lorde, Audre. 1984. *Sister Outsider*. Freedom, CA: The Crossing Press.

Murray, Kim. 1998. "An Activist Forum II: Fault Line." Pp. 131–132 in *Teaching for Social Justice*, ed. William Ayers, Jean Ann Hunt, and Therese Quinn. New York: The New Press.

Owens, Robert E., Jr. 1998. *Queer Kids: The Challenges and Promise for Lesbian, Gay, and Bisexual Youth*. New York: Harrington Park Press.

Percelay, James, Monteria Ivey, and Stephen Dweck. 1994. *Snaps*. New York: Quill William Morrow.

Perry, Theresa. 1998. "'I 'on Know Why They Be Trippin': Reflections on the Ebonics Debate." Pp. 3–15 in *The Real Ebonics Debate: Power, Language, and the Education of African American Children*, ed. Theresa Perry and Lisa Delpit. Boston: Beacon Press.

Perry, Theresa and Lisa Delpit, eds. 1998. *The Real Ebonics Debate: Power, Language, and the Education of African American Children*. Boston: Beacon Press.

Rofes, Eric. 1995. "Making Our Schools Safe for Sissies." Pp. 79–84 in *The Gay Teen: Educational Practice and Theory for Lesbian, Gay, and Bisexual Adolescents*, ed. Gerald Unks. New York: Routledge.

Sandoval, Chela. 2000. *Methodology of the Oppressed*. Minneapolis: University of Minnesota Press.

Savin-Williams, Ritch C. 1994. "Verbal and Physical Abuse as Stressors in the Lives of Lesbian, Gay Male and Bisexual Youths: Associations with School Problems, Running Away, Substance Abuse, Prostitution and Suicide." *Journal of Consulting Clinical Psychology* 62, no. 26: 1–269.

Smith, Ernie. 1998. "What is Black English? What is Ebonics?" Pp. 49–58 in *The Real Ebonics Debate: Power, Language, and the Education of African American Children*, ed. Theresa Perry and Lisa Delpit. Boston: Beacon Press.

Smitherman, Geneva. 1998. "Black English/Ebonics: What it Be Like?" Pp. 29–37 in *The Real Ebonics Debate: Power, Language, and the Education of African American Children*, ed. Theresa Perry and Lisa Delpit. Boston: Beacon Press.

Unks, Gerald. 1995. *The Gay Teen: Educational Practice and Theory for Lesbian, Gay, and Bisexual Adolescents*. New York: Routledge Press.

"Youth Voices." 1996. *Harvard Educational Review* 66, no. 2: 173–197.

C h a p t e r   N i n e

Bent as a Ballet Dancer

The Possibilities for and Limits of Legitimate Homomasculinity in School

Deborah Youdell

Introduction

•There is now a significant body of work concerned with sexualities and schooling. This work has detailed the discrimination faced by gay, lesbian, and bisexual students and examined the functioning of homophobia and assumptions about the normalness of heterosexuality—or heteronormativity—in school contexts. (See, for instance, Butler 1996; Epstein and Johnson 1996; Kehily 2002; Martino and Pallotta-Chiarolli 2003; and Mills 1999.) Recent research has also called into question the victimized, pathologized, or denigrated positions that are often ascribed to gay, lesbian, bisexual, and transgender students to consider if it is possible and, if so, under what circumstances, to be not-heterosexual in school *and* not be victimized, pathologized, or denigrated. Indeed, this work has asked whether, and how, queer[1] pleasure might be possible in school (Crowley and Rasmussen 2004).

My own research (Youdell 2004) has contributed to this work, and in this chapter I want to build on this to offer a self-consciously optimistic reading of the possibilities for queer inside school. Specifically, through a close reading of data generated through a school ethnography, I want to show how, despite the endurance of prevailing heteronormative discourses, non-heterosexual[2] selves (or subjects) might be not only recognized, but also taken as legitimate in school contexts. I draw on Judith Butler's (1997a) notion of performative politics in order to make sense of how this can happen and tease out the limits or costs that might be associated with this. By doing this I hope to offer methodological and analytical tools that researchers and educators in schools can use to understand their own and others' practices in new ways and to think about how they might practice differently.

Theory and Methodology

The research that this paper draws on was undertaken in London, UK, during the 1997/1998 academic year. Participants were students in their final year of compulsory schooling, aged 15 to 16, attending a government, coeducational, multi-ethnic, mixed social class, secondary school. In undertaking ethnography in school I draw on the approaches developed within critical school ethnography (Ball 1981; Delamont and Atkinson 1995; Hammersley and Atkinson 1996, Mac and Ghaill 1994) as well recent methodological debates informed by poststructural theory (Allvesson 2002; Silverman 1997; Stronach and Maclure 1997).

Borrowing Foucault's (1990, 1991) notion of discourse—multiple and shifting systems of knowledge that produce ideas as if these were truths being simply communicated—these methodological foundations suggest that ethnography is best understood as a practice that generates, rather than collects, data. It also suggests that analyses be concerned with those discourses that are embedded in, evaded by, and excluded from these data. The established strengths of critical ethnography include the rich, detailed, and contextually located data provided and the possibility of using these to test and generate theory (Hammersley 1992; Hammersley and Atkinson 1995). A poststructural ethnography, then, offers a valuable methodology for generating nuanced representations that allow for the examination of empirical examples of the circulation and function of discourse and the assessment of the usefulness of these theories to researchers and educators.

By looking at an extract of those data that I analyze in detail in the following section, this particular approach to ethnography can be seen.

Data from a Science Lesson

Scott is in conversation with the girls sitting at his table. He takes a pair of pink ballet shoes out of his bag. He holds the shoes in his hands and examines them while listening and contributing to conversation. Vici, Suzi, and I notice Scott examining his ballet shoes.

Vici: *[calls out]* Scott, are they your *en pointe* shoes?

Scott: *[looks over with a (feigned) surprised smile]* No, they're for footwork.

Vici: They're beautiful.

Suzi: *[chuckling]* Your feet must be so scummy!

Scott: *[nods and laughs]* They are. *[replying to VICI]* These are my practice ones, you should see my good ones, they're satin!

Rather than seeking to describe a "true" and "full" account of what "actually" happened in this classroom, this approach to ethnography sees data as a representation that can never be a true reflection of what really happened. This is because there is no single and final truth about this, or any other event; rather, multiple interpretations and possible representations are acknowledged. Most significantly, the research process and the data generated through it are considered not just in terms of what happened, but in terms of what discourses are circulating in and barred from the context, and what meanings these discourses bring to the events represented. In relation to the data above, then, this approach does not ask whether Vici really thinks Scott is examining his *en pointe* shoes; why Suzi considers them beautiful; or if Scott's feet are really made "scummy" by ballet. Instead, my analysis asks what it might mean for this male student to do ballet and to make this widely known to his classmates by taking out his ballet shoes in this science lesson, and to ask this by considering what discourses are being tacitly, or knowingly, drawn on by Vici, Suzi, and Scott, and any observers (including myself) to this scene.

This approach to ethnography also suggests a particular understanding of the person, or subject. The person is often understood, even if this is in a tacit or commonsense way, as an abiding, self-knowing, and rational actor—the Cartesian subject. With such an understanding, analyses might again ask what Vici, Suzi, and Scott really mean, or what they really want, from the encounter. The approach to the subject taken in the analysis offered below recognizes that the subject may well experience him/herself as rational, coherent, and self-knowing; however, it understands the subject to be the product of discourse even as discourse produces the subject as if s/he were an enduring Cartesian self. Such a subject is often said to be decentered (see Mansfield 2000).

Suggesting that the subject is a product of discourse—or discursively constituted—also suggests that the subject is constrained by discourse or, more specifically, the terms of those discourses through which s/he is located and produced. Such a subject cannot simply rationally identify what she/he means and wants and then pursue this. As a result, what the subject means and wants is neither at the center of analysis nor at its end point. Instead, analysis focuses on how those discourses that circulate in a context make possible and limit "who" the subject can be, what s/he can mean, and what s/he can make happen. In relation to the data above, then, Suzi, Vici, and Scott are understood to be produced in the terms of the discourses that are circulating in the context. Given that notions of identity and difference—categorized along axes such as sex, gender, and sexuality, as well as ability, disability, race, class—are deeply embedded within contemporary discourses, these remain crucially important to analyses of the decentered subject. Rather than seeing these categories as descriptive of a person who precedes them, however, these categories are seen as being fundamentally implicated in the production of the person in these terms. So the analysis asks how the discourses circulating in this moment constitute Suzi, Vici, and Scott as sexed, gendered, and sexualized as well as raced, classed, and embodied subjects, and what the implications of these constitutions might be.

In this discussion of the methodological significance of understanding the subject as discursively constituted, I have touched on the contribution made by Michel Foucault. These ideas, and their development by Judith Butler, are central to my analyses of the representations generated through my ethnography and so merit some further exploration here. My interpretation of these theorizations draws on my earlier detailed examination of this work (2000) and my subsequent reappraisals of this (2003a; 2003b; 2003c; 2004).

I touched above on Foucault's understanding of discourses as at once productive and unstable. Foucault (1990; 1991) also asserts that it is through discourse that power has productive effects, and this underpins Judith Butler's theorization of "discursive performativity" (Butler 1993, 13). Reflecting Foucault's understanding of discourse as productive, Butler takes up Austin's (1961) notion of performative speech acts to make sense of the decentered subject and to imagine how such a subject might be an agent for social and political change. Butler makes use of the understanding that the "performative functions to produce that which it declares" (Butler 1993, 107) to show that discursive practices that appear to *describe* a (preexisting) subject are *productive* of this subject. This is not a performative free-for-all; rather, Butler (1993) suggests that performatives are citational, that is, they cite existing discourses and so their meanings become sedimented. That the meanings of performatives become sedimented through their citation of prior discourses does not, according to Butler, cement or determine their meaning. Instead she turns to Derrida's (1988) insistence that performatives can always "misfire" (72) and so have unexpected effects, to show that performatives can mean something else and, therefore, the subjects produced through performatives can "be" someone else.

Butler elaborates her understanding of the performatively constituted subject through her work with Bourdieu's (1990) notion of bodily *habitus*. Bourdieu's idea of *habitus* is concerned with how ways of being and doing "become internalized as a second nature" (56) and sedimented in what Bourdieu calls the "bodily hexis" (Bourdieu 1991, 86) through the unrealizing taking on of the bodily dispositions of others. So when Butler suggests that the bodily *habitus* is "a citational chain lived and believed at the level of the body" (Butler 1997a, 155) that can be understood as a "tacit performative" (159–60), she is suggesting that it is at once formed by and *formative of* bodily conventions that are taken as natural and unremarkable.

Butler also extends her work on the performatively constituted subject by examining Althusser's notion of interpellation (Althusser 1971)—of naming—through the lens of discursive performativity. Butler suggests that being interpellated, or named, is necessary for being "*recognizable*" (Butler 1997a, 5; original emphasis) as a subject. As such, she argues that the names of categorical identities—sex, gender, sexuality, and so on—are performatives that produce the subject and make him/her intelligible (Butler 1997b). That I need to use the gendered third person pronouns "him" and "her" to explain this shows how categories of gender make the subject make sense.

That naming renders the subject knowable does not mean that the person named is at the whim or mercy of the subject by whom s/he is addressed. Instead, being named, and so made meaningful through naming, means that the named subject can name another. Judith Butler calls this "discursive agency" (Butler 1997a, 127). The notion of discursive agency is extremely significant because it insists that the performatively constituted subject can act with intent. Such acts are understood as deployments of discourse that circulate within a wider discursive field. Given this wider discursive field, those discourses deployed may, or may not, have the effects envisaged by the discursive agent. As such, discursive agency does not place the subject, or what s/he means and wants, back at the center of analysis. But it does demonstrate how, within the constraints of discourse, the performatively interpellated subject acts with intent and so continues to be a political subject. When Scott takes out his ballet shoes, then, he may well have the intention of producing himself in a particular way, but the success of this act remains uncertain.

A Politics of Performativity

Discursive agency is the foundation for Butler's understanding of political possibility and is crucial for my analysis of whether heteronormativity can be challenged in school and whether nonheterosexual students might be produced as legitimate subjects. Butler (1997a) suggests that the combined outcome of the potential for performatives to misfire and the discursive agency of the performatively constituted subject is the possibility of a *performative politics*. Specifically, Butler suggests that discursive agents can resist the sedimented meanings of performatives, they can deploy them in new contexts, and they can attempt to imbue them with new meaning such that sedimented meanings might shift. Butler writes: "The possibility of decontextualizing and recontextualizing . . . terms through radical acts of public misappropriation constitutes the basis of an ironic hopefulness that the conventional relation between [interpellation and meaning] might become tenuous and even broken over time" (Butler 1997a, 100).

The provisional success of this performative politics has been illustrated by the reinscription of the term "queer" and, more contentiously, the term "nigga,"[3] where terms that once constituted subjects as denigrated might no longer do so. This does not mean, however, that performative politics is simply a matter of asserting a new or altered meaning, because normative, sedimented meanings are likely to be resistant to reinscription. Yet they are never immune from it. The possibility of reinscription is intrinsic to the performative. Butler writes:

> [C]ontexts inhere in certain speech acts in ways that are very difficult to shake. . . . [but] contexts are never fully determined in advance . . . the possibility for the speech act to *take on a non-ordinary meaning, to function in contexts where it has not belonged*, is precisely the political promise of the performative, one that positions the performative at the center of a politics of hegemony, one that offers an unanticipated political future for deconstructive thinking. (Butler 1997a, 161, my emphasis)

Such a politics, it seems, takes hegemony (Gramsci 2003)—the broad take-up of ideas, practices, or values that are not in the interest of significant sections of the population that subscribes to these—to be produced through and productive of discourse. A performative politics of hegemony, then, would seek to trouble, undermine, or shift hegemonic discourse through the sorts of reinscriptions I have been discussing. If deconstructive thinking is concerned with the *reversal and displacement* of those embedded hierarchical binaries that Derrida (1988) sees as intrinsic to the inscription of power relations, then a performative politics of hegemony offers deconstructive thinking an unanticipated political future because it sets out discursive tools and strategies whereby these reversals and displacements might be achieved. Butler does not indicate whether she takes public acts of performative politics to be an individual or group practice. Yet it seems that it is at the level of both the individual and the group (whose organization, coherence, and longevity may well vary) that such practices are, and might be, deployed. A sole subject may engage in practices of reinscription, and these performatives may, or may not, achieve (be received by another subject as having) a nonordinary meaning. The discursive frame in which such reinscription is deployed will undoubtedly be crucial to their effect. The transformation of normative meaning, however, requires the non-ordinary meaning of the performative to become, at least in some contexts, ordinary. Such an alteration can only be effected through repetition and *re*citation. As such, the proposition of a politics of performative reinscription is not a renunciation of collective acts of resistance. As I will show in the following section, when Scott takes out his ballet shoes in a science classroom, it is a sole act, but as he engages in discussion with Vici and Suzi this becomes a communal and, it seems, knowing act. And Scott, Vici, and Suzi's communal act seems to resonate with the prior acts of these and, perhaps, other, unknown discursive agents who have resisted and perhaps shifted sedimented meanings here and in other contexts.

Discursive agency and the potential for the performative to misfire, then, is where the possibility for intentional acts of resistance and performative politics lies. This means that the performative may be strategically reinscribed, but also means that it might be recouped within authorized discourse. Performative names that ordinarily act to constitute a pathologized, victimized, or denigrated subject cannot simply be discarded. And attempts to silence or erase these names do not interrupt their capacity to constitute particular sorts of subjects; indeed, such attempts may contribute to these constitutions. Instead, a performative politics suggests that these names be retained, redeployed, and reinscribed: "[t]he word that wounds becomes an instrument of resistance in the redeployment that destroys the prior territory of its operation" (Butler 1997a, 163).

In the analysis that follows, I explore these possibilities through my reading of data generated in a London secondary school. I hope to show performative politics in practice and, therefore, demonstrate the usefulness of these ideas for researchers and educators concerned to contribute to a politics that undercuts homophobia and heteronormativity and promises alternative ways of being and thinking sex, sexuality, and the subject.

Resisting Subjugated Homosexuality, Reinscribing Gay Masculinity

I have indicated earlier that schools can be understood as heteronormative sites where particular modes of heterosexual masculinity and femininity are proliferated and homosexualities are (explicitly and/or implicitly) disavowed and subjugated (see, for instance, Kehily 2002; Nayak and Kehily 1996; Youdell 2000, 2004). As my discussion of performative politics suggests, however, this does not mean that these discourses cannot be resisted. In the remainder of this section I will make use of these ideas to analyze empirical data in the form of the two scenes offered below. Through my analysis I will argue that the scenes represent moments in which heteronormativity and the disavowal and/or subjugation of homosexuality (or compulsory heterosexuality [Rich 1980]) are resisted and reinscribed to produce an intelligible gay masculinity in the school context. That is, *the scenes can be understood as moments of a politics of performative reinscription.*

Bent as a ballet dancer

Scene 1.

> *Year 11 Science Lesson, mixed ability. DY is sitting at a table with VICI and SUZI (girls, white, aged 15/16). At the next table, SCOTT (boy, white, aged 15/16) is sitting with three girls (all white). The class is noisy and inattentive and the teacher seems unable to counter this. There is a relatively high level of movement around the room.*

Scott comes and stands next to the table where Vici, Suzi, and I are sitting. He leans down over the table, bending at the waist, and rests his elbows on the table-top. He takes Vici's hands and enthusiastically tells her about a dance performance that he took part in the previous weekend. Daniel (boy, Black) walks past the table and, while passing, says in a derisory tone but to no one in particular: "He's getting ready." Scott and Vici exchange a momentary look but do not acknowledge Daniel's comment verbally. Scott continues to recount his story and a minute or so later he returns to his seat at the next table.

Later in the lesson. Scott is in conversation with the girls sitting at his table. He takes a pair of pink ballet shoes out of his bag. He holds the shoes in his hands and examines them while listening and contributing to conversation. Vici, Suzi, and I notice Scott examining his ballet shoes.

Vici: *[calls out]* Scott, are they your *en pointe* shoes?

Scott: *[looks over with a (feigned) surprised smile]* No, they're for footwork.

Vici: They're beautiful.

Suzi: *[chuckling]* Your feet must be so scummy!

Scott: *[nods and laughs]* They are. *[replying to VICI]* These are my practice ones, you should see my good ones, they're satin!

Vici smiles at Scott and the conversation ends. Scott returns to his previous conversation and, while chatting, puts his ballet shoes on. He stands up and runs through a short sequence of classical ballet positions, before raising himself up onto his toes, his arms outstretched to the front and side. The girls sitting at the table with Scott watch and smile. Vici calls: "Beautiful, Scott" and begins a round of brief, delicate applause which Suzi and I join. Scott smiles and bows before sitting back down. He rejoins the conversation at his table. After a few minutes he takes off his ballet shoes and puts them on the table in front of him. A while later he returns his ballet shoes to his bag.

Scene 2.

Year 11 Leaving Day Show. The senior teacher with responsibility for the year group (Head of Year) has arranged a series of celebratory activities for the last day that Year 11 students are required to attend school for lessons. These activities include a Leaving Day Show in which staff and students entertain the year group and their teachers with songs, skits, poems, and dances. The show takes place in the Drama Studio. The auditorium has tiered seating on three sides arranged around a large empty floor space. The fourth side of this floor space is flanked by a low-level stage. The seating capacity of the Drama Studio is barely adequate to accommodate the entire year group. FORM TUTORS, members of the SENIOR MANAGEMENT TEAM, and STUDENTS are squashed together in their seats, with an overspill of STUDENTS seated on the floor at the edges of the central floor space. The HEAD OF YEAR, who is hosting the event, is on the stage. He also provides some musical interludes along with the school MUSIC TEACHER and a FORM TUTOR. The room is illuminated only by stage lighting on the stage and, when in use for performances, the central floor space.

The Head of Year announces that the next entertainment will be a dance by SCOTT. He introduces Scott as an "incredibly talented young man," reporting that Scott has recently been accepted into one of the UK's most prestigious dance schools. The Head of Year says that Scott was reluctant to perform in the Leaving Day Show, concerned over how his dance—which he performed for his successful audition—would be received.

The lights in the Drama Studio go out. A spotlight goes on and follows Scott as he enters and stands stationary in the middle of the central floor space. He is wearing a pair of white cotton-jersey tracksuit trousers. The trousers sit just below his hip-bones, the hems are turned up, exposing his ankles. This is the only garment that Scott wears. His feet are bare. His torso and arms are lean and well toned, with muscular and skeletal structure visible. He has a small, black Egyptian-style tattoo on one shoulder blade. The audience is momentarily silent, then gives light applause.

The spotlight goes out and contemporary classical music begins. Low-level lighting illuminates the central floor space and Scott begins to perform. The dance is tightly choreographed and professionally executed. The fast-paced dance and music convey a sense of peril, pursuit, and conflict. Scott's bodily movements are arresting. He sweeps around the entirety of the central performance space, sometimes lowering himself to the floor, sometimes leaping high into the air, sometimes lunging forward and imposing into the space of those seated in the front rows. The first time that Scott lunges in this way there is an audible gasp from the audience. As the dance ends Scott is spotlighted in a frozen pose on the ground. There is a moment of silence before the applause begins. The applause is loud but does not include the cheers, "boo boo boo's," or whistles that other students have received. Scott rises and exits the Drama Studio. The applause dies and there is silence punctuated by whispered conversation.

I have analyzed Scene 1 elsewhere in relation to distinct, but analytically resonant, practices inside a Sydney school (Youdell 2004). I return to these data here, offering an extended analysis that is crucial to making sense of the performative potential—specifically the possibilities for performative reinscription—of the performance represented in Scene 2.

Scene 1 represents a collection of discursive practices within the everyday context of a classroom. Leaning over a desk and resting elbows/forearms on the tabletop while talking to someone seated there is by no means exceptional. Indeed, this is a bodily practice that students and teachers engage in all the time. Yet when Scott engages in this bodily practice it seems to contribute to the ongoing constitution of his gay identity and precipitate a series of further practices through which intelligible sexualities are constituted and contested.

Scott is "out" within the school. A number of students in the year group identify as gay, lesbian, bisexual, and/or queer.[4] Of these students, however, Scott is the only one who appears to attempt actively to ensure that his nonheterosexual identity is known across the school. Scott, it seems, is engaged in ongoing, intentional constitutions of himself as gay. For instance, his school diary is decorated by images that cite and inscribe this gay identity and a gay aesthetic: a large rainbow flag sticker; red ribbon and World AIDS Day stickers; magazine clippings of monochrome images of semiclothed young men and dramatic landscapes. Inside the school Scott is rarely seen in the company of other boys and he is dismissive of Tom, the other boy in the year group known to identify as gay. However, he has a number of close friendships with girls. These friendships are tactile, affectionate, and include much verbal mutual admiration—citing and inscribing the gay man and straight woman (injuriously "fag-hag") relationship of popular and gay discourse. As indicated by Scene 2, Scott is a highly accomplished ballet dancer. This is an activity that he is well known for within the year group. Ballet dancing itself is intimately linked with Scott's gay identity both through his own practices and popular discourse that cites and inscribes the synonymy of homosexuality and ballet dancing—the male ballet dancer *is* homosexual.

In a context dominated by compulsory heterosexuality (Butler 1991) but in which Scott is "out," when he leans over the table, takes Vici's hands, and effusively recounts his recent ballet performance, it seems that his bodily and linguistic practices cite and inscribe his identity as the gay ballet dancer. This raises two related questions. First, are Scott's practices here any different to the multitude of leanings over tables and chattings that go on within the school every day? And second, how does Scott come to practice in the ways that he does? In answer to my first question, it seems that Scott's practices differ in small but significant ways from those of the boys around him. Chatting effusively about a ballet performance and holding the hands of the girl being spoken to (without this contact being sexually charged) are practices that are unintelligible within the terms of those heterosexual masculinities that dominate this context. And the *precise way* that Scott leans over the table—the placement of his feet, the straightness of his waist, the elegance of his back—while more difficult to differentiate from the ways that other boys might lean, has a grace (that of a [gay] ballet dancer?) not seen among the other boys.

This begins to indicate a possible answer to my second question. Scott's bodily practices here might be understood, in part, as the dispositions of a particular bodily *habitus*.[5] In positing this, I am not suggesting that these are the dispositions of a *habitus* inculcated primarily within the home during early childhood, as Bourdieu's (1990,1991) work might suggest. Rather, I am suggesting that the dispositions of this *performative habitus* are constituted and constituting on an *ongoing* basis (Butler 1997a). Such dispositions might be unknowingly inculcated through images and representations of gay icons and a gay aesthetic; the gay scene; and the ballet school. The constituting and constitutive dispositions of such a performative *habitus* might be unintentionally cited *and* intentionally mimicked. Scott's bodily practices here, then, can be understood *at once* as the disposition of a particular performative *habitus* and the intentional mimicry of a particular modality of gayness.

As Scott leans over and talks to Vici, his practices cite and inscribe his gay identity—he displays publicly an identity that is disavowed by compulsory heterosexuality. By being "out" and displaying this "outness," Scott potentially reinscribes homosexuality as intelligible and legitimate. Returning to Derrida's notion of the reversal and displacement of hierarchical binaries that deconstruction seeks, this reinscription of homosexuality can be seen to expose the Same/Other relationship of heterosexual/homosexual and to provisionally displace this. It is this reinscription of the disavowed homosexual Other and the exposures that it effects that inspires, or even compels, Daniel's censure.

When Daniel announces "He's getting ready" he does not address Scott directly, nor does his comment make any explicit reference to homosexuality. Indeed the comment does not make explicit *what* Scott might be getting ready for.

The comment can be understood as a (verbally incomplete) citation of the homophobic insult that insists that if a man or boy who is known or even suspected to be homosexual bends over, then he is preparing for/inviting anal penetration—to complete Daniel's colloquialism, "He's getting ready" "to take it up the arse." This understanding is reinforced by the derisory tone in which the comment is delivered. The oblique/ incomplete nature of the comment does not negate its potential to performatively constitute Scott in particular ways. Indeed, that it is unnecessary to utter the assertion in its entirety highlights the enduring historicity of authorized (heteronormative/homophobic) discourses of homosexuality. This comment cites the obsession within authorized discourse with the homosexual man who receives anal penetration and inscribes receptive anal penetration as synonymous with male homosexuality (the mystery of who might penetrate remains unresolved with this discourse). In this way, Daniel's comment also cites and inscribes the normative constitution of homosexuality as a poor imitation of the (illusory) heterosexual original (Butler 1991).

In an apparently more benign reading of the comment "He's getting ready," Daniel might be taken to have observed Scott's interaction with the girls and anticipated the impromptu ballet exercises to come later in the lesson. Scott might, therefore, be "getting ready" "to perform ballet." Understanding Daniel's comment as an anticipation of Scott's later dance might seem to lessen its homophobic force/intent. Yet, that the male ballet dancer is synonymous with the male homosexual in popular discourse suggests that, understood in this way, Daniel's comment remains at least implicitly homophobic and threatens to constitute Scott's homosexuality in particular ways. Furthermore, the comment might simultaneously suggest the (imagined) sexual practice *and* the ballet exercises. Within the heteronormative discursive frame that Daniel cites, these are both key markers of the subjugated homosexual whose lack of masculinity is exposed through the constellation of his bodily practices, whether these practices are sexual or otherwise. Daniel's comment then is a potential and provisional performative constitution of Scott as (a particular) homosexual.

Daniel is not potentially interpellating the denigrated homosexuality of a boy whose bodily dispositions have unwittingly failed to cite heterosexual masculinity. Scott deploys his discursive agency to performatively constitute himself as (a particular) homosexual, but this is by no means the same identity that Daniel's comment cites and inscribes. Scott's bodily practices cite, inscribe, and celebrate the sexual identity that he seeks to constitute. Scott may not have sought Daniel's comment, but this comment confirms Scott's self-constitution. This is not to suggest that Daniel's comment is welcome. It is an injurious interpellation that potentially constitutes Scott as the disavowed and subjugated homosexual. In this sense, the mundane moment of leaning over a desk and a comment being passed can be seen as a skirmish over the limits of intelligible masculinity, homosexuality, and gay identity.

Later in the scene, Scott takes out and examines his ballet shoes; engages (across the space between two tables) in a (mildly) camp discussion of his good satin ballet shoes and the state of his feet; and offers the girls an unbidden impromptu performance. Scott's practices here can be understood as a hyperbolic masquerade (Butler 1990) of the subjugated homosexual that Daniel (provisionally) constituted him as. His practices might at the same time be seen to mimic and so constitute himself as a gay identity that is legitimate outside the school context but subjugated within it. As such, these practices have the potential to recoup Daniel's constitution and reinscribe gay. The participation of the girls is significant. Vici and Suzi's questions, and the appreciative audience that they and the other girls form, guarantee Scott a positive reception that contributes to his reinscription of the legitimacy, intelligibility, and desirability of his gay identity.

Daniel does not appear to acknowledge or respond to Scott's performative performance.[6] The homophobia of Daniel's comment that I have outlined might lead to the expectation that Daniel will retaliate, perhaps aggressively or with physical violence, to Scott's sequence of ballet exercises. I suggest, however, that a number of factors protect against any such retaliation.

First, the specific context of the classroom in which the dance takes place appears significant. This is a classroom where the teacher consistently lacks control and the students appear to have a tacit agreement to regularly challenge the teacher's authority and disrupt the lesson. In this specific context it may be that doing ballet exercises gains acceptability, and even kudos, by contributing to this ongoing challenge and disruption.

Second, Scott has many friends and allies among girls in the year group and a number of these make up Scott's audience within this classroom. These are the very girls who, within the terms of heteromasculinity, Daniel is likely or expected to pursue. The continued approval of these girls is highly important. By drawing attention to and denigrating Scott's homosexuality, Daniel asserts his own heterosexual masculinity. In this sense the comment may have served its purpose in the moment of its utterance. Indeed, Scott's subsequent ballet exercises are performative in their constitution of Scott's gay identity *and* Daniel's heterosexual masculinity. In these terms, Daniel need take no further action and to do so may well be counterproductive.

Third, despite his homosexuality, Scott has significant capital within the institutional discourse of the school—he is white, middle-class, high attaining, even "talented." Daniel, on the other hand, is Black and has a history of disciplinary conflict with the school. In such a context, even if Daniel wanted to censure Scott more strongly (which I suggest is not the case anyway), to do so would be to guarantee the full weight of institutional retaliation. (See Youdell 2003a for an extended discussion of the constitution of Black students as unacceptable learners.)

Fourth, the "wisdoms" of pop-psychology/sexology (themselves appropriated within gay discourse)—that suggest that those individuals who are most ardent in their criticisms of homosexuality are, in fact, the "closet" homosexuals—may well have percolated into the discourses of the mainstream student subculture. If this is the case, it may render it possible to protest against homosexuality, but not too much.

Finally, the broader pop-cultural context may bar Daniel from denigrating Scott's homosexuality through any more explicit practices than his partially expressed comment. In recent years gay culture has attained a new degree of exemplary "chic" within pop culture. This can be seen through discourses of the "pink pound" and "lesbian chic"; exemplary gay, lesbian, and transsexual celebrities (think Tatu, and Lilly Savage); the endorsement by heterosexual icons of ultra-fashionable gay exemplars (think Madonna and Jean Paul Gaultier); and the prominent role of gay culture in popularizing the dance and rave scene (think ultra-camp Culture Club singer turned ultra-cool Ministry of Sound DJ Boy George). It is arguable that within this broader pop-cultural context, Year 11 students attending a large, London comprehensive school in the late 1990s may well have recognized, at least partially and tacitly, the "cache of queer," the "cosmopolitan" requirement to be unfazed by and accepting of difference.

In a context framed by these various discourses, gay bashers are uncool and may well be hiding their own homosexuality. The cool man must constitute himself as absolutely heterosexual and dismissive of but unthreatened by the homosexual man.

If Daniel had not made his potentially constituting comment, Scott may or may not have engaged in these practices. The elapsed time between the comment and the exchange that leads up to the impromptu ballet exercises obscures any explicit intent by Scott to retaliate/recoup. This elapsed time also protects Scott from becoming involved in a direct confrontation with Daniel. Irrespective of intent, Scott's practices potentially recoup the denigrated homosexual that Daniel's comment cited and inscribed as well as provisionally reinscribing gay *again differently*.

Scene 2, Scott's contribution to the Leaving Day Show, represents an exceptional moment in this performative reinscription of gayness. Scott's foremost intention in performing in the Leaving Day Show may well be the display of his dancing accomplishment. As my analysis of Scene 1 demonstrates, however, Scott's identity as ballet dancer and gay man interact both within the popular discourses that pervade this context and his own practices.

In understanding this scene it is useful to consider Scott's audience and how he is located institutionally and in relation to student subcultures. The dance can be understood as being performed for two overarching audiences—teachers and students. The student audience is by no means homogeneous. Rather, it is self-consciously categorized along biographical and subcultural lines, with social class acting as a key axis of differentiation. Likewise, the teacher audience is differentiated, for instance, along biographical, cultural, and professional axes. As already noted, Scott is a white, middle-class, high attaining student. His interacting biographical and learner identities combine with his disavowed and subjugated sexual identity to constitute him as outside the mainstream student subculture.

Although the reasons for Scott's reluctance to perform are not specified, it seems reasonable to conjecture that this is due to his awareness of the explicit and implicit homophobia within the mainstream student subculture. Scott is guaranteed a positive reception by the middle-class student minority who form an alternative student subculture (see Youdell 2003c), as well as by those girls with whom he shares a close friendship. The teachers' professional identities demand their support. Furthermore, that the Head of Year has persuaded Scott to participate suggests that there is genuine support for him among the staff. In addition, if student attainment is understood to be a central official concern of the school, then any implicit homophobia among staff is likely to be outweighed or neutralized by Scott's exceptional success. This is not to suggest that the acceptability of Scott's gayness among teachers is necessarily generalizable. Indeed, as a white, middle-class, high attaining student, Scott's gayness might simply be overlooked and/or understood (constituted) as exemplary (Connell 1995).

Yet by dancing in this public arena that has, at least in part, been captured by/surrendered to the students, Scott risks the possibility of vigorous and aggressive censure by the student majority. It seems, however, that it is the potential constitutions of this audience that Scott may be concerned, tacitly or intentionally, to recoup and reinscribe.

The majority of these students has never been and never will be his friend or ally. He is already exiled. It seems that Scott may have little or nothing to lose by performing. And once again, Scott enjoys the institutional protection that bars an outright rejection by his student audience. Furthermore, those mediating popular discourses of urban street cool, gay cache, and homophobia as a mark of the closet that were discussed in relation to Scene 1, act further to subdue the audience.

Social class differences, and the cultural capitals—understood as familiarity with and competence in cultural forms that vary across social groups and that are differently valued across groups and contexts (Bourdieu 1990)—that these are constitutive of and constituted through, are also likely to be significant here. The largely working-class student audience is unlikely to be exposed regularly to any form of ballet. At the same time, they are undoubtedly familiar with such forms of dance and are likely to recognize these as pursuits (as dancers and audience) of, and belonging to, the upper-middle and upper-classes. Furthermore, working-class students may understand, albeit with resentment and/or attempts to recoup this, that within certain discursive fields (and perhaps ones that "count"), ballet is superior, or of greater value, than pop-cultural dance forms. This uncomfortable knowing—which can be understood as a tacit or explicit recognition that even as particular cultural capitals are their preserve, others are all but unattainable—may well act to silence, subdue, or discomfort the pupil majority. That is, the social class differences between Scott and the majority of his audience may well contribute to the intelligibility and legitimacy of his gay identity, even as this provides the very terms by which this gay identity might be recouped.

In the formal market of the Leaving Day Show and broader hegemonic markets, then, the high value of the cultural capital cited and inscribed through Scott's biographical and learner identities—including his identity as a (gay) ballet dancer—is likely to mitigate any enduring performative force that the constitutions of the student majority might have. That is, it may be Scott's interacting whiteness, middle classness, and ableness that allow him to constitute the "out" gay ballet dancer as intelligible and legitimate.

Yet the audience does not need to do anything as overt as heckle for their reception of Scott's dance to be mediated by, and in turn inscribe, particular enduring discourses. Within authorized discourses of compulsory heterosexuality and oppositional man-masculine/woman-feminine, the homosexual man is (although impossibly within this discourse) *not* man. In this discursive frame, the homosexual man is constituted as (un)masculine/feminine, physically (and psychologically) weak, a poor imitation of the (illusory) heterosexual man whom he (fails) to imitate (Butler 1991). Scott's bodily practices and his body itself within his Leaving Day Show performance resist these constitutions of the homosexual man. Scott's body is strong, muscular, controlled—he is indisputably masculine. Yet his dance is also that of a classically trained ballet dancer and the popular discourse that frames this context insists that the male ballet dancer is homosexual. As such, the dance recoups the incommensurability of masculinity and male homosexuality and reinscribes *again differently* a gay identity that is at once masculine *and* homosexual. This underscores the inseparability of sex, gender, and sexuality.

In my previous work (Youdell 2003b) I examined Butler's (1999) discussion of whether it is possible, in the contemporary moment, to separate sex-desire and jettison categories of sex and sexuality. Butler (1999) asserts that the possibilities for thinking bodies and pleasures separated from categories of sex, gender, and sexuality that are often sought, after Foucault (1990), by queer politics and theory are extremely limited in the current discursive context. This is due, she suggests, to the fact that sex and desire are entwined in prevailing discourses so deeply that they remain fundamental to the constitution of intelligible subjects. The citational chains of sex-gender-sexuality constellations (Youdell 2003b) are evident in Scott's practices. These reinscribe homosexual, but this is in part effected through simultaneous inscriptions of normative masculinity and the masculine body. This is not to suggest a simple citation—the normative masculine body is necessarily heterosexual. Scott's sex-gender-sexuality constellation couples homosexuality and masculine physicality and is, therefore, intrinsically troubling.

Scott's performance, then, is a moment of defiant, triumphant, and celebratory homosexual masculinity. It insists that this is legitimate and arguably, at the level of the physicality of the male body at least, superior to the heteromasculinities that it is accused of failing to approximate and by which it has been disavowed and subjugated. Scott's resistances and reinscriptions may well be at once intentional *and* tacit. The fact of the dance, and Scott's bodily performatives within it, do not reinscribe once and for all those popular and enduring discourses that constitute the homosexual man as (un)masculine/feminine; the male ballet dancer as homosexual; and the homosexual as disavowed and subjugated. But his dance does trouble these constituting discourses. The audience's silence as he enters; audible gasp during moments of the dance; silence as he finishes; loud but polite and formal applause; silence and whispered conversation after his exit, all imply this trouble. Scott's performance is at once intelligible and unintelligible. It at once confirms what the audience "knows" about the gay ballet dancer and unsettles this "knowledge." It is a moment of performative politics.

Conclusion

The analysis that I have offered demonstrates how the minutiae of Scott's practices—from his particular way of leaning over a table and his mode of animated engagement with a female friend; to the hyperbolic masquerade of an impromptu show in a science classroom; and the challenge of a performance, for an audience of school peers, of modern ballet and masculine physicality—act to reinscribe gay.

These practices effect this reinscription in two key ways that reflect Butler's (1997a) suggestion that performative politics be concerned with discursive practices taking on nonordinary meanings and functioning in contexts where they have not belonged. First, these practices cite an easily recognizable pop-gay identity that, while perhaps reflecting a restricted notion of gayness, renders this legitimate inside the school. That is, gayness is constituted as an intelligible and legitimate identity in a context where it has not previously belonged. Second, these practices inscribe a modality of gayness that is likely to have been unknown, or even unintelligible, in the discursive frame of the school. That is, gayness takes on a meaning that is nonordinary in this context.

More broadly, this analysis demonstrates the usefulness of school ethnography informed by poststructural theory for generating representations of school life that allow the analysis of discursive practices, as these produce particular subjects of schooling. It also shows how understanding the subject as discursively constituted but with discursive agency posits a decentered subject who is framed but not determined by discourse and who retains intent and, therefore, the potential to act politically. And it offers insights into how the practices of students and schools are implicated in producing particular sorts of subjects including, optimistically, legitimate gay-masculinity. By offering these analyses I hope that the chapter is able to contribute tools for researchers and educators to understand the potential, limits, and costs of their own and other practices, retaining the possibility for intent, political acts, and thinking and being differently.

The analysis also shows, however, how the reinscriptions of performative politics are, like the discourses through which they are effected, discontinuous and subject to shifts and slippages. This acts as a reminder that performative reinscriptions are neither guaranteed nor final, and that they may well also inscribe the terms by which they can be recouped and redeployed. This is not a failure of performative politics, rather it is its necessary terrain.

Notes

1. Reflecting the Foucauldian framework that guides this study, I use the term queer as a verb in order to denote and posit the possibility of practices that might have queer effects, rather than exclusively as a noun to indicate a queer identity.
2. I am provisionally using a notion of nonheterosexual to avoid pre-empting what "sort" of nonheterosexual this might be (for instance gay, lesbian, bisexual) and excluding the possibility for nonheterosexual to be otherwise.
3. I suspect that the differential assessments of these reinscriptions might reflect the status of "queer" as academic-intellectual-political counterdiscourse, while the reinscription of "nigga" (note also the respelling here) has emanated from subcultural practices, most notably rap and hip-hop. As such, the role of the academic/intellectual in resignifying "nigga" has predominantly been one of response and/or commentary.
4. Used here by the students as a noun to indicate a particular identity.
5. I have some discomfort in suggesting a gay bodily habitus—it might be taken to infer a "gay body" that, while perhaps not natural or innate, could precede the designation, the "coming out," of this body as gay. Furthermore, it seems to risk a citation and inscription of the much denigrated homosexual "camp," thereby inscribing the intrinsic (un)masculinity/femininity of the gay man within authorized discourse.
6. I make a distinction here between a performance, which is necessarily enacted knowingly and with intent, and a performative, which may be deployed intentionally but which is often a tacit or unknowing practice.

References

Allvesson, Mats. 2002. *Postmodernism and Social Research*. Buckingham, UK: Open University Press.

Althusser, Louis. 1971."Ideology and Ideological State Apparatuses." Pp. 170–186 in *Lenin and Philosophy*, trans. Ben. Brewster. London: Monthly Review Press.

Austin, John L. 1961. *How To Do Things with Words*. Oxford: Clarendon Press.

Ball, Stephen. J. 1981. *Beachside Comprehensive: A Case Study of Secondary Schooling*. Cambridge: The University Press.

Bourdieu, Pierre. 1990. *The Logic of Practice*. Stanford: Stanford University Press.

———. 1991. *Language and Symbolic Power*. Cambridge, Mass.: Harvard University Press.

Butler, James. 1996. "The Poof Paradox: Homonegativity and Silencing." Pp. 131–150 in *Schooling and Sexualities: Teaching for a Positive Sexuality*, eds. Louise Laskey and Catherine Beavis. Geelong: Deakin Centre for Education and Change.

Butler, Judith. 1991. "Imitation and Gender Insubordination." Pp. 13–31 in *Inside/Out: Lesbian Theories, Gay Theories*, ed. Diane Fuss. London: Routledge.

———. 1993. *Bodies That Matter: On the Discursive Limits of "Sex."* London: Routledge.

———. 1997a. *Excitable Speech: A Politics of the Performative*. London: Routledge.

———. 1997b. *The Psychic Life of Power: Theories in Subjection*. Stanford, Calif.: Stanford University Press.

———. 1999. "Revisiting Bodies and Pleasures." *Theory, Culture and Society* 16, no. 2: 11–20.

Connell, Robert W. 1995. *Masculinities*. Cambridge, UK: Polity Press.

Crowley, Vicki, and Mary Louise Rasmussen. 2004. "Wounded Identities and the Promise of Pleasure (Special Edition)." *Discourse* 24, no. 4.

Delamont, Sara, and Paul Atkinson. 1995. *Fighting Familiarity: Essays on Education and Ethnography*. Cresskill, N.J.: Hampton Press.

Derrida, Jacques. 1988. "Signature Event Context." Pp. 1–23 in *Limited Inc*. Jacques Derrida. Evanston, Ill.: Northwestern University Press.

Epstein, Debbie, and Richard Johnson. 1996. *Schooling Sexualities*. Buckingham, Eng.: Open University Press.

Foucault, Michel. 1990. *The History of Sexuality Volume 1: An Introduction*. London: Penguin.

———. 1991. *Discipline and Punish: The Birth of the Prison*. London: Penguin.

Gramsci, Antonio. 2003. *Selections from the Prison Notebooks*. Trans. and ed. Quintin Hoare and Geoffrey Nowell Smith. London: Lawrence and Wishart.

Hammersley, Martyn. 1992. *What's Wrong with Ethnography?: Methodological Exploration*. London: Routledge.

Hammersley, Martyn, and Paul Atkinson. 1996. *Ethnography: Principles in Practice*. 2d ed. London: Tavistock Publications.

Kehily, Mary Jane. 2002. *Sexuality, Gender, and Schooling*. London: Routledge Falmer.

Mac an Ghaill, Martin. 1994. *The Making of Men: Masculinities, Sexualities and Schooling*. Buckingham, Eng.: Open University Press.

Mansfield, Nick. 2000. *Subjectivity: Theories of the Self from Freud to Haraway*. Sydney: Allen Unwin.

Martino, Wayne, and Maria Pallotta-Chiarolli. 2003. *So What's a Boy?* Buckingham, Eng.: Open University Press

Mills, Martin. 1999. "Homophobia and Anti-Lesbianism in Schools: Challenges and Possibilities for Social Justice." *Melbourne Studies in Education* 40, no. 2: 105–125.

Nayak, Anoop, and Mary Jane Kehily. 1996. "Playing it Straight: Masculinities, Homophobias and Schooling." *Journal of Gender Studies* 5, no. 2: 211–230.

Rich, Adrienne. 1980. "Compulsory Heterosexuality and Lesbian Existence." *Signs* 5, no. 4: 631–660.

Silverman, David, ed. 1997a. *Qualitative Research: Theory, Method and Practice.* London: Sage.

Stronach, Ian, and Maggie Maclure. 1997. *Educational Research Undone: The Postmodern Embrace.* Buckingham, Eng.: Open University Press.

Youdell, Deborah. 2000. *Schooling Identities: An Ethnography of the Constitution of Pupil Identities Inside Schools.* Ph.D. Thesis, University of London.

———. 2003a. "Identity Traps or How Black Students Fail: The Interactions Between Biographical, Sub-Cultural, and Learner Identities." *British Journal of Sociology of Education* 24, no. 1: 3–20.

———. 2003b. "Sex-Gender-Sexuality: How Gender and Sexuality Constellations are Performatively Constituted in Schools." Paper presented at the American Educational Research Association Annual Meeting, Chicago, April 2003.

———. 2003c. "Shazas 'n' Bazas and Dir'y 'ippies: Pupil Sub-cultures and the Production of Classed Selves in the Classroom." Paper presented at the British Educational Research Association Annual Conference. Edinburgh, September 2003.

———. 2004. "Wounds and Reinscriptions: Schools, Sexualities and Performative Subjects." *Discourse* 24, no. 4.

C h a p t e r   T e n

Melancholy and the Productive Negotiations of Power in Sissy Boy Experience

David McInnes

Introduction

This chapter considers the sissy boy and schooling, and begins some theorizing of the sissy boy experience. To date, little theoretical work has been done in the arena of queer theory about sissy boys. Yet, in considering the experience of sissy boys, a political potential emerges that extends beyond liberal notions of inclusion, tolerance, difference, or diversity to more disruptive and lively engagements with gender as a cultural formation. Notions of tolerance and inclusion work on the assumption that there is an outside to power—a place where all of us can be accepted, equally and in celebration of our difference. These ideas ignore the necessity of power in the formation of gender and sexuality. Against this liberalism, the chapter argues that keeping in view the (per)formative production of gender prior to the mobilizing of discourses of tolerance, demands that the recognition of who young men and boys are be uneasy and contingent. An uneasy recognition is politically useful because it refuses the naturalness of gender and foregrounds the processes through which gender is formed and valued.

Sissy boys are those boys at schools who have "gentle and sweet" voices, who "avoid sports and all roughness," and who play with girls. They cry a lot when they get hurt, they can't throw balls, and sometimes they like to put on girls' clothing. This sketch of the gender nonconforming performance of the sissy boy is provided as an account, by the author, of his own experience (Rofes 1995, 79). Eric Rofes describes this gender nonconforming behavior as "heresy" and declares "heresy was me" (79). Rofes' piece makes important points about gay men ignoring their sissy pasts. Though this is a useful and provocative reclamation, sissy boys are not necessarily protogay youth: not all sissies grow up to be gay. And, whether or not the sissy grows up to be gay, the sissy boy experience is one that deserves theoretical attention. Rofes' agenda is not only to acknowledge the heritage of sissy for gay men, but to recommend ways in which schools can be made safe for sissies. He concludes with a three-point plan for school responses to the persecution of sissies: to reduce bullying, to give boys alternative activities and to honor nontraditional achievements for boys.

In contrast to this agenda but without suggesting that safety is unimportant, this chapter considers sissy boy experience and theorizes it outside of and resistant to questions of gayness and discourses of homophobia. The discussion here is positioned at a point prior to the overdetermination that issues of sexuality demand in discourses of homophobia and, instead, proposes a theoretical account of what the sissy boy's gender-nonconforming experience is about. This will keep the formation of gender in view and uneasy, and provide the potential to work pedagogically in ways that resist reinscribing values around the performance of gender by young men and boys.

Distinctions

Two distinctions serve as starting points in theorizing about the politics of sissy boys in this chapter. The first is a distinction between homophobic discourse and discourses of homophobia. *Homophobic discourse* is understood to be that set of things that are possible to say about sexuality and those things that cannot be said because they are "homophobic": that is, statements, ideas, ideals, principles, omissions, silences, and repudiations that marginalize, vilify, ostracize, abuse, demean, humiliate, and render "other" those who have same-sex sexual attachment or desire. The *discourse of homophobia,* on the other hand, is the second order discourse, about homophobic discourse that is found in policy documents, antidiscrimination policy and legislation, the media, and, of particular interest here, in school-based resources about the experience of same-sex attracted youth (SSAY), their experience of homophobia (homophobic discourse), and what might be done about it.

This distinction between homophobic discourse and the discourse of homophobia is made because, while the first is something to combat and to treat critically (Dempsey, Hillier and Harrison 2001; FPA Health 2000; Hillier, Harrison and Dempsey 1999; Mason and Tomsen 1997; Plummer 1999, 2001a, 2001b), the second, generated as it is to deal with the first, overrides and overdetermines much in relation to young people, sex, sexuality, gender, and schooling. Drawing the distinction here, at the outset, is necessary so that there is clarity about the damage done by discourse that is homophobic; this discourse vilifies and abuses those who are same-sex attracted. This homophobic discourse is distinguished here from the damage, differently but relatedly produced, wrought by discourses *about* homophobia. This second order discourse— in which homophobic discourse is targeted—does its own kinds of damage by the assumptions and determinations it makes.

To consider and theorize the sissy boy's experience, a further distinction is made between sexuality and gender. Surprisingly, this distinction is not made often in discourses of homophobia (or in homophobic discourse). Gender and sexuality are interrelated but, in the discourses of homophobia, sexuality (as sexual attachment, sexual attraction, sexual desire, or sexual practice) operates as a defining term, overriding considerations of gender and conflating issues of gender into and under the umbrella of sexuality. Clearly, homophobic discourse does this too, and this means that teasing these apart in either discourse is not easy. But, such unraveling is essential if understandings about the political potential of gender nonconformity are to be developed. So, throughout this chapter, same-sex attraction will be differentiated from nonconforming performances of gender. In other words, same-sex attracted youth and sissy boys will be seen as referring to different subjectivities and as different experiences, even if there are instances where the experiences and subjectivities reside with the same individual. The distinction between sexuality and gender is being maintained in order to propel a theoretical discussion that could ultimately have an impact on pedagogical interventions.

Safety in Our Schools

Safety in Our Schools: Strategies for Responding to Homophobia (Ollis, Mitchell, Watson, Hillier and Walsh, undated) is a booklet produced in 2002 by the Australian Research Centre in Sex Health and Society at La Trobe University in Melbourne. The booklet "provides a summary of issues to help make schools safer for gay, lesbian and bisexual students and staff, so that they can participate and achieve in the full range of school programs and activities" (2). The booklet positions those it seeks to help or make safe as "same-sex attracted," but it also includes as its concern those that experience homophobic discrimination "based on a perception that they are gay or lesbian" (3).

The authors clearly state that the need for safety for all students in schools is based on the proposition that feeling safe contributes to "well-being" (2). They further claim that same-sex attracted youth are at risk of vilification, discrimination, verbal and physical abuse and that they are at risk of higher-than-average substance use (5). Their aim parallels that of other antidiscrimination agendas and strategies: "A society may discriminate against lesbian women and gay men and deny them the rights enjoyed by other members of society. Learning to recognize and understand difference is a first step towards countering homophobia" (quoted by Ollis, et al. from *Mates: HIV Related Discrimination*, NSW Department of School Education, 1994).

For the authors of *Safety in Our Schools*, a key component of countering homophobia is to create and maintain a safe and supportive "whole school learning approach." This involves "acknowledging diversity" as a "positive way to address discrimination or harassment. Education programs which affirm the sexual diversity of students have the potential to affect the educational opportunities of these students and improve many aspects of their health and safety" (9). To acknowledge diversity in the reduction of discrimination, the authors outline a set of strategies for the classroom, one of which is to set "ground rules," which include "no put-downs." Put-downs include discriminatory name-calling. Once the ground rules are set and the ideas of nondiscriminatory language are outlined, the use of put-downs, they suggest, should be met by references to the "ground rules" and then, subsequently, disciplinary procedures. The booklet focuses on language as a mechanism of abuse and as a means of countering homophobia. Discriminatory language is, they imply, to be replaced with other forms of language that are not discriminatory. This, again by implication, will reduce discrimination and increase safety for SSAY.

This put-down-free aim, though useful to some extent, is imbued with the notion of an ideal school world in which there is an acceptance of diversity and the absence of verbal abuse. The aim of developing a school environment where there are no put-downs raises the question of what happens when one set of words is removed or replaced by others. Take, for example, the word "gay." Its shift in meaning can be broadly described as one moving from pejorative (in the 1950s and 1960s) (Simes 1996), through phases of political self-declaration (gay liberation of the 1970s) (Simes 1996), and into a period of use in which, in some contexts, it has a more neutral, less pejorative meaning. Its contemporary less-pejorative uses, though, still involve a negotiation of power, albeit different to that of earlier meanings and contexts. Gay is a concept located in late Western capitalism. As an adjective and as a classifier of sexuality it allows for the silencing not only of some of the pejorative and hate speech dimensions of its use, but also of aspects of what it might mean that could confront, challenge, or disrupt (McInnes 2002, 1997). To be called a "nancy," "poof," "fudge-tunneller," among others, is still an experience of vilification, but it is also an experience, by its very quality as hate speech, that calls forth and into view aspects of a heteronormative and masculine world still threatened by male-to-male sexual desire and sexual practice. This same world is less threatened and destabilized by the "gay" man who dresses well, is educated, and who is not "out there" or "in your face" about his sex life. My point is this: when one word goes or its meanings change, questions need to be continually asked of the shifts in signification involved. Language is always loaded with both spoken and unspoken organizations of value and power. Power is continually enacted and negotiated through language and other semiotic systems by the production of difference by sign and by structural and contextual differentiations of value. The next section of this chapter will focus on the process of "put-down" or linguistic violence in the designation of "sissy boy."

Sissy Boy Shame

Case Study One: You are conducting a continuum activity with year 8 students responding to the statement "girls get it easier at school than boys." One boy goes to the "strongly agree" end of the continuum. You ask him why and he replies, "Some boys get it easy too, Matt gets it the easiest but he acts like a girl."

—Ollis, et al. undated

The above case study scenario comes from a section of the booklet *Safety in Our Schools* called "In the Classroom," which provides scenarios and strategies for intervention in relation to homophobia in classrooms. It provides a frame for ground rules and, in a structured way ("So what to do if . . . "), examples of homophobia and a set of strategies for intervention. I will return to the interventions at the close of this chapter.

In this text, a question of gender nonconformity (the substance of the boy's declarations concerning Matt) has been placed under the umbrella of homophobia. This conflation of gender behavior and sexuality happens often and, though in some cases homophobia is seen to police masculinity (Plummer 1999, 2001), it is nevertheless the acceptance or tolerance of homosexuality that is the key focus of solutions or strategies. The nesting of issues of gender nonconformity for young men under the umbrella discourse of homophobia obfuscates the threat of nonmasculine boys to the social ordering of gender. Without a focus on gender, the issue becomes one of tolerance of the diversity of sexuality and moves discussion to questions of pride, in which questions of the value of femininity in relation to masculinity are avoided. Femininity is powerfully disruptive to the fragile enterprise of masculinity, and its containment away from, outside of, and in service to the masculine is a major component of masculine domination (Bourdieu 2001, 7–8). If that which is supposed to be masculine is (in part) feminine, the threat to masculinity becomes more intense. Sissy boys are a threat, not to men, but to the formation of masculinity because they destabilize the logic involved in assuming that specific genders are written onto and through certain kinds of bodies.

The declaration that "[Matt] acts like a girl" is performative in the sense that the statement does things when it is spoken. It enacts linguistic violence by a form of hate speech (Butler 1997a). Matt is positioned as other, as nonmasculine, and by being "like" a girl he is positioned socially in a less powerful and less valuable position than other boys. Because sissy boys are boys that act like, appear like, perform like, or speak like girls, they are sissies. They do not conform to expectations of what boys, as masculine, should be like. To be, like Matt, declared a boy who acts like a girl (to be named a sissy boy) is a process of being othered and is an experience of shame. Shame is a negative affect (Tomkins 1962, 1963). In that shame usually involves a turning away or a lack of reciprocation in interaction, it necessitates an attenuation of positive affect such as interest or enjoyment, but not a removal of these positive affects. For Matt, his interest or enjoyment in the sociality of the school would be attenuated by the above kind of declaration. But, he would retain some interest in belonging and in the sociality of the school environment. He experiences a shaming, as "acting like a girl," as a boy who is classified as different and problematically feminine.

Generally, and here in relation to gender, shame operates as "feedback" (Sedgwick and Frank 1995a, and b). It provides a policing of behavior through the management of connection to sociality and as such works to order and maintain how boys and girls should be.

> Shame becomes the most social of negative affects because it modulates, regulates, impedes, contains, the interest and enjoyment that powers all sociality. Just as the experience of shame pulls us from social interaction, it calls attention to and helps define social interaction. (Nathanson 1992, 251)

Shame, brought by the linguistic violence of being declared "like a girl," manages Matt's place in his social world by impediment and containment. But, it is precisely because one retains a desire to belong or to have a place socially that shame works so powerfully: "If shame is the affect of withdrawal, of sinking down and slumping, of physiological removal from interaction of the face, it is still always an affect made painful only to the extent that interest and enjoyment remain" (251).

Many of the strategies in resources like *Safety in Our Schools* are designed to produce a safe place or space for same-sex attracted young people. Safe spaces in these contexts are both spaces free from physical threat and abuse and from verbal and emotional abuse. So they work to offset the kind of shame that comes from being pushed from sociality or being relegated to a marginal and less valued place in a social domain such as the school. A sissy boy's shame happens because of the loss of attachment to, or inclusion in, the social world of the school. Shame is a very powerful modulator of the social performance of selves. It serves to include and exclude, to fold-in socially or render as other. The "simplest" solution to such shaming processes in the management of the gendered order of a school would be to develop a school environment in which diversity is embraced and difference is celebrated: in other words, to develop a culture in which young boys are not shamed because of their gender nonconformity. As will be clear when considerations return to the *Safety in Our Schools* booklet later, this is a common strategy, though in resources such as this one it is in relation to sexuality.

Sissy boy shame is an indication of a disruption, and sissy boys make different responses to this shame. Strategies such as those suggested in *Safety in Our Schools* do not engage with this disruption because they concentrate instead on neutralizing the context. This kind of strategy does not embrace or use the kinds of disruptive potential available in sissy boy shame, responses to it, and dynamics that might unfold from it. The next section develops further ideas about the position of the sissy boy in the school. In order to theorize the political potential inherent in this position, not as about tolerance or diversity but as a form of ambivalence and a resistance to foreclosure, the work of Judith Butler on melancholy is drawn into the discussion.

Melancholy Gender

In *The Psychic Life of Power*, Judith Butler suggests that melancholia as ungrievable loss and unbroken attachment is an essential part of the formation of gender. She suggests that "the positions of 'masculine' and 'feminine' are established in part through prohibitions which *demand the loss* of certain sexual attachments, and demand as well that those losses not be avowed, and not be grieved" (1997b, 135). An unavowed and ungrieved loss is the substance of melancholy. Butler suggests that, as one cannot take the parent of the same sex as an object of sexual attachment *and* the very possibility of such attachment can *never* be acknowledged, "the loss of homosexual objects and aims would appear to be foreclosed from the start" (139). So, the loss that cannot be grieved is (and ungrievable because it is) a sexual attachment to the same sex. This is ungrievable and unable to be acknowledged because of the prohibition (a preestablished foreclosure in Butler's words) against same-sex attraction. Thus, "masculinity" and "femininity" are "formed and consolidated through identifications which are in part composed of disavowed grief" (139). Gender is composed of precisely what remains inarticulate in sexuality and, therefore, is founded on a renunciation of attachment and loss.

Butler (1997b) considers the lack of renunciation in gay male sexuality as a disruptive potential. Gays in the military, for example, are a presence of what is repudiated and as such disrupt the circuit of renunciation on which masculinity is built (139). This analysis is profound and useful in the manner in which it ties anxieties about homosexuality to the fundamental anxieties present in the formation and ongoing process of consolidating masculinity. However, there is more to be considered about melancholic gender than that which can be articulated by a focus on homosexual attachments or desires.

There is, as stressed above, a shame or shaming experienced by boys who "act like girls." Sissy boys who don't like to do things that boys are supposed to do are declared other to the masculine norm and are thus aligned with the feminine. This kind of shame disciplines subjects and is part of a process of producing a proper world in which boys and girls are properly gendered. This, as Butler suggests, does require a renunciation of same-sex sexual attachments, but it also requires that boys act like boys and that girls act like girls in many other ways.

Butler's ideas about gender melancholy can be usefully extended to think about the other ways in which gender nonconformity work beyond and around sexual orientation: Part of the renunciation that affords "proper" masculinity would be the renunciation of a performative identity that is "feminine." To be "properly" masculine would involve both a nonarticulation of same-sex sexual attachments and a nonarticulation of a self that is gendered as other than that predicted by biological sex. These two, of course, are interrelated in ways that are difficult to tease apart. But, the difficulty of teasing them apart often leads to a collapse of one into and as the other; that is, gender nonconformity is often assumed to mean homosexual attachment. This collapse means that Matt's declaration in Case Study One, above, is understood in terms of homophobia.

Eve Kosofsky Sedgwick engages the space between gender performance and sexuality/sexual attachment in her discussion of "How to Bring Your Kids up Gay" (Sedgwick 1993). Her analysis centers on the way in which psychiatric texts have negotiated the "de-pathologizing" of homosexuality. The texts in focus for Sedgwick include the *DSM III* (American Psychiatric Association Staff, 1980) and Richard Friedman's *Male Homosexuality: A Contemporary Psychoanalytic Perspective* (1988). These texts, she suggests, manage to be happy with gay as long as gay means already grown-up and masculine. In her discussion, she warns against "distinguishing between gender and sexuality" because "while denaturalizing sexual object choice, it radically *re*naturalizes gender" (73). In the textual domain of Sedgwick's concern (psychiatric literature), the problem of gender disorder for effeminate boys—when boys act like (or want to be) girls—is coupled with the problem that, because of this, they might turn out to be gay. The texts on which she focuses claim that these problems can be remedied by active social recognition of effeminate boys as masculine and that this recognition should come from other men. In other words, effeminate boys, those gender "disordered," can be aided in becoming "ordered" if men (and pointedly not women) affirm them as masculine. This solution, as Sedgwick points out, renaturalizes and enforces gender assignment (73).

The sissy boy is a melancholic figure because he is an expression of what should be inexpressible. In this expression, he is a presence of disorder, not disorder in himself or his gender, but a presence of disorder in the school. Once drawn from the discourse of homophobia, gender nonconformity has a troubling, disruptive potential and offers an opportunity to critique and keep unstable the delicate reproduction of orders of gender in school environments.

Heresy

In 1997, the Australian *60 Minutes* (Nine Network Australia, aired July 1997) aired a story titled "Pride and Prejudice." The story was about Chris Tsakalos, a young man who, because he was "afraid to go to school," sued the New South Wales Department of School Education because they had not provided him a safe place to go to school. Chris was "bashed up" and "roughed up" at school for being a "faggot." The reporter on the story, Jeff McMullen, explained at the outset that Chris' teachers "have told him, the way out is to tone down his flamboyance."

Chris' experience is presented (by himself and others in the story, including the journalist) as tightly bound to questions of his sexuality and, as such, the story is narrated through the discourse of homophobia; that is, the second order discourse that configures both the problem of homophobia (the discourse that vilifies and abuses those same-sex attracted) and its solution via tolerance and the acceptance of diversity. Chris' gayness is the central issue or problem for Chris, his mother, the journalist, and for Derek Williams, who was at the time the head of a group called Gay and Lesbian Teachers and Students Association (GALTAS). But what emerges as the most significant problem, flagged at the outset by the journalist, is Chris' flamboyance and effeminacy.

Derek Williams describes Chris as a "stereotypical effeminate gay boy." Chris' account to the reporter of his school principals' advice is centered, not on his gayness, but his gender performance: "Chris, you're instigating most of it, the way you act, the way you walk, the way you speak, the way you wave your hands, the way your appearance is." The principal, Mrs. McNally's, own account suggests "everybody has to work on their interpersonal skills. It's part of the learning process in a school." As much as Chris is gay, he is also a sissy and it is his nonmasculine and effeminate performance of gender that is a core problem in this story. Gender nonconformity so flagrantly performed is a problematic and disruptive force and runs counter to the "learning" of "interpersonal skills" that are appropriate for young men in school contexts.

This story outlines and exemplifies a homophobic discourse. In this discourse, Chris' gender nonconformity is the basis for the assumption of his homosexuality and this leads to verbal and physical abuse and to shame. Other parts of the story are an illustration of the discourses of homophobia in which this homophobic discourse is figured and a solution to it is presented—most of the story, told from various perspectives, is understood to be the story of a boy who, because of his gayness, is abused, vilified, and ostracized and, most crucially, the discussion of Chris' gender nonconformity is as that which unsettles the possible resolution he might find in being accepted as gay.

Chris causes trouble because he is so flagrantly "gay," so effeminate, open, and demonstrative. If the issue of sexuality is suspended from the question of Chris' gender performance, gender nonconformity is exposed as very troubling, even for a gay young man: boys should act like boys and effeminacy (on the wrong body) draws (negative, critical, and shameful) attention to itself. That Chris, or any other sissy boy, discomforts the gendered order of the school signals that the "natural" order in which girls act like girls and boys act like boys appears real because it appears ordered; it appears ordered because, by mechanisms like shame, disorder is minimized and silenced (disavowed, denounced).

Butler suggests that in the face of conventionally produced gender norms, a melancholic presence, one that refuses closure and that sustains ambivalence, is mobile and lively: "We are made all the more fragile under the pressure of such rules, and all the more mobile when ambivalence and loss are given a dramatic language in which to do their acting out" (1997b, 150). Chris' acting-out, on one hand, is *not* ambivalent in terms of sexuality, but, on the other, *is* ambivalent in terms of gender. His gender nonconformity makes mobile the possibilities of his own identification, and this is frustrating for the world around him. This frustration is what makes him so fragile: he is hard to "know" (hard to recognize in the categories available) and he is vulnerable. Two things emerge here. One is that there is a difficult and risky mobility and fragility for Chris as "sissy," and two is that the severity of attempts to contain and know him in other, equally foreclosing terms, makes visible the mobility and fragility of the order in which he stands as other.

Chris is a visible manifestation of that which needs to be disavowed, denounced. He is to the gendered order of the school world what a gay man is to the heterosexual masculinity of the military, metaphorized throughout this chapter as the position of melancholia. The melancholic's "rebellion" is embodied in their refusal to grieve—to lose and to accept the loss of either sexual object or gender performance. This, as rebellion, is in the form of a rejection of "reality," a resistance to closure, discomforted by and discomforting of the "reality" of gender. The next section further theorizes this rebellion in sissy boy experience.

Frustrating Foreclosure:
The Liveliness of Heresy

The discursive foreclosures that produce gender and sexuality are *frustrating*. They powerfully reproduce, as reality, the orders of gender that mean that some are "disordered" and others aren't—Chris and Matt are "disordered." But foreclosures of this kind can also be *frustrated*. They can be frustrated if they are seen to be moments of iteration that invoke or realize valued distinctions of gender and sexuality rather than being seen as "natural" or "real." If Matt and Chris' experience is understood as only about sexuality, the process by which they are declared disordered because of their performance of gender is obscured. If attention is paid to the moments of foreclosure when such declarations of disorder are made, there is the possibility of strategies other than acceptance or tolerance

The process of iteration is never completely foreclosed, and moments of iteration (performative speech acts, like being called a "sissy boy") are places where semiotic codes can be questioned, where they call attention to themselves or can even be redrafted, rewritten, recontextualized. These ideas draw heavily on the work of Judith Butler, especially her insistence in *Excitable Speech* that "the [performative] speech act is one whose contexts are never fully determined in advance, and that the possibility for the speech act to take on a non-ordinary meaning, to function in contexts in which it has not belonged, is precisely the political promise of the performative" (1997a, 161). The moment of declaration or recognition of sissy boy is a moment of foreclosure—it predicts and instantiates a system of gender and of value. Yet, these moments of declaration are also a moment available for disruption. The sissy boy declaration or recognition, its shame and its melancholy frustrate foreclosure and may be exploited further in this enterprise of frustration. Chris and Matt are both disruptions to the performance of gender by those understood as biologically male.

Melancholia has been used throughout this chapter as a metaphor for describing the way in which the sissy boy is a presence of what should be silenced and, as such, disrupts the circuit of repudiation involved in the formation of gendered identity. The sissy boy experience is interpreted as unsettling the real and reality-producing construction of masculinity. In melancholia ambivalence is kept lively and active. An active ambivalence performs a disruption because it does not settle, does not resolve or achieve closure, either to gender or its appropriate silences around normative gender/body alignments. The sissy boy, as a performance that speaks this lack of resolution, remains ambivalent because the sissy boy is neither boy nor girl, masculine nor feminine. The disruptive potential of ambivalence also keeps shame operative. Gender melancholy in the sissy boy experience, with its active, dramatic language, is a shameless acting out, calling attention to itself and to the context of its production.

Discourses of homophobia operate to overwrite and overdetermine sissy boy gender nonconformity as an issue of sexuality, obscuring what else might be going on. In this way, discourses of homophobia reduce, by subsuming, the productive and disruptive possibilities of the sissy boy experience. Both homophobic discourse and the discourses of homophobia police masculinity. Both these discourses, differently but powerfully, iterate formations of masculinity in processes of shame. But, if we do not tease the issue of gender out from under the rubric of homophobia, then masculinity (as Sedgwick suggests in relation to appropriate grown-up gayness in psychiatric literature) becomes renaturalized, accepted as real and appropriate for certain (male) bodies. The sissy boy experience, as one about gender, reveals the iteration of masculinity as one that is fragile and uncertain.

According to Plummer, "homophobia is a mobile polymorphous prejudice that incorporates a range of meanings, many of which are nonsexual" (1999, 302). Citing Rofes (1995), he elsewhere suggests that "homophobic terms are gendered from the outset" (2001a, 60). Plummer's book is called *One of the Boys: Masculinity, Homophobia and Modern Manhood*. The title implies a principle of social inclusion as part of what homophobia does—being one of a group, designated masculine. Earlier comments in this chapter about the operation of shame in relation to sociality and social inclusion related to gender nonconformity share this perspective. Inclusion into manhood or the masculine is managed by the threat of shameful exclusion. Another paper of Plummer's is called "Policing Manhood." Here again, homophobia, as prejudice, demonizes "non-conformists who 'betray' or who fail to 'measure up' to collectively authorized standards of masculinity" (2001a, 12). Plummer describes this as an *intragender* divide; where boys and men police how it is that their fellows measure up to their collectively held ideas of masculinity (6).

Plummer downplays the issue of gender nonconformity in both these texts. Having suggested that his project "has identified aspects of homophobia that do not seem to be directly related to gender" (1999, 9), he concludes his book by suggesting that through a "homophobic passage," experienced through developmental periods of a boy's or man's life, the meanings of homophobia develop from the meaning of "you were a bit of a girl" (2001a, 61, quoting from a participant) into sexualized meanings. This homophobic passage, Plummer argues, is *into* manhood. He goes on to conclude in his book that homophobia's "true logic lies in its negative bias, its relationship with 'otherness,' and its antithesis to masculinity" (1999, 305).

Masculinity and masculine domination depend on the construction of the other as nonmasculine (often feminized). This *is* about gender nonconformity (the logic of a negative bias toward the nonmasculine, as Plummer suggests). Why apply the term "homophobia," especially as it directs discussion, both in terms of growth and development and in terms of school-based interventions, to issues of resolving and affirming sexual identity and acceptance of the diversity of different sexualities? The sissy boy is lost in this analysis because his experience is moved on into later, sexualized meanings of homophobia in the homophobic passage to manhood without adequate attention being paid to either the experience and conditions of gender nonconformity or to its political potential. Attention should be paid to the positioning and strategic maneuverings of sissies within and in contradiction of the orders of gender in the school.

This chapter has argued that there is political potential available in sissy boy experience because it calls attention to the formation of gender. The declaration "sissy boy" ("bit of a girl," "acting like a girl") is a moment when discourse forecloses around gender by signaling very powerfully that boys should act like boys and that girls should act like girls. If, rather than making these moments of foreclosure about sexuality (a process that works in both homophobic discourse and discourses of homophobia), they are considered as processes of shaming due to "disordered" gender performance, then their uneasiness and the uneasiness of those that witness them can be interrogated. In other words, politically useful attention can be paid to the sissy boy experience by asking: How do sissies get to be sissies? How is this experience dealt with on a day-to-day basis in the school environment? How are sissies figured and understood as part of the school? What roles do sissies play? What other fields and discourses do they have dispositions toward or against? How do sissies move from their in-school positioning to extraschool experiences, either while they are at school or after? Do sissies figure as influences from or toward powerful discourse outside the school?

These questions, generated to interrogate sissy boy shame, are "political" because they all inquire about the complexity of power within and without the school, and link gender to other discursive formations. In asking these questions, there is an acknowledgement that there is no "outside" to power. Rather, these questions assume that power is produced in each iteration, in each maneuver. This kind of thinking is a necessity if the way gender nonconformity impacts on or is impacted by other aspects of schooling is to be adequately understood. For example, in other analyses (McInnes and Couch, 2004), the alignment of sissy boys with knowledge production through epistemophilia (the love of knowledge and of knowing) has been interpreted as a strategic masquerade that, while not "redeeming" a boy from his status as sissy, describes the way discourses of academic knowledge are powerfully deployed and exploited by some sissy boys. This inverts assumptions about power and discursive positioning because the hitherto "powerless" sissy aligns himself with the power of knowing and knowledge, a power and value that extends beyond the bounds of the school. The sissy boy's negotiations can be strategic, and powerful because of their very liveliness, because of their discomforting of category or type, and by their dynamic engagement with discursive power. The melancholic figure of the sissy boy refuses the circuit of renunciation, retaining and using ambivalence, and resisting foreclosure.

Conclusion

Attempts to map gender nonconformity into an issue of sexuality without adequate attention to the masquerade of gender, risks reproducing categories of gender unproblematically and reproducing the political landscape of the school. More than this, though, paying critical attention to sissy boy shame, prior to its surrender to discourses of homophobia, can yield a different kind of politics in the school.

In *Safety in Our Schools* the case study involving the declaration that Matt "acts like a girl" is framed within the following problem-solution genre:

7.ii So, what to do if . . .

Someone makes discriminatory comments?

One of the most effective and immediate challenges to homophobia in the school culture is to challenge homophobic language. Try the NAC approach:

1. Name it: "That's a problem"

2. Refer to Agreement: "Our ground rules state no-put-downs"

3. Give consequences: "If you use a put-down again you will have to follow disciplinary procedures." (Ollis, et al. 13)

The NAC strategy, aimed as it is on reducing the violence of hate speech, seeks to reduce homophobia by reducing the use of homophobic language. Elsewhere in the booklet, the authors recommend processes that not only reduce discrimination but work toward acceptance. Following Case Study One, referred to earlier, they suggest that you can "process the statement [Matt acts like a girl] with the whole class, exploring and questioning students on the implications of the statement for all those involved." Following the logic of the booklet, "implications" refers to a lack of safety for some and a need for acceptance by others. The arguments made in this chapter about resisting the collapse into discourse of homophobia and their liberal ideas of tolerance would suggest, in contrast, that keeping the gender nonconformity issue alive, rather than collapsing into homophobia, and working with rather than removing foreclosures enacted through put-downs, would allow for a critical engagement with gender in the school, using the deconstructive potential available in the sissy boy experience. If sissy boy negotiations from their melancholic positions reveal how identity is a negotiation with and about the powerful operation of various interconnected discourses, then there is a different kind of educational potential available in these moments. To explore the implications of the arguments made in this chapter for the school, the discussion now turns to the consideration of classroom strategies.

In the *Safety in Our Schools* scenario, the disciplining and governing of students to avoid "put-downs" works on the principle of tolerance and diversity. As already argued, it seeks to include those whose sexuality is different and, by doing so, assumes that the formation of gender and sexuality through various discourses can be avoided or managed. In this scenario, Matt would be free to behave like a girl and would not be verbally abused because of his gender nonconformity, because his acting like a girl is a consequence of his sexuality. If his sexuality is accepted, then his gender nonconformity is accepted. Questions of gender—what is valued and powerful and what is not— are left without critical attention in this scenario and, as such, the idea of what is right and wrong in gender performance for young men is left intact. Boys act like boys, except when they are gay and this is okay because we can tolerate their sexuality.

The young man who declares that Matt acts like a girl does so not only because boys should act like boys, but because the shaming of Matt as a sissy reflexively produces the value of his own kind of masculinity and keeps the "ordered" relation between bodies and gender stable. The declaration "sissy," as with any performative speech act, takes place in a context that demands that the one declaring and the one declared both recognize the declaration. It also rests, for its effectiveness, on the witness of others. In other words, the social context of declared, declarer, and witness authenticates the declaration. In terms of gender non-conformity and schools, this means that all in the classroom in which Matt is declared to "act like a girl" are witness not only to Matt's status as sissy but to the formation of the other male student's masculinity and, further, to the reinscribing and revaluing of gender, especially in terms of appropriate (or ordered) masculinity.

The shaming declaration of sissy is a reiteration of the difference in value between masculinity and femininity, and between the different possible performances of gender by those considered biologically male. It is important to keep in mind, that the power of gender is that it comes to rest without question on certain bodies and their performances, and that this is self-evident (Sedgwick http://www.duke.edu/sedgwic/WRITING/GOSH.htm). The moments when Matt and Chris are declared other because of their gender nonconformity are moments when the easy categorizations of gender are unsettled. The declarations happen in order to rework the system of category and of value—pointing out disorder, of course, identifies and values order. Instead of telling the student who declared that Matt "acts like a girl" that he would be disciplined if he used "put-downs," this moment could be used in the classroom to reflect on why he has made the declaration and to further question whether or not there is such a sharp distinction between the way boys act and the way girls act. Perhaps asking why he needs to make the distinction and what this does for him would be both pedagogically and politically useful in that it resists the self-evidence of the production of gender. Pedagogically and politically this makes the uneasy production of gender visible, the formation of masculinity fragile, and leaves unresolved questions of how young men and boys "should" be.

Discourses of homophobia, as often deployed and reworked in relation to school experience, do not allow for or embrace the disruptive potential of the sissy boy experience, because these discourses assume the possibility of resolution (as masculine, as appropriately gay) and, by resolving in this way, they are intolerant to ambivalence.

Further, the focus on sexuality with which they are structured avoids the risk to masculinity of gender nonconformity.

Sissy boy melancholia and its formative shame are instantiations of the tension and frustrations of gender foreclosure. They offer a productive and disruptive ambivalence in their very iteration *(if we take note)* by exposing the fragile achievement of masculinity. More than this, though, if we take note, we can question and use the disruption further. Discourses of homophobia provide a "way out," an easy exit from debates about gender order or disorder, in that the collapse to gay and to sexuality provides a nameable identity category, a type of person that has rights and can be accepted as part of difference and diversity. These closures distract from the iterative process of practice/ing gender.

What is proposed here is a risky and difficult load to bear for gender nonconforming boys, for sissy boys. But, if paid attention to, the negotiations made from the shameful recognition of and as sissy boy would offer a capacity to negotiate other dimensions and aspects of power in the school context. These areas of productive, nongender normalizing strategic operation and the boys that enact them deserve much greater theoretical and empirical attention.

References

American Psychiatric Association Staff. 1980. *Diagnostic and Statistical Manual of Mental Disorders, 3rd Ed.* Washington, D.C.: American Psychiatric Association.

Bourdieu, Pierre. 2001. *Masculine Domination.* Cambridge, UK: Polity Press.

Butler, Judith. 1997a. *Excitable Speech: A Politics of the Performative.* New York and London: Routledge.

———. 1997b. *The Psychic Life of Power: Theories of Subjection.* Stanford: Stanford University Press.

Dempsey, Deborah, Lynne Hillier, and Lynne Harrison. 2001. "Gendered (S)explorations Among Same-Sex Attracted Young People in Australia." *Journal of Adolescence* 24, no. 1: 67–81.

Friedman, Richard. 1988. *Male Homosexuality: A Contemporary Psychoanalytic Perspective.* New Haven, Conn.: Yale University Press.

Hillier, Lynne, Lynne Harrison, and Deborah Dempsey. 1999. "Whatever Happened to Duty of Care? Same Sex Attracted Young People's Stories of Schooling and Violence." *Studies in Education Special Issue, Sexualities and Education* 40, no. 2: 59–74.

Mason, Gail and Steve Tomsen, eds. 1997. *Homophobic Violence.* Annandale (NSW): Australian Institute of Criminology and the Hawkins Press.

McInnes, David. 1997. "Into the Queerzone: Iterative Potential and Semiotic Tensions." pp. 27–36 in *Queer Zone, Working Papers in Women's Studies, Feminist Cultural Studies Series*, no. 4., eds. Jane Hobson, David McInnes, Linnell Secomb, and Kaye Shumack. Sydney: University of Western Sydney, Nepean.

———. 2002. "Thighs and Sighs: A Sissy Boy's Take on Rugby League's Gay Hero." *word is out* e-journal, no. 4, http://www.arts.usyd.edu.au/publications/wordisout/front.htm.

McInnes, David, and Murray Couch. 2004. "Quiet Please! There's a Lady on the Stage: Boys, Gender and Sexuality Non-Conformity and Class." *Discourse: Studies in the Cultural Politics of Education, Special Issue, Wounded Identities and the Promise of Pleasure*, 24, no.4.

Nathanson, Donald. L. 1992. *Shame and Pride: Affect, Sex and the Birth of the Self*. New York: Norton.

Ollis, Debbie, Anne Mitchell, Jan Watson, Lynne Hillier, and Jenny Walsh. Undated. *Safety in Our Schools: Strategies for Responding to Homophobia*. Melbourne: Australian Research Centre in Sex, Health and Society.

Plummer, David. 1999. *One of the Boys: Masculinity, Homophobia and Modern Manhood*. New York: Hawthorn Press.

———. 2001a. "Policing Manhood: New Theories about the Social Significance of Homophobia," Pp. 60–75 in *Sexual Positions: An Australian View*, ed. Carl Wood. Melbourne: Hill of Content.

———. 2001b. "The Quest for Modern Manhood: Masculine Stereotypes, Peer Culture and the Social Significance of Homophobia." *Journal of Adolescence*, 24, no. 1: 15–23.

Rofes, Eric. 1995. "Making our Schools Safe for Sissies," Pp. 79–84 in *The Gay Teen: Educational Practice and Theory for Lesbian, Gay and Bisexual Adolescents*, ed. Gerald Unks. Routledge: New York.

Sedgwick, Eve Kosofsky. 1993. "How to Bring Your Kids up Gay." Pp. 69–81 in *Fear of a Queer Planet*, ed. Michael Warner. Minneapolis: University of Minnesota Press.

———. "Gosh, Boy George, You must be Awfully Secure in Your Masculinity!" http://www.duke.edu/~sedgwic/WRITING/GOSH.htm, accessed November 20, 2003.

Sedgwick, Eve Kosofsky, and Adam Frank. 1995b. "Shame in the Cybernetic Fold: Reading Sylvan Tomkins." *Critical Inquiry* 21: 497–522.

———. 1995a. *Shame and Its Sisters*. Durham, N.C.: Duke University Press.

Simes, Gary. 1996. "'Gay's The Word': A History of Gay in Dictionary Form." Pp. 303–347 in *Gay and Lesbian Perspectives III: Essays in Australian Culture*, ed. Gary Wotherspoon. Sydney: Department of Economic History and The Australian Centre for Lesbian and Gay Research, University of Sydney.

Tomkins, Silvan. 1962. *Affect, Imagery, Consciousness, Vol. 1*. New York: Springer.

———. 1963. *Affect, Imagery, Consciousness, Vol. 2*. New York: Springer.

Notes on Contributors

SINE ANAHITA is Assistant Professor of Sociology and Women's Studies at the University of Alaska, Fairbanks. Her research and teaching interests include the sociology of sexuality, sex and gender, race and ethnic relations, organizations, and sociological issues of Alaska and the Circumpolar North. Her dissertation research focused on contemporary U.S. landdyke communities, and two articles based on this research are forthcoming in sociological journals.

MOLLIE V. BLACKBURN is Assistant Professor in Literacy, Language, and Culture in the College of Education at The Ohio State University. She completed her doctoral studies at the University of Pennsylvania in 2001, where she received an award for writing a dissertation that works for social justice. Her research is critical and activist in nature and works to explore the ways in which youth engage in literacy performances to construct their identities and work for social change. Her work has been published in such journals as *Teachers College Record* and *Research in the Teaching of English*.

JACKIE M. BLOUNT is Associate Professor of Historical, Philosophical, and Comparative Studies in Education at Iowa State University. She has written *Destined to Rule the Schools: Women and the Superintendency, 1873–1995* (SUNY Press, 1998) and *Fit to Teach: Same-Sex Desire, Gender, and School Work in the Twentieth Century* (SUNY Press, 2004).

ANDREA COLEMAN is a doctoral student in Curriculum and Teaching at Teachers College, Columbia University, researching queer activism in public education. She currently serves as Director of Education and Youth Services at FEGS, a health and human services agency in New York City.

MARY EHRENWORTH is a doctoral student in Curriculum and Teaching at Teachers College, Columbia University, and a staff developer in the New York City public schools. Her book *Looking to Write: Students Writing through the Visual Arts* describes ways to engage students with the visual arts in order to write narratives of love and desire.

JEN GILBERT is Assistant Professor in the Faculty of Education at York University in Toronto. Her research interests include the representation of adolescence in literature, models of sex education, and psychoanalytic theories of learning.

VALERIE HARWOOD lectures in foundations of education in the Faculty of Education, University of Wollongong. Her research interests are in the areas of youth studies, the construction of psychopathology, and methodological applications of Foucault's critical thought.

NANCY LESKO teaches in the areas of curriculum and gender and cultural studies at Teachers College, Columbia University. Recent publications include *Act Your Age! A Cultural Construction of Adolescence* (Routledge, 2001) and *Masculinities at School* (Sage, 2000). Her work in progress investigates citizenship and curriculum in the context of social crises.

DAVID MCINNES has a Ph.D. in Semiotics from The University of Sydney and lectures in English, Text and Writing at The University of Western Sydney. His research interests include gay sexual and community politics in Australia, the Australian community-based response to the HIV epidemic, and the analysis of health promotion and education.

MARY LOUISE RASMUSSEN is a lecturer in the school of Social and Cultural Studies in Education at Deakin University, Victoria, Australia. Currently, her research interests are focused on the nexus of pedagogies, popular cultures, and globalization.

ERIC ROFES is Associate Professor of Education at Humboldt State University in Arcata, California, 300 miles north of San Francisco. A long-time community organizer, he has served on the boards of the National Gay and Lesbian Task Force, the National Lesbian and Gay Health Association, and the OUT Fund for Gay Liberation. He was an openly gay middle school teacher in the late '70s and early '80s and teaches a course focused on gay and lesbian issues in schools. At Humboldt State, he teaches courses in community organizing, the sociology of education, and qualitative research methods and directs a credential program for elementary school teachers.

SUSAN TALBURT teaches courses in curriculum theory, anthropology of education, and feminist and poststructural theory at Georgia State University. She is the author of *Subject to Identity: Knowledge, Sexual-*

ity, and Academic Practices in Higher Education (SUNY Press, 2000) and co-editor of *Thinking Queer: Sexuality, Culture, and Education* (Peter Lang, 2000).

DEBORAH YOUDELL is a lecturer in Education at the University of Cambridge, UK. Her work covers a range of issues concerned with education policy, social justice in education, and the ways that schools are implicated in producing and policing the subjectivities of students. Her publications include *Rationing Education: Policy, Practice, Reform and Equity* (co-authored with David Gillborn).

Index

CPSIA information can be obtained at www.ICGtesting.com
Printed in the USA
LVOW092136210512

282712LV00005B/14/P